Chinese and Americans often unwittingly communicate at cross-purposes because they are misled by the cultural trappings of talk. This book aims to clarify their misunderstandings by examining their different ideals and strategies of talk. It draws on cultural, philosophical, and linguistic insights and traces the development of Chinese communicative strategies from Confucius through the "eight-legged essay" to the boardrooms and streets of Hong Kong. Its formal analysis of taped interchanges and in-depth interviews reveals Chinese speakers' distinctive ways of communicating and relating. *Crosstalk and culture in Sino-American communication* will alert people to the pitfalls of cultural misunderstandings and the hidden assumptions and expectations underlying talk.

Studies in Interactional Sociolinguistics 10

General Editor: John J. Gumperz

Crosstalk and culture in
Sino-American communication

Studies in Interactional Sociolinguistics

Crosstalk and culture in Sino-American communication

LINDA W. L. YOUNG

CAMBRIDGE
UNIVERSITY PRESS

Published by the Press Syndicate of the University of Cambridge
The Pitt Building, Trumpington Street, Cambridge CB2 1RP
40 West 20th Street, New York, NY 10011-4211, USA
10 Stamford Road, Oakleigh, Melbourne 3166, Australia

First published 1994

A catalogue record for this book is available from the British Library

Library of Congress cataloguing in publication data

Young, Linda Wai Ling.
    Crosstalk and culture in Sino-American communication / Linda W. L. Young.
        p.   cm. – (Studies in interactional sociolinguistics; 10)
ISBN 0 521 41619 1
    1. Chinese language – Social aspects. 2. Intercultural communication.
    I. Title. II. Series.
PL1074.Y68   1994
495.1 – dc20   93-3980 CIP

ISBN 0 521 41619 1 hardback

Transferred to digital printing 2003

BS

For my parents

In the beginning was the Word
(Gospel of St. John)

Dao (道) which can be spoken (道)
is not constant Dao (道)
(*Dao De Jing*)

Contents

Foreword
by John J. Gumperz

The last few decades have seen a dramatic increase both in the amount and in the quality and intensity of communication among individuals of different cultural background. In the ever expanding global marketplace where national economies co-exist in close interdependence, international organizations and multi-national companies proliferate, boundaries become more and more porous and populations increasingly mobile. People who grew up in distant parts of the world under historically quite distinct circumstances must now work together as part of the same labor force, jointly participate in local community affairs and compete for access to public facilities. So that, regardless of whether we live abroad or in our own familiar home environment, we are all more and more likely to come into direct contact with others who do not share our basic assumptions and perspectives. Intercultural communication is well on its way to becoming an everyday phenomenon.

Questions of culture have, to be sure, not escaped scholarly attention. A number of first rate ethnographic descriptions and cultural analyses incisively document the far-reaching differences in worldview, beliefs, and value systems among the various peoples of the globe. As a result, many of us have become aware of the complex, previously unsuspected, and often quite subtle ways in which our own perceptions of reality are constrained by taken for granted culturally specific presuppositions. Yet descriptions so far available concentrate almost exclusively on one single cultural tradition at a time. The very term multi-culturalism which has been so useful and important in countering the constantly re-emerging prejudices against the foreign minorities in our midst, and has by now become an integral part of our everyday language, nevertheless seems to imply that today's issues of cultural diversity can be viewed in terms of finite sets of co-existing, qualitatively distinct unitary systems.

Yet the problem of how this diversity affects everyday communication is still far from well understood. Today's minority groups are after all to a large extent bilingual and bicultural. They cannot therefore be treated as total communicative isolates. We know from experience that it is on the whole easier to get things done in situations where all involved share the same basic background. In culturally diverse communicative environments hidden, normally unnoticed differences in perspectives may bring about radically conflicting interpretations of what is happening. Miscommunications are likely to proliferate and become difficult to repair even when the same language is used and participants seem to agree on what is to be accomplished. What is it about communication and culture that brings about this effect?

There is relatively little in the way of published material available on this issue, at least nothing that even remotely approaches the depth and theoretical sophistication of existing single culture studies. Most of the published materials we have either take the form of relatively abstract quantitative studies or of practical manuals and "how to do it" books. The latter offer essential information on manners and principles of etiquette not usually found in the scholarly literature and frequently illustrated by means of interesting and quite revealing anecdotes. They also provide helpful pointers on what to do or how to behave in typical situations. Yet such practical guides are by their very nature limited to generalized descriptions of behavioral norms. Moreover they tend to presuppose a view of intercultural communication as typically associated with the brief instrumental encounters characteristic of tourist or business travel, where communicative goals are relatively transparent and verbal communication relies in large part on formulaic phrases. Participants in such encounters are cognizant of the fact that they meet as strangers who may have only a limited knowledge of each other's linguistic background. Miscommunications are expected, and when they occur they can, for the most part, be readily attributed to insufficient knowledge of vocabulary or grammar.

It is evident that such simple models cannot account for the communicative requirements of the post-industrial market place. Note that along with the ever increasing diversity, the very nature of interactive tasks has also undergone significant change. Increasingly such more or less organized events as meetings and group discussions or negotiations, as well as employment, counseling and social service interviews of various kinds, both formal and informal, have come to constitute a significant part of the communicative routine both at work and in public life. These play a key role in decision making of all kinds and are therefore particularly important both for individuals and for the economic success of an enterprise. In contrast to tourist encounters, gatherings of the latter kind tend to involve longer often highly complex interactions where delicate power relations must be kept in balance and conflicting interests reconciled. Cognitively and socially demanding problems are likely to arise that place a premium on rhetorical skills and may make it difficult to reach agreement or achieve understanding even when language and culture are shared. Active participation in such situations presupposes functional control of a single language so that intelligibility at the level of grammar and lexicon as such is often not the issue. The basic question is more commonly one of rhetorical effectiveness and it is in this connection that the most serious problems arise. This is not to say that grammar and vocabulary are not important. Rhetorical effectiveness obviously presupposes knowledge of linguistic form. The point is that because of their complexity, problems of misunderstanding are most fruitfully examined on the basis of everyday talk.

Experience with intercultural communication indicates that the most tenacious and troublesome interpretive difficulties tend to arise in the course of the process of communicating as such and often for reasons that participants immersed in the interaction, and intent on formulating their own arguments, tend not to be consciously aware of. To understand the communicative mechanisms involved, it becomes necessary to look more closely at the way speech exchanges work. Face-to-face communication, as we all know, is always a collaborative endeavor requiring active contributions from speakers as well as from listeners. This means that in exercising their right to speak individuals take on obligations towards their partners that require them to do more than merely put information into words. Whatever is said must somehow fit into or be relatable to themes established in the course of the preceding talk. Regardless of whether or not speakers agree, some degree of topical or thematic continuity has to be maintained. To begin with, whatever one speaker says sets up expectations for what is to follow, and this has significant consequences for discourse organization. Questions call for answers, requests or suggestions need to be acknowledged, and assertions need either to be confirmed or contradicted. Furthermore, turns at speaking must be co-ordinated both to allow for speaker change and to give those who hold the floor a chance to complete their arguments. To give just one more example, a simple declarative sentence such as "last night we went to town" often serves as a lead-in to a personal narrative, and those who understand it this way are expected to allow the speaker space to develop his or her story. In sum, conversationalists need to know not only what to say, in the sense of putting their ideas into words. They also have to know how and in what style to express their ideas and how to time their contributions in such a way as to maintain the flow of the interaction.

Complex as it is, conversational collaboration is normally achieved automatically without conscious reflection, as is also the case with the production of grammatical sentences. Yet since the conditions of contextual relevance that affect conversational inference are subject to regular change as the interaction progresses, the co-ordination process cannot be described in terms of grammar-like rules, valid without regard to context. We must assume that conversationalists plan their talk while the interaction is in process on the basis of what they see and hear in the encounter. In doing this they rely on their perception of certain signalling mechanisms called contextualization cues – including among others such features of conversational style as speech rhythm and tempo, intonation, choice of vocabulary or pronunciation – as well as on the content of the talk. In this way they simultaneously assess the significance of the talk at hand in relation to the interaction as a whole and determine what is intended by any one utterance.

Conversational inference is culturally specific in two respects.

First, cultural knowledge is a significant constituent of the background knowledge that we draw on in interpreting what we hear. Secondly, contextualization conventions are acquired in the course of home, school, peer communicative background. When speakers' inferences do not accord with those of other participants, the resulting discrepancies may violate the latter's expectations and conversational collaboration may be affected. Presumed violators may be seen to be interfering with others' rights, and those affected could take offense. The offender might be said to speak too much, fail to respond as expected, be rude or inconsiderate. In other words, not realizing that undetected differences in inferential practices could be at work, we react to violations of conversational expectations as we would to inappropriate language or other violations of accepted etiquette, attributing the problem to a person's ability or personality characteristics.

When inferences clash and background is shared, participants can draw on their knowledge of others' histories to find reasonable explanations for what is happening and thus give each other the benefit of the doubt. Moreover, the problems that arise are often readily repaired. But where the necessary shared background experience does not exist, difficulties arise. Miscommunications become more difficult to repair, since we tend to rely on indirect and therefore culturally specific ways of talking in making good a *faux pas* so as to avoid giving offense. This may raise additional comprehension problems and misunderstandings are likely to be compounded. A frequent end result is that participants lose their sense of what is going on. They may understand individual sentences but cannot fit them into a coherent argument. In the absence of any reasonable explanation there is a tendency to blame the other and fall back on interethnic stereotypes one might not ordinarily use to make sense of what is happening and preserve one's sense of control.

The interactive bases of intercultural misunderstandings were systematically investigated in a series of comparative studies of contacts between native speakers of English and English-speaking native speakers of South Asian languages and African Caribbeans in Britain. Analysis of recordings made in industry, counseling centers, employment offices, and similar institutional settings revealed that even though non-natives had good functional control of English grammar, their interactions with native English speakers showed a much higher rate of miscommunications than native-native encounters. Miscommunications were especially frequent in longer encounters, when speakers engaged in intricate communicative tasks such as arguing a point, explaining cognitively complex facts, or defending a controversial point. Here non-natives, even those who speak English well, tended to fall back on rhetorical and contextualization conventions characteristic of their own home language and community. The mismatch in communicative style seriously interfered with conversational collaboration and as a result both sets of speakers felt a loss of control. A number of individuals reported that they felt lost. Customary persuasive strategies did not seem to work, and attempts at repair strategies proved ineffective. Unable to see that the problem was in large part communicative, members of each group tended to blame the other. South Asians, for example, complained they were rarely given an opportunity to say what they wanted to say, that interlocutors were not interested in their problems and made no effort to see their point of view. Native English speakers saw the Asians as uncooperative, unable to respond to questions, not trying to understand what was really wanted, being longwinded and vague in their arguments and in general either unable or unwilling to cooperate. The problems were so great that they seriously interfered with assessments of personal ability in interviews and other situations where communicative effectiveness was important.

In the present volume Young applies a related communicative perspective to the study of Chinese–Western relations. Arguing that interpersonal communication plays a much greater role in creating and reinforcing pejorative intercultural stereotypes than has commonly been assumed, she begins by examining a number of anecdotal Western reports about the Chinese that have been appearing at frequent intervals over the last century. The remarkable similarity in the stereotypes reflected in accounts written at different periods of time suggests that these have their origin in Westerners' reaction to Chinese use of native language discursive strategies in their English talk. In the rest of the book Young turns to a detailed discussion of the differences between Chinese- and English-based discursive practices, using as her point of departure tapes of natural interactions recorded in a variety of institutional settings. Included in the analysis are grammar, discourse markers, discourse organization, rhetorical strategies, and cultural ideology. The treatment of the last two topics is of particular interest. In the West, classical Chinese culture is usually discussed from a historical perspective. Young demonstrates that many of the same principles and modes of interpretation continue to survive in the English language use of Chinese in Western academic and technological settings.

By the end of the book the reader will have obtained a unique picture of the Chinese discoursive and cultural tradition as an integrated system, of the ways in which it differs from English, and of how these differences affect everyday talk. It would be too much to claim that a book such as this can give detailed guidelines for everyday interaction. In specific encounters a host of unforeseen problems tends to arise that cannot be predicted in advance. What the book does is to provide the basic background knowledge to enable us to recognize communicative problems for what they are, to become aware of the ever-present danger of stereotyping, and perhaps avoid some of the grossest misjudgments.

Preface

Chinese and Americans often approach each other with very different assumptions and perceptions. These contribute significantly to the difficulties persistently marring Sino-American interactions. They have inspired, in turn, stock American images of the inscrutable Chinese.

This complex issue is the most prominent yet least understood chapter in US–China relations. The bewildering uncertainty bedeviling exchanges between Chinese and Americans regularly occurs across a range of international and national settings despite dramatic shifts in historical, ideological, and political winds. It also reappears in the cross-cultural interactions of Americans with some of the English-speaking children and grandchildren of transplanted Chinese in the United States. Surprisingly enough, despite historic recognition of the issue, and despite a large literature on the subject, the process by which it occurs and continues to occur has not received systematic attention.

This book represents my attempt to come to grips with this recalcitrant issue. What I shall describe, analyze, and explain are some underlying sources and typical displays of Chinese communicative behavior. What I am interested in are some of the wider implications for the pattern of perceptions and interactions that exists between Chinese and Americans; that is, for the way in which they come to view each other.

We can break this discussion down as follows: What are some prominent features of Chinese communicative strategies? How do these features relate to presumed Chinese personality characteristics? To what extent do these culturally based communicative patterns provide a justifiable basis for some of the images and stereotypes that arise in Sino-American interactions? In examining these issues, we will also be grappling with the following questions: What Chinese cultural ideals of interpersonal interaction influence the conduct and manner of their verbal output? What do Chinese strategies of face-redress reflect about how Chinese visualize and enact social relationships? Furthermore, how do cultural, inter-actional, and linguistic systems interact to affect the interpretation of messages? How do the systems fit together? Why do they fit together in certain patterns? What holds the patterns together? We shall also raise the following kinds of questions: What cultural ideals influence the layout, makeup, and playout of ideas? What sorts of information do conversational participants rely on to signify intent and decipher messages? What forms do these signals take? How do these signals function in the cross-cultural inter-pretation of meaning?

By the end of the book, the reader should have developed a finer-tuned understanding of why Chinese and Americans are so often so ill-attuned to one another, and an appreciation for why Western perceptions of Chinese inscrutability have lasted so long.

Acknowledgments

I owe thanks to many people for helping me with this undertaking. Detailed work like this makes it easy to lose sight of the forest for the trees. In my case, I was more often stranded on a limb or entangled in the roots. When this happened, I was rescued by John Gumperz and Roger Ames. They graciously showed me their *Daos* so that I can walk my own; for that and for the pleasures and examples of their scholarly vigor and sensitivities, I am most grateful. David McCraw kindly helped remove some boulders and fill in the potholes to smooth my way. I also thank Celia Roberts and Deborah Davison for providing me with the tapes for analysis, and Jim Matisoff, linguist extraordinaire, who told me a long time ago to "stick by your guns." Per Gjerde, Pan Chia-hua, Joan Fujimura, Claudia Carr, Donn Kessler, Suzanne Scollon, Karen Watson-Gegeo, David Gegeo, Annette, Willy, and Midnight Young gave inspiration and assistance in different ways.

1

The Ps and cues of Chinese inscrutability

Introduction

The image of the inscrutable Chinese runs deep in Western imagination. The inscrutable Chinese, i.e., mysterious, unfathomable, inexplicable, is a powerful image because it represents the many aspects of Chinese culture which Westerners find unaccountable and difficult to understand. But in fact, as we shall see, inscrutability is often just another way of saying that the unstated, culturally defined expectations which Chinese and Westerners bring to their face-to-face interactions do not coincide.

One conspicuous element making up Western images of the inscrutable Chinese has been the way Chinese talk and respond in conversations. The distinctive features of Chinese speech have been commented upon many times by many people of different cultures in very different contexts. Particularly in Western writings, the Chinese approach to talk has been viewed with profound ambivalence. Many report, for example, that Chinese rely on suggestive or illustrative statements, are apt to clarify and explain by example and analogy, and do a great deal more beating around the bush than do Americans. Former Secretary of State Henry A. Kissinger's admiring account of his first encounter with the late Chinese leader Mao Zedong is typical: "The cumulative effect was that his key points were enveloped in so many tangential phrases that they communicated a meaning while evading a commitment. Mao's elliptical phrases were passing shadows on a wall; they reflected a reality but they did not encompass it. They indicated a direction without defining the route of march" (Kissinger 1979: 1059). Continuing, he writes: "Later on, as I comprehended better the many-layered design of Mao's conversation, I understood that it was like the courtyards in the Forbidden City, each leading to a deeper recess distinguished from the others only by slight changes of proportion, with ultimate meaning residing in a totality that only long reflection could grasp" (1061). Another American has written less admiringly of his cross-cultural experience with Chinese while working at the Foreign Language Press in Beijing: "It took me a long while to learn the [Chinese] custom of starting with a little polite palaver, then sidling up to the problem and circumlocuting all around it, before actually identifying it and diffidently suggesting a solution. I still don't do it very well. I considered it pussy-footing, over-emphasizing the saving of face, a fear of coming to grips with conflict" (Shapiro 1979: 78).

The special characteristics of Chinese talk often appear as significant points of friction alongside other serious difficulties in trade and diplomatic negotiations. The literature is filled with references to this issue and references, moreover, which are consistent. Almost invariably, inaccurate assessments and images have led to distortion and misperception of the goals, intentions, and actions of each side, thus adding a discordant element or exacerbating a genuine conflict. Often, in technical and commercial exchanges, Chinese and Americans talk at cross-purposes, even in so simple a matter as thinking Chinese mean "yes" when in fact they mean "no." In a questionnaire survey conducted at the start of China's Open Door policy, American companies singled out a number of cultural factors that contributed to the success or failure of their negotiations with Chinese. They include, in descending order of significance: communication breakdowns (39.1%), business practices (36.3%), negotiation styles (34.7%), social customs (13.1%), cultural differences (12.4%), and ideological differences (12.3%) (Tung 1982, chapter 3). More detail about the communicative failures affecting Sino-American business relations appears in the following report on management characteristics in the People's Republic of China:

communications in the Chinese enterprises tend to be "vague" or "ambiguous"; implicit communications are generally adopted through "cues" and "indirection." Although implicit communications are more flexible, they are considered "ambiguous" from a Western point of view which emphasizes "clearness," "certainty," and "directness." Because of these differences, misunderstandings and disputes often arise between Chinese enterprises and foreign companies.   (Mun 1986: 319)

The distinctiveness of Chinese ways of speaking has also been viewed against the background of the ethnic experience and economic opportunities of Asians in America. In a number of writings on this issue, Chinese are often described as prone to an "antipathy towards articulation," an "aversion for assertion," and a "weakness in argumentation." Furthermore, they have tended to cluster around occupations and career choices that require few verbal and persuasive skills.

To be sure, Chinese are no longer shut out of as many primary labor markets as before; in fact, they are widely represented in a variety of challenging professional and technological fields. Witness also the slew of articles in the popular press about the many academic and economic successes of newly arrived Chinese and other first or second generation Asian Americans. Nonetheless, communicating in a distinctively Chinese way continues to carry a hefty social price and subjects Chinese – and other Asians – to special varieties of rejection in America. For one thing, it presents them with a handicap in education. This happens no matter if they are recent immigrants: "These difficulties were so familiar to the staff at the University of California at Berkeley that Asians enrolled in 'Subject A' (remedial English) often received an 'Oriental D'" (Kim 1978: 321); or if they are native born:

Not only recent immigrants but also native-born Asian Americans whose families have lived in America for two, three, or more generations still manifest limited communicative skills in higher education environments . . . The contrast between Asian Americans' achievement in quantitative fields and their avoidance of and difficulties with fields that demand well developed verbal skills is stark among recent immigrants and still noticeable after several generations among the native born.   (Hsia 1988: 164)

For another, it puts them at a disadvantage in the job sector:

The Asian American English "problem" is generally cited as the major stumbling block to occupational success, the reason why many Asian Americans are relegated to low-level clerical and technical work, in accounting and engineering, and in other occupations requiring little public contact, decision making, or supervisorial duties . . . Numerous claims of discrimination against Asian Americans applying for promotion within the San Francisco City Civil Service System have been filed with the city's Civil Service Commission. Many Asian Americans who passed their written test, all university graduates, were denied promotion primarily on the basis of the oral interview. (Kim 1978: 322)

Although among the best educated and most credentialed of Americans, Asians, native-born or newcomer, confront slower salary increases and limited career advances in government and academe. The situation is much the same in industry and corporate America: upward-bound Asian Americans often find themselves stalled in their climb to the executive suite. Hughes Aircraft Company's David Barclay, vice-president for workforce diversity, summarizes reasons perceived by Hughes' white senior executives and Asian American employees. They include "poor language and communicative skills, rigidity (particularly among women), inflexibility, authoritarian traits, lack of motivating and management skills and an overly reserved approach" (*Transpacific*, July/August 1992, p. 35).

The distinctiveness of Chinese cultural characteristics has also been recognized in other ways. For example, a revised version of the Minnesota Multiphasic Personality Inventory (MMPI), which had been carried out nationwide in China in 1980 by the Chinese – and replicated with similar results in Hong Kong (Cheung 1985) – identified some character traits that contrasted with those of Americans. In particular, the Chinese are described as:

emotionally more reserved, introverted, fond of tranquility, overly considerate, socially overcautious, habituated to self-restraint, and so forth. These character traits are not only manifested in the test results but are also corroborated by the daily lives of Chinese people. Therefore, we believe that the two peaks on the profile types do not indicate that Chinese people are of a more depressive or more schizophrenic character than Americans. They are simply reflective of the differences between the national characters of the two peoples. (Song 1985: 53)

By contrast, in a study comparing American therapists and Chinese-American therapists on their perceptions of Chinese patients, American clinicians unfamiliar with Chinese cultural differences saw their Chinese patients as less socially poised with little interpersonal capacity, and, by inference, interpreted the differences as signs of "social introversion, withdrawal, and even depression" (Li-Repac 1980: 339).

Certainly, it is well known that Chinese and Americans hold

very different assumptions about how persons should present themselves in relation to one another. These differences, in turn, are rooted in the different cultural assumptions and social emphases underlying social relationships and self-presentation rituals in general and, further, call into play formal procedures of action and expression that some Americans will find at best remote and at worst alien. In particular, as part of their constant attention to deference and demeanor, Chinese concerns with maintaining one's own face is equally matched by their concern to publicly give – and leave – honor to the other's face (see Hu 1944). By and large, face-saving strategies figure rather prominently in Chinese ritual expression, and, moreover, are signalled in ways and occasions which Americans are not familiar with. In fact, the ways in which face-saving strategies are signalled, the occasions which call for their appearance, and the reasons why they must be expressed in the Chinese cultural tradition are critical sources of confusion for most Americans. For the most part:

Chinese people still appear to whites as being exaggeratedly humble and deferent, and as oblique or devious in their business and other communications and interactions. They are too much given to face-saving devices, in order to avoid embarrassment or discomfort either to those they are speaking to, or to themselves. In general, they are more concerned about shame (*being seen* to be wrong) than about guilt (*feeling* that one is wrong). Because they have different ways of expressing emotions from whites, they still seem to us inscrutable and reserved. (Vernon 1982: 16)

On the Chinese side, we find the basic cultural differences expressed as a result of their very specific vulnerabilities in American life:

The Chinese tend to be withdrawn and non-aggressive. They consider it to be in bad taste to be "forward" or assertive. Except among friends, they tend to be reticent and constrained . . . They hesitate to speak up or even to ask questions. This is not altogether due to language difficulty. Much of it comes from the habit of refraining from aggressive speech or action. Chinese courtesy puts a premium on reservedness and deference, or avoiding to be the first to speak or act. Such a characteristic becomes a handicap in an open and competitive society in which an individual tends to gain by taking the initiative in personal relations and bold action to assert his rights. (Chen 1976: 46)

That Chinese experience a particularly intense frustration when the appropriateness and relevance of Chinese conventions decrease is apparent in the emotionally tinged recollections of the Hong Kong-reared, movie director Wayne Wang (of *Chan is Missing* and *Dim Sum* fame):

After his graduation from a Jesuit school, Wang's parents sent him to California. At Foothill College in Los Altos, a white, upper-middle-class suburban community college, Wang was one of ten Chinese students, all foreign students. "I really wanted to become a part of that whole scene so badly. I did everything I could to blend in, to be All-American. And it was very painful!

Chinese are always more reserved, more polite, never say no to anything. Americans are not like that. They are very direct, very aggressive, very assertive. I didn't know how to respond, how to become a part of it." ("Datebook" section, *Sunday San Francisco Examiner and Chronicle*, July 4, 1982, p. 22)

Wang's plight gains greater clarity when we attend to the following description of communicative behavior in Taiwan:

Formosans are reluctant to state what they think they deserve for their efforts or services, they talk as if forced by circumstances to express themselves, they are hesitant in voicing opinions, they apologize before giving speeches in front of others, they underplay emotions of joy or sadness, and, when receiving an invitation, will frequently say "no" first out of politeness, allowing the offerer to insist or force them into acceptance. (Schneider 1985: 277)

As one example of Chinese politeness and face-saving strategies, consider the following rejection letter to a British author by a journal published in the People's Republic of China:

We have read your manuscript with boundless delight. If we were to publish your paper it would be impossible for us to publish any work of a lower standard. And as it is unthinkable that, in the next thousand years we shall see its equal, we are, to our regret, compelled to return your divine composition, and beg you a thousand times to overlook our short sight and timidity. (Sociologists for Women in Society [SWS] Network, 1982)

As another example, consider the scrupulous care in traditional China to modify direct address such as "I" or "you" and substitute instead third person reference such as "humble person" to refer to oneself and "gentleman" or "sir" to refer to the addressee;

as in Japan, a speaker customarily raises the addressee and correspondingly lowers him (or her) self in polite discourse when both are of equal standing. This is part of the knack Chinese – and other Asians – develop for making people feel important. Chester Holcombe (1895: 262), an interpreter and Acting Minister for the United States in China, describes one such encounter. The words may be dated but the spirit persists:

> What is your honorable cognomen?
> The trifling name of your little brother is Wang.
> What is your exalted longevity?
> Very small. Only a miserable seventy years.
> Where is your noble mansion?
> The mud hovel in which I hide is in such or such a place.
> How many precious parcels (sons) have you?
> Only so many stupid little pigs.

In the traditional Chinese cultural context, harmony and cooperation had been key symbols in a communally oriented, heavily populated, agrarian-based society where, for much of its recorded history, social proprieties and familial obligations ranked high. The constant stress on harmony and expressions of appropriate conduct in family and society is reflected in the fact that considerable portions of the 10,000 volumes of the Qing dynasty encyclopedia had been directed to aspects of *li*, glossed variously as 'rites,' 'propriety,' 'decorum,' or 'manners.' Generally speaking, *li* was a body of norms, conventions, and mores which influenced all secular and sacred aspects of social living in traditional China. According to historian Richard Smith:

Testimony to the enduring value of *li* in traditional China may be found in the venerated classic texts *I-li* (*Etiquette and Ritual*), *Chou-li* (*Rites of Chou*), and *Li-chi* (*Record of Ritual*), which together exerted a profound influence on the Chinese elite from the Han period through the Ch'ing. These three works alone provided hundreds of general principles and guidelines, as well as literally thousands of specific prescriptions, for proper conduct in Chinese society. For hundreds of years the Chinese commonly referred to China as "the land of ritual and right behavior" (*li-i chih pang*), equating the values of *li* (禮) and *i* (義) with civilization itself. (1983: 6)

But what is little understood about harmony in Chinese terms is the fact that it has been consistently paired with diversity since

ancient times. Human diversity is accepted as a basic condition of
social life, and the point of harmony is to minimize the conflict
that comes along with diversity. Indeed, the greater the diversity,
the greater the harmony sought and generated. Harmony, in fact,
is a recognition of diversity in unity; diversity is respected or
tolerated so long as actions are aimed toward the broader good.
Participating in *li* or ritual action is the means by which harmony
is articulated, and Confucius is the person most often credited
with envisioning *li*'s potential as a dignifying and integrating force
in human relations.

That *li* is enshrouded by a sense of sacredness is due partly to
the fact that it involved religious rites by China's ancient rulers
and specialists and grew to encompass all forms of conduct and
development that foster interpersonal relations. Significantly, the
character *li* (禮) originally meant 'sacrifice' and is made up of two
parts: the left part of the character means 'a stand to display
offerings to the spirits' and later evolved to mean 'to show'
or 'to display,' whereas the right part of the character means
'sacrificial vessel.' Together, they portray the sense of ceremony
and forms of restraint guiding civilized conduct; one "sacrifices"
for the moment by putting others before one's self in the interest
of pursuing a larger (or later) good, and one "shows" this through
forms of deference. Understood this way, observing *li* is a profoundly communal act and one that brings order and demonstrates cohesion in a society that has traditionally respected the
ceremonies and conventions of rank and relation.

In addition to courtesy and deference, Chinese put great store
on what ethnographer Olga Lang has described as their "moderation displayed . . . in interpreting all rules of behavior" (1946: 53).
These range widely across a complex of communication forms
from styles of dress and modes of talk, to the movements of facial
and body parts, and is further reflected in the development of
a complex of social institutions where balance and moderation
became key operating themes. Whereas any casual observer of
the Chinese in their natural, intimate social contexts can see
immediately that Chinese enjoy talking and talking boisterously
and with great mirth, nonetheless, in both the old and new Chinese
milieus, formal Chinese public manners emphasize modesty,
restraint, and cooperation. Conversely, Chinese frown on aggres-

sive displays; they actively discourage expressions of open competition, overt conflict, and direct confrontation, despite the violence and abuse cutting across all levels of Chinese life (see Lipman and Harrell 1990).

In general, Chinese learn ways of communicating and relating that contrast with American experiences. For one thing, each person is firmly embedded in a network of (largely kin and usually enduring) bonds. From early on, children are taught to feel a connection to others and to constantly nurture and subtly communicate these bonds in face-to-face engagements; they learn to look to and include others in their communications and decisions. In particular, they are expected to develop a capacity to attune their selves and actions with others and to develop acuity in discovering or anticipating the other's wants or moods. Furthermore, they are taught the advantages of cooperation and humility and shown the limits of self-indulgent behavior. In short, children are expected to develop the ability to get along well and smoothly with others; sometimes, parents take harsh physical action to drive the point home. These abilities are expected to sustain them and continue with them into adult life.

At the same time, children also develop a sensitivity to risk and ridicule; they resist attracting attention to themselves or their actions and refrain from imposing on or burdening others. They learn to feel a sense of restraint, that is, to hold back from hurting others or revealing too much of themselves that would allow others to hurt them. They also learn to feel a sense of shame and to avoid blame or damage to face. And, as part of the dominant cultural theme of indirection, children are taught to work around obstacles and issues rather than to take the initiative and confront them. Although the literature on Chinese socialization practices remains sparse, there seems to be some evidence that children learn similar strategies for the conduct of talk at home and at all levels of education as well.

In addition, most Chinese adults have a sense of power balance or imbalance in daily life because of their childhood experiences in power relationships. A series of Thematic Apperception Tests (TAT) and indepth interviews with a number of Chinese men raised in late imperial China leads political scientist Richard Solomon to observe that parental authority is traditionally rein-

forced by the prerogative to initiate talk and to give opinions and
orders:

The giving of opinions, like the giving of food, is an activity where adults,
certain adults, have precedence and take initiative. Children are made to
feel that they are incompetent to develop their own opinions, that they
"don't understand," and lack sufficient experience in society and hence
should rely for guidance on the adults who do have the proper understanding and experience. The communication pattern which the growing
Chinese child learns is thus nonreciprocal. Parents are the ones with the
authority to give, whether the giving concerns food, opinions, or orders;
there is no "giving back" on the child's part; he has to learn to "take in"
what is given to him in proper fashion. (Solomon 1971: 49)

   Moreover, Chinese have been consistently exposed to messages
in various forms that view individual expression, individual
recognition, and individual fulfillment to be of secondary importance. As an example of this phenomenon, one investigator
reports that academic materials and teaching methods in Taiwan
regularly direct the student away from independent action:

This morals training is at times highly specific with stories in reading texts
consciously constructed to elucidate moral rules. For instance, in an
elementary level text book used on Taiwan there is a story of a small
goose who flies away from the rest of the flock (*Kuo-li Pien I Kuan* 1964).
Twice the small goose does this and twice other members of the flock fly
after him to attempt to persuade the small goose to return. The third time
that the small goose departs, however, a hawk spies and seizes him. The
admonitions given by other members of the flock to the small goose
during this story contain injunctions such as, "such wild flying is not
permitted," "you must follow the rules of the group," "being with the
group is most important," and, of course, the tragic ending is designed to
provide confirmation that departing from group rules and norms is highly
undesirable and dangerous. However, stories such as this one are not
simply childhood parables. When the official in charge of compiling these
textbook tales was queried concerning the story of the small goose, he
replied that this parable had been deliberately chosen since the formation
that geese fly in is roughly the same as the Chinese character for people
[*ren* 人]. In class, therefore, the teacher could use this character as a
simple device to bring the story of the small goose into a human context
and thus impress upon the children the importance of proper group
behavior. (Wilson 1981: 123–124)

   Geese flying in formation, just like minnows darting, are frequently invoked as an image of spontaneous, communal harmony.

Socializing children to be responsive to others and to participate with others towards a common goal is captured in the following matter-of-fact response by a mainland Chinese preschool teacher to anthropologist David Wu's query about the practice of herding youngsters in groups to the communal restroom, an open trench: "(A)s a matter of routine, it's good for children to learn to regulate their bodies and attune their rhythms to those of their classmates" (in Tobin, Wu, and Davidson 1989: 105).

By and large, Chinese children are systematically yet subtly steered towards cooperative behavior, whether in play: "One recent American visitor to a Chinese nursery school reports noticing that the blocks seemed awfully heavy for the small children. 'Exactly!' beamed the teachers. 'That fosters mutual help'" (Dollar 1985: 130); or engaged in classroom language learning:

Language teaching... is centered on encouraging children to express that which is socially shared rather than, as in the United States, on that which is individual and personal. Preschool teachers... use the techniques of choral recitation and memorization of stories much more than in the United States, where teachers spend a larger proportion of their time working with children individually, coaching them in how to express their personal thoughts and beliefs. (Tobin, Wu, and Davidson 1989: 191)

American anthropologist Frances Hsu, China born and reared, has commented on these differences in an earlier account:

[A]merican schools foster a desire and a skill for self-expression that is little known in the Chinese schools. Even in nursery schools American children are taught to stand up individually to tell the rest of the class about something they know – perhaps a toy or an outing with parents. When I compare American youngsters with those I have known in China, I cannot help being amazed at the ease and the self-composure of the former when facing a single listener or a sizable audience, as contrasted with the awkwardness and the self-consciousness of Chinese youngsters in similar circumstances... In modern Chinese schools after 1911, public appearance came into vogue. But even then the responsibility usually fell on the shoulders of the selected few, and practically all of the public oratory in trade and high schools was performed by rote, prepared in advance, and corrected by teachers before delivery. (Hsu 1981: 93–94)

Many of these and other factors combine to give a unique cast to Chinese ways of talking. Yet, partly as a result of not recognizing these factors, some Westerners have engaged in speculations about the reasoning processes and personality characteristics of

Chinese. Time and again, investigators have come up with notions about the "Chinese (or East Asian) mind" (see, for example, Moore 1967, Abegg 1952) along with proposals that the grammatical and other linguistic features of Chinese are influential in shaping Chinese cognition (see, most recently, Bloom 1981). Further, the fact that Chinese lean towards allusive, suggestive statements rather than sharp, clear statements has led some to the suggestion that there is something in the Chinese language which prevents concise, clear, and logical presentations. And yet, what must be pointed out about these efforts is that neither cognitive characteristics nor grammatical or other linguistic elements can predict the actual behavior or response of any Chinese interactant on any given occasion.

When Chinese present ideas and information in English, moreover, Westerners have noted that many of their constructions are foreign-sounding, giving rise to various statements about "limping sentences," "fractured syntax," and "drifting words." What is not noted is that these constructions are largely reflective of the fact that the linguistic system of Chinese provides an altogether different way of producing sounds, connecting utterances, and indicating grammatical relationships. For one thing, Chinese is a tonal language with a different phonemic inventory and syllabic structure, which, in turn, gives rise to a variety of accented English where there is the frequent substitution of "r" or "n" for "l," as in "fry" for "fly," and the mispronunciation and misspelling of "gassee" for "gas" or "roase beef" for "roast beef." (I recorded the latter two from a hand-lettered gas station sign "No More Gassee," and a butcher's meat display sign, respectively, in Oakland, California.)

Further, the Chinese have a unique way of sequencing information, connecting ideas, highlighting points, and shifting emphasis; these in turn are partially influenced by fundamental typological differences between Chinese and English (see chapters 2, 3, and 6). For example, Chinese is viewed as a topic-prominent language as compared to a subject-prominent language such as English. It is also distinguished by an aspect system as compared to the tense system of English. Furthermore, it makes no distinction between singular and plural, and the same word can function as noun, verb, or adjective, depending on the context. From the

Western standpoint, however, upon first encountering Chinese ways of speaking, they are often startled into maneuvering through a maze of ideas which appear to be loosened from familiar logic and connected in novel ways.

Yet, the issue goes beyond sound differences and accents or the very real differences in grammar and sentence structure. What both Chinese and Americans do not recognize is that they also have substantially different conceptions of how talk is to be conducted and of communicative strategies in general. For one thing, communication in their respective cultural milieus assumes forms and purposes with utterly different strategies for engagement and strikingly different dimensions, intensity, and emotional charge. For another, they have vastly different cultural beliefs about what should or should not be verbalized, what should be elicited and responded to in interactions, and what is polite or impolite to state directly. As we shall see, Chinese and Americans enter into conversation where they mistakenly assume that the strategies for discourse and interaction are mutually understood and observed. The confusion is compounded in those instances where English is employed. This condition arises because, paradoxically, the use of a supposedly common language code obscures cultural and subcultural differences in patterns of language use, leading Chinese and Americans to evaluate and respond to each other under the misconception that they share similar inferential processes. Taken together, these differences in the strategies and features of talk cause large blind spots that lead to distortion, to the emergence of stereotypical notions such as inscrutability, and to the creation and perpetuation of cultural boundaries.

Theoretical orientation

How can we sharpen our understanding of Chinese communicative behavior in cross-cultural interactions? How can we approach cultural differences in discourse and interaction with enough detail and sophistication to get us beyond apparent differences and clichéd generalizations?

I suggest that recent work in interactional sociolinguistics will help us answer these questions. This work anchors itself on actual taped conversations and seeks insight into the linguistic details and the interactional ends or consequences of talk. It reveals the nuanced and often unnoticed ways in which different discourse strategies and interpretive conventions can distort and confuse encounters between conversationalists who do not share similar social and cultural backgrounds.

More specifically, this work looks into the inner workings of ordinary conversation to develop understanding of its interpretive and interactional achievements. It examines how grammar, culture, and interactive conventions affect conversationalists' competence to make inferences and negotiate intent. It looks beyond individual words, utterances and the things they signify to just how they are used and perceived within the turns and sequences of an exchange – that is, in their links, contexts, and interdependence – and within these turns and sequences, what signalling mechanisms are crucial to the operation, success, or failure of an exchange. Though the focus is on exceedingly subtle matters, it is precisely the details that cause misplaced interpretation.

As background to this method of analysis, we need to under-stand what various researchers have said about talk and conversa-tion in general. In the first place, ethnographers of communication have made it clear that talking takes on different functions in different situations in different cultures. So, in fact, does silence. Participants also have mutual expectations and perceptions about how to conduct and experience talk. They share sociocultural and situational assumptions about the obligations of gender, status, and relationship, the conventions of power, performance, and participation, the nature of the communicative task and how it ought to be achieved and enacted, the various strategies, choices, and options guiding the production and perceptions of talk (Bauman and Sherzer 1974). Participants know that there is a time to speak, a tone of voice to be used, and a moment to pause just as they know the split-second to drop (or raise) their eyes and the right instant to nod, smile, or bow. However, an action that is natural and necessary in one culture may be considered a *faux pas* in another. Anthropologist Edward Hall long ago pointed out in *The Silent Language* (1959) and other books how ingrained cultural habits of space, gaze, posture, and gesture can undermine communications cross-culturally. For instance, a Chinese or Japanese subordinate who sits rigidly and stares fixedly at some point on a superior's neck or over his or her shoulder as a respectful sign might, in American eyes, appear unbecomingly timid. Conversely, American speakers who insist on making eye-to-eye contact might seem brazen, even threatening, to these same Asians.

Apart from this, once talk begins, participants use unawares a whole complex of multisensory procedures involving elusive and ephemeral phenomena. Kinesicists, for example, point out how interactional partners fall into a rhythmic synchrony by subconsciously making constant and delicate adjustments to one another's movements (Condon and Ogsten 1969, Birdwhistell 1970). From a different perspective, research by social psychologists on impression formation has consistently pointed out how readily people use cues to classify and stereotype persons into groups and categories (Giles and Powesland 1975). In socially strained situations, these microfeatures can take on macro-importance and cause alarming consequences.

As an example, let us look at anthropologists Frederick Erickson and Jeffrey Schultz's (1982) work on linguistic mis-evaluations and "gate-keeping" encounters; their work reveals how inadvertent misassessments of the smallest details in face-to-face exchanges can compound and perpetuate social disadvantages. Following kinesicists, they show how interlocutors' speaking and listening behaviors take on an extraordinary coordination; without realizing it, interlocutors develop a rhythmic synchrony and move together almost as if they were participating in a per-fectly choreographed piece. Erickson and Schultz go on to stress that without this synchronization, the rapport in encounters can suffer; a sense of disharmony can amplify to the extent that communicants fall prey to distorted evaluations. The situation worsens when communicants with different backgrounds assume that because they share the same grammar and lexicon, they share the same cues for listening and speaking. That this is not the case is revealed in Erickson and Schultz's frame-by-frame analysis of black student–white counselor interviews in which such barely perceptible asynchronous miscues contribute to an overall sense of interactional dissonance, ultimately sabotaging students' efforts to secure information needed for career advancements.

Conversation analysts, meanwhile, have shown that conversations everywhere are governed by universal principles of interactional ordering, so that participating in a verbal encounter involves more than simply putting one's own ideas into words. Conversing must be viewed as a cooperative activity where speakers must work to gain others' attention and maintain what sociologist Erving Goffman has called "conversational involvement." Talk when seen from this perspective is thus sequentially organized in accordance with local principles, such as those governing changes of speakers at appropriate points in a conversation (Sacks, Jefferson, and Schegloff 1974). Interpretation, moreover, depends on the "contextedness" of actual talk – that is, on the position of utterances in a sequence – and on listener's determination of how what is said in one part of an exchange implicates what has or is about to be said in another (Atkinson and Heritage 1984).

By and large, conversation analysts examine how speaker's and listener's implicit understandings of the intent and content of each other's responses show up internally in subsequent responses; conversationalists' subsequent responses, in turn, display their mutual expectations and agreements about the purpose and direction of the discourse. What's more, their expectations and agreements about its purpose and direction keep evolving and changing as conversation proceeds. Conversations move along on constantly shifting ground: conversationalists keep apace with one another by adapting to each other's shifting perspectives and by interpreting how messages combine to form coherent themes. As talk flows on, participants jointly negotiate and arrive at interpretations of communicative intent; they establish conversational involvement and keep conversations fluent by working together to decipher the spirit and intent of each message.

Other researchers concerned with interpretation, such as philosopher H.P. Grice (1975), argue that all communication is intentional communication and that, in fact, understanding is a matter of interpreting what is intended rather than of decoding the referential meaning of utterances. Furthermore, in these interpretive processes, people always rely on extralinguistic knowledge not overtly expressed in utterances; that is, people make indirect inferences about intent by bringing in cultural and other background knowledge that is not contained in the literal meaning of words.

How exactly do conversationalists infer what each is intending to convey and negotiate implicit agreements about intent? Building on the above and related traditions, anthropologist John Gumperz addresses these issues through his concept of "conversational inference" which he explains as "the situated or context bound process of interpretation by means of which participants in an exchange assess each other's communicative intentions (i.e., the illocutionary force of what is conveyed) and on which they base their responses" (1982a, 1990, 1992). By their very nature, these inferences are not available for direct inquiry. Rather, they are indirectly examined by focusing on the semantic ties between subsequent responses and their coherence to other responses to see how they contribute to the thematic progression of an exchange. In his view, participants' ability to make such situated inferences and negotiate agreements about communicative intent presupposes a shared system of cues or contextualization conventions. Along with nonverbal cues, contextualization conventions function as conversational guideposts, affecting and channeling interpretation; they work closely with the lexical–grammatical systems, along with knowledge about settings and participants and other cultural background information, to activate interpretive frames and prompt tentative assessments about such matters as speaker turn, relative emphasis or formality, topic change and likely outcomes. Like grammatical knowledge, contextualization conventions are deeply rooted and operate without conscious effort; yet, while they are empirically detectable, they are not like the stuff of grammar in that they are not interpretable nor definable in isolation. Instead, they function relationally, co-occurring with a variety of other cues at multiple signalling levels, and range widely from prosodic phenomena to rhetorical structure to code-switching and formulaic expressions. Indeed, they involve the entire array of lexical and nonlexical verbal signs – including pauses, tempo, overlap, synchronicity, tone, word choice, volume shift and other expressive cues – that enable participants to retrieve the presuppositions necessary to assess what a speaker intends to convey at the time of speaking and to understand and maintain conversational involvement.

Gumperz's view is noteworthy because he and his colleagues were able to demonstrate through comparative studies of intra- and interethnic encounters that knowledge of contextualization cues is culturally specific. In particular, they were able to show in great detail how interpretive conflicts emerge interactively among culturally (or subculturally) different speakers (for example, speakers of Filipino, West Indian, East Indian, Black, British or American Englishes) (1982b, with Roberts 1991). Like the Chinese in our study, these different English-speaking populations may draw from the same pool of lexical–grammatical materials yet routinely rely on different contextualization conventions and interpretive practices to achieve their interactive ends. Since these differences are often obscured, the result is an unwitting breakdown of communication: conversational casualties pile up as the signalling details for implicit understandings go wayward. And yet, as Gumperz *et al.* discovered, participants in these cross-cultural exchanges experiencing constant communicative distress rarely identified the linguistic bases of mistaken inferences and misconstrued intentions as sources of their distress. Instead, they consistently erred by misjudging their distress in terms of a speaker's competence or personal characteristics, ultimately vivifying cultural stereotypes, or, worse, perpetuating discriminatory decisions and reinforcing existing socioeconomic divisions.

Anthropologists Penelope Brown and Stephen Levinson's (1987) book on politeness phenomena provides us with basic insight into the interactive principles that govern interpersonal communication. Although they use the term politeness, what they actually refer to are the universal principles of sociability that govern the conduct of conversations. They begin with the view that every society honors specific verbal strategies designed to respect the personal images of others and to minimize potential face-threats; however, the linguistic forms and signs of face-redress are differently realized and standardized due to culturally different interactional requirements. They use pan-cultural parallels in the linguistic details of politeness to argue for three basic super-politeness strategies, each of which is influenced by culturally rooted considerations of relative power, social distance, and rank or degree of imposition. The variety and combinations of these strategies contribute to those differences in interactive style which they call the ethos – i.e., "the general tone of social interactions" – of particular societies or groups.

Brown and Levinson's analysis rests on the assumption that directness is the basic communicative norm – that is, they treat directness as the default in communication. As they admit, this very matter of directness is based on norms that govern communicative conduct in Western European cultures. But what information we have from languages in Asia (see Ide 1989 for Japanese) and Africa (see Albert 1972 for Burundi) reveals that this is by no means universal. In Asia and Africa, the reverse is more often the case: indirection plays a greater role in these cultures. The problem of indirection is perhaps one of the most important reasons for misunderstandings between East and West and forms an important topic in this book.

We must also keep in mind that, for Chinese, politeness rituals in formal terms involve much more than the norms and strategies of social interaction. Indeed, *li* or ritual action, as Confucius visualized it, lies at the very core of person-making; in Confucius' eyes, ritual refines and regulates human dispositions and human conduct. Moreover, in Chinese terms, face goes beyond Brown and Levinson's description of a "public self-image" that is satisfied, preserved, enhanced, or threatened in interactions; rather, face is social capital and can be either "thick" or "thin," weighed, contested, borrowed, given, augmented, diminished, and so on. Face goes deep to the core of a Chinese person's identity and integrity. And, since a Chinese person's identity and integrity are entwined with others', face then becomes "collective property" (King and Bond 1985). For Chinese elders to admonish "Don't lose face for us" exemplifies this thinking.

Combined, these various approaches enable us to penetrate some of the cultural conflicts underlying Chinese and American interactions in a powerful and rigorous way. My aim, therefore, is to wed sociolinguistic analysis with indepth cultural analysis (supplemented with philosophical insights) to illuminate the cultural trappings of talk and uncover the linguistic details of the cultural impasse between Chinese and Americans. To this extent, then, Chinese communicative behavior serves less as a focus of analysis in its own right than as an entrance into a broader understanding of one of the most prominent patterns in Sino-American interactions.

Chapter overview and considerations

In the chapters that follow, I shall examine instances of Chinese
engaged in talk among themselves and with an American, in
English and in Chinese. I shall look at them from a variety of
perspectives and with considerable help from a great many
Chinese and American informants. By so doing, I shall dissect
the multifaceted puzzle of Chinese inscrutability into manageable
pieces so that selected pieces can be examined with greater clarity
and depth in separate chapters.

Very briefly, I approach and analyze the data collected in these
chapters as follows:

I work primarily from a data base of audiotaped conversations
with English-speaking Chinese participating in focused encounters.
(The passage to be examined in chapter 5, an exchange in Chinese
between a Chinese subordinate and his superior, is a notable
exception.) The Chinese conversing on these tapes live and work
in Hong Kong or Taiwan; at least one was born and raised in
China. I also use taped materials of English-speaking Chinese
gathered from archival oral history interviews, broadcast news
interviews, and academic conferences to evaluate the reliability of
my findings.

I begin by examining the audiotapes myself, searching for
recurring patterns, ambiguous points, and potential troublespots.
I rely for insight on my familiarity with a number of Chinese
dialects, coupled with my experiences interacting with Chinese
peoples and informally observing them in interaction with
Westerners in Hong Kong and in the People's Republic of China,
among other places.

I submit the tape recordings either to native Chinese speakers
(chapter 5) or to both Chinese- and English-speaking natives
(chapers 2 and 6) to elicit in detail their intuitions and assumptions about the exchanges. Throughout, I keep in mind that
the speakers on the tapes are interacting persons operating from
specific cultural assumptions. Thus, I make it a point to ask each
informant what these assumptions might consist of and what
significance they hold for these interactions. I also search in informants' remarks for perceived differences between Chinese and
American communicative behavior. I test the reliability of this

interview data against independent observations and published works on Chinese communicative practices.

I want to point out that the chapters analyzing particular conversations use different sets of informants due to constraints upon their time, availability, and expertise. Like the Chinese conversing on the tapes, all the Chinese informants were born and raised in China, Hong Kong, or Taiwan. These informants come from different walks of life. Many Chinese informants were affiliated with universities as employees, faculty, or as students in business or political science; others include civil service employees or small business owners. American informants ranged from business consultants to police dispatchers to university faculty and students.

I also want to stress that during my interviews with informants, the discussion is always oriented toward the cultural ends of interaction rather than toward questions of individual temperament, prejudice, and attitude which members of different cultures may bring to a conversation. Such an orientation is appropriate since we are not concerned with issues of individual motivation but rather with systematic cultural differences in interpretation that develop from the dialogue itself.

Working from actual taped exchanges and indepth interviews with both Chinese and Americans allows me to avoid the error of mistaking native speakers' ideological accounts about communicative behavior from behavior they actually produce. Likewise, in the case of Chinese, it eliminates another wrinkle since they can unwittingly accept the stereotypes imposed on them or, conversely, may advantageously manipulate them. In addition, Americans may hold conflicting images of the Chinese, as newspaperman Harold Isaacs (1958) reports from his interviews; evidently, Americans hold several stereotypes which they can refer to depending on the occasion.

Our argument enables each chapter to expand and develop the one before; each chapter uses a slightly different approach to understand Chinese communicative behavior. Chapter 2 sets up the discussion for the next three chapters whereas chapter 6 puts the variety of cultural obstacles examined in the earlier chapters into interactive perspective.

In chapter 2, I analyze a taped interchange among English-speaking, Hong Kong Chinese middle managers and show how significant features of their discourse differ, point after point, from standard American discourse practices. I show, in particular, how Westerners find the logical form and explanatory value of their responses to be inappropriate. I next discuss Chinese philological and philosophical insights to suggest that many of these differences can be traced to a specifically Chinese sense of causality and order informing their ways of discourse and interaction.

In chapter 3, I turn to the linguistics literature on Chinese to seek other avenues of construing and analyzing the same data examined in chapter 2. I discover important parallels and links across linguistic levels. In addition, I observe that Chinese have an altogether different way of organizing and linking their ideas in an overall framework. I suggest that these differences are influenced by fundamental typological differences between Chinese and English. I suggest, moreover, that these differences help explain why Americans so often fail to penetrate and identify Chinese points of view effectively.

In chapter 4, I shift our focus from the routine to the ideal by taking a broad-gauged look at indirection in Chinese rhetoric and examining how its evocative and participatory import conveys classical Chinese ideals. I attend, in particular, to these ideals' social and cosmic resonances in Chinese language, thought, and literary forms, with special emphasis on traditional Chinese poetry and on Confucius' thinking regarding the centrality of communication (via speech, ritual, and the metaphor of music) in the development of one's humanity. There is a lot of ground to cover; consequently, this chapter is longer than others.

In chapter 5, I return to everyday discourse to elaborate on the communicative means by which a speaker signals status and power differences. I analyze a natural audiotaped interchange between a Chinese male subordinate and his immediate superior to demonstrate Chinese understandings and concerns about face and form and the ritual requirements of social deference. At the same time, I show how the evocative–participatory thrust described for traditional Chinese poetry and literature is generalizable to ordinary talk.

Chapter 6 makes explicit how unrecognized cultural differences in communicative strategies have immediate and far-ranging effects. Here I take two nearly identical instances of face-to-face encounters between Hong Kong Chinese police officers and an American. I show how the cross-cultural encounters are marked throughout by significant distortions and misjudgments which in turn are fueled by strikingly different cultural ideals and strategies of interaction. At the same time, I trace how Western perceptions of Chinese inscrutability can become animated and affirmed.

Chapter 7 pulls together the diverse threads discussed in preceding chapters that contribute to American perceptions of Chinese inscrutability and ends with a brief statement about inscrutability's vigor.

All chapters except chapter 4 emphasize what I will call, for convenience, the "because...so..." construction, which appears frequently in Chinese taped responses. Examining this Chinese construction proves enlightening, as it not only explains some critical instances of confusion and stylistic differences between Chinese and English but also helps reconstruct their speakers' culturally divergent interactional goals. The "because...so..." construction in fact represents the typologically distinctive topic-comment construction, a grammatical feature that Chinese shares with most of its close Asian neighbors. As grammatical and lexical stimuli, or, "contextualization cues" in John Gumperz's terminology, "because" and "so" function in tandem with the system of culturally specific interactive signs and conventions which often complicates and distorts interactions between Chinese and Americans.

There are a few matters to be disposed of before we can proceed. Clearly, the Chinese are a highly diverse group with a great deal of geographical, class, and dialectal variability and regional stereotyping as well (see, for the latter, Eberhard 1965 and Moser 1985). This diversity, when coupled with the different political ideologies and rapid economic and social changes which many Chinese populations are currently undergoing, makes it difficult to generalize about Chinese communicative behavior. Nonetheless, these Chinese populations share characteristics of discourse and interaction which make them different from non-Chinese. This unifying set of characteristics arises in part from a common literary tradition, in which texts on rites and etiquette play an important role, and a common underlying linguistic system. In regards to the latter, linguist Charles Li (1984: 307) has stated that all members of the Chinese language family are distinguished by their "isolating status" in that there is "no inflection," "no morphological markers or processes denoting number, gender, person, tense, grammatical role or parts of speech," and "no concordance between parts of a constituent." These conditions support my presumption that we are dealing with conventions that form a homogeneous entity.

Even so, I have deliberately construed the focal groups narrowly, in large part confining the inquiry to the speech of Chinese and Americans engaged in formal encounters. This ensures us settings where participants give serious care to their speech. In using the word "formal," I am referring to what might be more technically described as an increase in the structure and convention of discourse and situation (Irvine 1979). This shifts our discussion towards positional and public expression representing a consensus of shared cultural knowledge rather than towards aspects of private identities.

Definitions apart, I acknowledge that a wide variety of communicative styles exist in any one society, to say nothing of the different styles representing regional, class, age, and sex groupings. While taking this into account, I further acknowledge that Chinese styles of discourse are constantly undergoing various changes, partly as a result of internal forces among Chinese populations, partly in response to repeated contacts with the West and other societies, and in the case of English-speaking Chinese, partly as a result of their different exposure to and experience in Western-oriented settings. To complicate matters even further, all these styles co-exist; an able Chinese can freely switch from one to the other depending on situation and context. (There is also the situation where, sometimes, due to cultural lag or as a response to conditions of ethnicity, Chinese outside of China may show more traditional Chinese characteristics. Other times, as in the case of hyphenated Chinese, such as Chinese-Americans, some are still importantly American but deeply Chinese. American newswoman Connie Chung, for instance, admits: "I think I am very American but also extraordinarily Chinese. I *think* Chinese..." [*US News and World Report*, April 2, 1984, p. 47].) Nonetheless, I submit that when Chinese try to speak formally in English or when

Chinese and Americans face each other in serious talk or public interaction, a particular style emerges that often distinguishes one from the other.

I emphasize Chinese perceptions and experiences in this book because far less information is available for their part. I have two other pertinent reasons for doing this. First, I feel it important to ask what non-native speakers experience in using a second language. As speakers of a second language, Chinese are more sensitive about how it contrasts with their native language. Of course, second language experiences do not always harden into practical knowledge; Chinese can see the differences and explain them, but to perform well as a fluent bicultural is a different matter. On the other hand, Chinese may not be fully aware of fundamental differences, having only a hazy, casual, uncritical acceptance of surface similarities or having fixed their attention solely on the sentence level. Both situations are represented in the chapters to follow.

Second, Chinese discussants' comparisons and critiques reveal their strong views about American communicative behavior. Chinese read into this foreign discourse norm their own philosophical and social views about discourse. Although often grounded in misunderstandings, their interpretations are illuminating. In addition, our study in reverse lets us uncover the values and assumptions upon which American communicative strategies depend, and, further, lets Americans see themselves as others see them.

I have chosen to leave the Chinese speakers' words in their original state, first to retain the flavor and vividness of Chinese discourse and, second to maintain a faithful transcription. Since this procedure leads to occasional awkwardness and misinterpretation, I have added bracketed matter for clarification. In presenting the linguistic material for analysis, I abide by conventional guidelines used in linguistics: (1) I follow the Pinyin system of romanization for Chinese words. (Other systems of romanization used are left as the original authors present them.) Depending on the context, the English gloss appears directly under the Chinese word, or it is enclosed within single quotation marks beside the Chinese word. (2) Empty parenthesis ( ) in numbered sets or interview statements indicate that the word or phrase proved

unintelligible during the transcription process; pauses and un-
finished statements by informants are indicated by two and three
consecutive dots, respectively.

Throughout our discussion, the People's Republic of China will
be referred to as China, and the Republic of China will be referred
to as Taiwan. Unless otherwise identified, "Chinese" refers to
what I consider to be key cultural symbols and expressions shared
by members of diverse Chinese populations. "English-speaking
Chinese" primarily refers to those Chinese whose mother tongue
is not English. In this regard, we should also note that some
Chinese who speak a heavily accented English are able to use and
understand it like a native English speaker. Others who speak
English fluently like a native may still retain Chinese habits of
thought and action and fall back on these habits in situations of
distress or when lengthy discussion or persuasion is required. The
term "Westerner" refers to those educated Americans (or Anglos)
from mainstream backgrounds. (Sometimes, I switch freely between "Westerner" and "American"; I am actually referring
to English-speaking natives of European ancestry.) With the
exception of *Analects* 2/14, 6/30, and 13/23, reference to the
Confucian *Analects* draws from D. C. Lau's (1979) translation.
The Latin word *Analects* means "collection" and consists primarily of (remembered) conversations between Confucius and his
followers. In discussing Confucius' thoughts, I borrow key words
and ideas from Hall and Ames' (1987) argument and mix them
with others' explanation and my own understanding. In particular, I have appropriated their use of the terms "quality person,"
"ritual action" and "participatory ritual order" as they stress
nicely the fact that ritual was not facade but foundation for
human(e) engagement and spiritual development in the relationally based, person-making task envisioned by Confucius.

Finally, at a number of points along the way, I shall briefly
refer to a few pan-Asian features insofar as they relate to the
material under discussion. This excursion is necessary, I believe,
because a number of East Asian and Southeast Asian societies
employ similar strategies and features of talk. These features
sometimes parallel the typological features of language which
divide this area of the world from the Indo-European family and
give rise to the oft-stated East–West dichotomy. While much is

yet to be discovered, overt similarities in communicative strategies across East Asian and Southeast Asian cultures partly account for Americans' similar predicaments when dealing with members of these different societies. (The reverse is also true: many Asians find themselves in similar predicaments when dealing with Americans and other English-speaking natives.) In the pages that follow, I shall only make brief statements about these features.

While examining the data, we should keep in mind that the variables in any cross-cultural interaction are so complex that it will never be possible to diagnose all the points that can fail. Moreover, differences in linguistic and cultural backgrounds cannot explain away every conflict in Sino-American interactions. Nevertheless, our approach can take what some Americans see as strange or inscrutable in the Chinese way of doing things and give it a brand new twist which will perhaps make Chinese people more scrutable for Western readers and vice versa.

Plumbing the depths of Chinese inscrutability is no easy task but we can at least find the thread to unravel a part of its mystery. We turn now to this task.

2

Deceptive cause

What links the missionary generation of China sojourners to the recent crop of eager, China-bound entrepreneurs is their profound sense of disorientation when engaged in conversations with Chinese. Their disorientation has led to some interesting rhetoric and to recurring Western claims about the peculiarities of the Chinese mind. Hence the following:

> There are few things more amusing, and at the same time more exasperating, to a European than the utter confusion of thought which characterizes the Chinese as a race... There seems to be a looseness of reasoning, a want of consecutiveness, in the mental process of the Chinese which argues for an internal defect in their constitution. (Ball 1903: 166, citing Balfour, n.d.)

The passage is old but its contents wear well. Despite the intervening decades, the current literature on Sino-American commercial negotiations raises similar concerns, albeit more vaguely stated. Thus, we see that a number of American companies with extensive trading experience with China continue to complain that Chinese are "indirect and like to ramble" (DePauw 1981: 52).

In this chapter, I use taped conversations to identify some inconsistencies in the surface phenomena and underlying presuppositions of talk that may go unrecognized and so jeopardize understanding between Chinese and Americans. Although my data encompass a variety of formal speech encounters, I focus primarily on a role play of a business meeting among English-speaking, Hong Kong-based Chinese managers. These contact settings are essentially nonantagonistic; I presume therefore that the participants share a mutual interest in achieving and

sustaining cooperation. Since most are produced spontaneously
and naturally in the course of exchanging ideas about other matters, these contact settings may also be freer of extralinguistic
concerns such as the assymmetry of relative power and cultural
dominance which can play a determining role in many interethnic
interactions. This procedure enables us to throw Chinese cultural
ideals and strategies into sharper relief.

In general, the total configuration of the Chinese responses in
the following conversational exchanges reveals a distinct tendency
in the production and management of discourse. In most cases,
the Chinese discourse patterns seem to be the inverse of English
discourse conventions in that definitive summary statements of
main arguments are delayed until the end. Thus, as we shall see,
"because" and "so" are used, respectively, in Chinese discourse
to initiate the discussion and mark the transition to the definitive
summary statements.

The first example comes from a recorded discussion of a group
of Chinese who manage the various units of a major Hong Kong
business corporation. The chairman of the meeting is Chinese.
They are discussing the qualities desired in a good salesman. The
discussion is capitalized, summary statements are italicized.

(1) CHAIRMAN   Oscar, anything else to add? Your line of business is,
                again, quite different from what PK and Tony have.
                And, in your line of business, I presume market infor-
                mation will be quite important.
     OSCAR   Yes. What have been mentioned previously by the three
                gentlemen, I think, they are quite sufficient to cover all
                the basic requirement of a salesman.
                My business is textile. The salesman is . . . the quality
                of the salesman, need something different. BECAUSE
                THE VOLUME OF MAKING A SALES IS ABOUT, AT LEAST
                TO OVER TEN THOUSAND US DOLLARS, SOMETIMES. SO
                THAT IS THE PROBLEM. THAT IS, WHENEVER ANYBODY
                WHO MAKES A DECISION TO BUY SUCH . . WILLING TO
                PAY SUCH AMOUNT, WE'LL MAKE SURE THEIR FINANCIAL
                AID IS STRONG AND, THEN, SUCH . . . SOMETIMES THE
                MARKET MAY SUDDENLY DROP IN TEXTILE. MAYBE
                WE'RE WILLING TO BUY ONE MONTH AGO, BUT MAY NOT
                BE BUYING . . WANT TO BUY . . THINGS LIKE THAT. *So,
                the, so, for a salesman, always have to understand
                about the financial situation and things like that.*

The second example comes from an audiotaped oral history interview with a Chinese gentleman in his seventies who had resided in the United States for more than forty years. The interview appears in the archival records of the University of California's Bancroft Library.

(2) AMERICAN Do you have any opinions about intermarriage or inter-racial dating and marriage?

    CHINESE Ah, well, this is very hard to say. BECAUSE TO THE CHINESE, IF YOU WANT TO KEEP IT TO THE CHINESE CULTURE ... I AM IN FAVOR OF THE CHINESE MARRIED TO THE CHINESE. BUT, ON THE OTHER HAND, TO THE INDIVIDUAL, FOR THE ONE THAT YOU LOVE, IT DOESN'T MAKE ANY DIFFERENCE. AH, BECAUSE IF YOU FIND A CHINESE WIFE, AND IF SHE DOESN'T LOVE EACH OTHER, WELL, IT'S NOT GOING TO BE A HAPPY FAMILY. SO THE INTERMARRIAGE WILL COME IN, AH, MUCH BETTER. _So, it depends on which point._

The third example comes from a role play by a young business student born and raised in Hong Kong and educated in secondary schools there. Upon my request, he gave two presentations, one in Cantonese and one in English. (The English version is given below. However, I shall have occasion to refer to his presentations in the next chapter.) His task was to initiate a proposal to his superior that would revamp the antiquated student registration system at a place called Klum gym:

(3) CHINESE Mr. Wang, lately, a lot of students are complaining about the registration system at Klum gym. And, BECAUSE THEY THINK IT'S A WASTE OF TIME, AND, WELL, BECAUSE THEY HAVE TO WAIT IN LINE TO GET INTO THE GYM TO REGISTER. AND, THEN, AS SOON AS THEY GET IN, THEY HAVE TO LOOK FOR THE COURSES THAT THEY WANT TO ENROLL. WELL, THEY HAVE TO WAIT IN LINE AND ... WELL, BY THE TIME THEY GET TO THE FRONT [OF THE LINE], PROBABLY THE COURSE CLOSED, SO THEY MIGHT GO THE OTHER LINE TO LOOK FOR ANOTHER COURSE. AND, IT'S JUST A WASTE OF TIME. AND, IT'S REALLY MESSY. MAKE THE GYM AND EVERYBODY RUNNING AROUND. AND, REALLY, EVERYBODY SEEMS TO BE VERY WORRIED ABOUT TAKING [BEING ABLE TO SIGN UP FOR] THEIR COURSES. IN ADDITION, ALSO THE WORKERS. BEFORE, THEY HAVE

TO PLAN THE WHOLE THING FOR THE REGISTRATION. WELL, OF COURSE, THEY NEED A LOT OF WORKERS TO ACCOMPLISH THIS JOB. AND, ALSO, THEY NEED TO HAVE A LOT OF TRAINING. AND, [THERE'S] LOTS OF WORK THAT NEEDS TO BE DONE. AND, WELL, IT'LL BE VERY EASY TO MAKE MISTAKES, TOO. *So, I was thinking, if possible, maybe we can think of other alternatives. Like, maybe we can use a computer to replace manwork. Because a computer would be more accurate and would be more faster and convenient. Well, so maybe, I think, if possible, the university would go purchase some computers for the registration staff. I hope this is going to work. I think that's all I have to say. Mr. Wang, I hope you can think about my idea, and, if you like it, maybe I can help you to organize this job. I hope this is going to work out.*

Although illustrations can be multiplied from other taped inter-changes involving native Chinese speakers, these examples suggest that a systematic pattern in the organization and presentation of information exists. Specifically, Chinese seem to prefer to steadily unravel and build up information before arriving at the important message.

These remarks set the scene for the following, more detailed analysis of data collected from a simulated budget meeting. The participants are primarily Cantonese-speaking middle managers who are local Hong Kong people employed by British-owned, Hong Kong-based companies. As middle managers who work under senior managers – nearly all of whom are native English speakers – they are expected to conduct their business transactions and meetings in English. To improve their English, these middle managers are enrolled in a British-run, upper intermediate/advanced Business English course. In the exercise we are about to discuss, they were each given a card listing who they were to play and the basic position they were to argue. Since they are in reality working managers, I would argue that the exercise was closer to a re-creation of their own experiences in such meetings than a normal role play. (There is, of course, the possibility that the circum-stances of a role play and the fact that they were not using their own materials may influence how these middle managers structure their arguments. Nonetheless, as managers who do have to use English at work and who have encountered similar budget meetings there, it is more than likely they will draw on habitual rhetorical strategies to present their arguments, despite their role playing. My premise that they will rely on these habitual strategies is supported by spontaneous talk collected elsewhere and presented below.)

There were five participants, one of whom chaired the meeting, and all of whom, for the unique purposes of the simulated budget meeting, adopted the roles of Westerners. The chairman opened the meeting by announcing that there was an excess sum of one hundred and eighty thousand pounds in the budget and asked how it should be distributed. Several of the participants, for various reasons, requested a portion of the fund for their unit.

There is a remarkable coincidence in the presentation of requests. Each began by stating the reasons or justifications for his request; each established the situational framework for the request first. In more prosaic terms, the listener is given a build-up before the punchline is delivered. The following example comes from the tape.

(4)   THETA   One thing I would like to ask. BECAUSE MOST OF OUR RAW MATERIALS ARE COMING FROM JAPAN AND ( ) THIS YEAR IS GOING UP AND UP AND, UH, IT'S NOT REALLY, I THINK, AN INCREASE IN PRICE, BUT, UH, WE LOSE A LOT IN EXCHANGE RATE. AND, SECONDLY, I UNDERSTAND WE'VE SPENT A LOT OF MONEY IN TV ADS LAST YEAR. _So,_ *in that case, I would like to suggest here: chop half of the budget in TV ads and spend a little money on Mad magazine.*

Note that, as in examples (1), (2) and (3), the subordinate marker "because" initiates the discussion while the conjunction "so" signifies the transition to the main information. Between the two markers are several independent clauses, connected by the conjunction "and," which itemize the reasons. The example presents a series of conjoined sentences that provide the context for evaluating the significant information to follow. A similar rhetorical structure is represented in the next two examples. Note that in examples (5) and (6), "as (you know)" seems to take the place of "because." Note also that this rhetorical pattern is followed by a similar construction in each of those speaker's responses. (I have marked off this phenomenon visually by putting them into separate paragraphs.)

(5) CHAIRMAN   I would like to have your opinion on how we should
                utilize the extra amount of one hundred eighty thou-
                sand pounds to improve ... (Beta's answer follows
                another person's presentation).

     BETA   AS YOU KNOW, I HAVE SPENT FIVE HUNDRED AND
                SEVENTY THOUSAND POUNDS LAST YEAR TO .. ON THE
                MACHINERY AND COMPONENTS. AND, AH, IF, AH, IF
                MR., AH, LINCOLN WOULD LIKE TO INCREASE THE, AH,
                PRODUCTION IN AH, THROUGH THE COMING YEAR, I
                THINK WE HAVE TO MAKE OUR BUDGET TEN PERCENT ON
                TOP OF THE AMOUNT FIVE HUNDRED AND SEVENTY
                THOUSAND POUNDS BECAUSE THERE WILL BE A TEN
                PERCENT ON UH INCREASE IN PRICE ON AVERAGE. AND,
                UH, *in other words, I need another sixty thousand
                pounds to buy the same material and quality.*
                And, AS YOU KNOW, WHENEVER THERE'S A
                SHORTAGE OF COMPONENTS ON THE ( ) AMOUNT
                OF TIME, AND, AH, ALTHOUGH WE HAVE ARRANGED
                DELIVERY OF NORMAL SUPPLIES FOR FOR FOR AT LEAST
                SIX MONTHS, BUT WE STILL NEED AH AN EXTRA MONEY
                TO BUY AH THE REPLACEMENT, WHICH COST US FIVE
                HUNDRED MORE. *So, in other words, I need at least six
                hundred thousand, sorry, six hundred thousand pounds
                for an extra uh extra money for the for the new ah
                budget for for our component.*

(6) CHAIRMAN   Uh, Mr. Lincoln, do you think the new machinery that
                you just mentioned that will cost us sixty thousand
                pounds will cater for the the ( ) the new model, that
                is, the portable TV set that was just mentioned by Mr.
                Jeffrey?

     ALPHA   I think this new machine will certainly reduce the pro-
                duction cost. And uh, AS WE HAVE AN EXTRA
                BUDGET OF ABOUT ONE HUNDRED EIGHTY THOUSAND
                POUNDS STERLING AND WE JUST SPENT ABOUT ONE
                THIRD OF THE TOTAL AMOUNT BUYING THIS NEW
                MACHINE AND AS THE SALES OF IT INCREASING THE
                PRODUCTION OF HOURS, *therefore, I think it is very
                worthwhile at minimal to invest in this new machine by
                buying a sixty thousand pounds sterling new machine.*
                I have also one thing to say. BECAUSE THE
                PERSONNEL MANAGER, HE MENTIONED A FEW DAYS
                AGO THAT, UH, THERE ARE SOME DIFFICULTIES IN THE
                EQUIPPING MORE NEW WORKERS AND ASK THE EXISTING
                WORKERS TO WORK OVERTIME BY PAYING THEM SOME

> EXTRA MONEY, *therefore,* *I* *think* *that* *we* *have*
> *no alternative but to buy a new machine or otherwise*
> *incur a lot of cost by using the existing one.*

What is striking about the data is the similarity in the presentations, the smoothness of the interactions, and the evident ease of comprehension among the participants. Apparently, the Chinese participants on the tape treated the discussion as a natural way of proceeding; not only did they appear to follow the same discourse principles, they also seemed to have no problem in understanding and responding to each other's strategies and signals. It is, therefore, unlikely that these patterns are simply chance occurrences or idiosyncratic examples.

Nevertheless, Americans asked to listen to the tape experienced many difficulties. A chief distress sprang from their inability to separate supporting information from a central idea. Adding to their confusion was a lack of understanding of how the important information was highlighted. In fact, their appreciation of the significance of any one feature proved elusive. Here are some sample evaluations:

I can understand his point, but I don't know how he got there.

I found it hard to listen to this because I didn't have an overall view. I didn't know exactly what he was saying until the end.

The organization of thoughts is messy. It's difficult to pull out the major ideas.

That Americans did not understand what the Chinese were arguing for is not the issue. On the contrary, they eventually caught the main drift of each argument. But the point is just *that.* To Americans, it seemed as though the Chinese were simply drifting. They found the organization of ideas messy and vital information buried in that mess. Here is one illuminating response: "In English, it's statement and explanation or statement and context, whereas in Chinese, there is context and at the end comes statement. That's not good." Having also listened to the tape containing example (1), he used it to point out that:

There's basically one message to all of this, which is, the salesman in certain industries must also know the financial situation. However, the way this message comes at us is that, first of all, he goes into a fairly lengthy explanation of the things that affect the trade – they're seasonal, and someone who wanted to buy, say, six months ago may not want to buy something now, and the price fluctuations, and go through all of that. The real thesis to this whole comment, the one sentence that labels it, that makes it easy to understand and digest, is at the very end; so, "a good salesman must be aware of the financial situation."

and, continuing with his explanation, concluded that it was not "titled fairly clearly and cleanly in the beginning":

From an efficiency of communication standpoint, he needs to get that statement up to the beginning: "A good salesman also needs to be aware of the financial situation. For example, in *my* industry . . ." And, then, he probably could cut down the description of the various odds and ends, the technical material that filled up the first half of this . . .

Essentially, what he is saying is that the opening lines of the Chinese discourse did not provide a thesis or preview statement which would have oriented a listener to the overall direction of the discourse. The other Americans agreed, adding that, from their sense of organization and style, a clear and concise overview statement would have made the Chinese presentations "more precise," "more dramatic," and "more eloquent." As it was, in their view, the clarity, conciseness, and forcefulness of the main points were obscured. Worst of all, the lack of precision and the failure to address the point led to suspicions that the Chinese speakers were beating around the bush.

A closer look at the data brought out other factors which confounded Americans. For instance, sentence connectives, which play an essential role in guiding the listener's journey through the discourse, had been used in ways which are somewhat different from their usual associations in English. Specifically, the listeners were not fully aware of the fact that the Chinese often employed single word items such as "because," "as," and "so" to replace whole clause connectives commonly used in English, such as "in light of this," "to begin with," or "in conclusion." It seems, moreover, that the single word items may have Chinese antecedents. "Because" and "so," in fact, form a connective pair – notably, "*yinwei* 因為 . . . *suoyi* 所以 . . ." – and constitute one of a number of fixed constructions in Chinese; they have specific clausal positions and serve to signal the relationship between clauses.

To illustrate, let us take example (6). An English speaker would normally associate the second "as" in the sixth line with the "therefore" in the seventh line. However, this is not the case here. The "therefore" is conceptually linked to the entire paragraph, starting with the first "as" in the second line. The unusual position of the connectives undermines Americans' ability to keep statements related or separated. Confusion and ambiguity result because the conceptual linkage between statements cannot be predicted as it is ordinarily when "as" and "therefore" are in immediate proximity.

Another complication for Americans turns on prosody. As reported, the American informants had difficulty with the way Chinese set the main point apart for special emphasis. More specifically, they could not locate signs of any significant shift in prosody taking place. But in fact a shift of pitch level has already begun to show up in the final portion of the discourse. The conjunction "so" is revealing in this respect because it intersects with the shift to a slightly lower pitch register in some examples.

If we seek to understand prosody's role here, we could give two plausible explanations. The first would be a commonsensical one: a lowered pitch or volume towards the end of a thought may be a common technique for approaching the conclusion of one's speech. However, in looking at previous discussions of low pitch in Chinese, I note that this feature may be a highly conventionalized technique used to call attention to matters of serious concern. The eminent linguist Y. R. Chao (1968: 43), for example, reports that the significance of low pitch in Chinese sentences indicates seriousness or great feeling. This feature has been remarked on elsewhere in less detail. For instance, one observer of Chinese negotiating practices has stated that "the Chinese often express their serious interest with a soft expression" (Pye 1992: 71, citing Kawasakiya [1979: 15]). As another instance of the significance of low pitch or volume, Sinologist Kenneth DeWoskin (1982: 161) points out that in ancient times, Chinese ritual and musical performance ideals evolved towards lesser volume and non-sounds altogether; minimalization was at a premium.

Chao's, Kawasakiya's, and DeWoskin's observations are significant for this inquiry, particularly when we compare examples (5) and (6) with example (4). It is obvious from their content – and from the group laughter on the tape – that the discussant in example (4) had been speaking in jest. More important, I could detect no lowering of pitch in example (4) such as is apparent in examples (5) and (6). Seen in this light, a lowered pitch or volume at the key information point is culturally significant. The American misperception stems from a failure to appreciate that the prosody of Chinese discourse runs opposite to an American preference to use high pitch and loudness to indicate emphasis or comparison.

More questions directed to Americans provoked comments that Chinese tend to minimize confrontation in formal encounters. Recall, for instance, their remarks about the indirection of Chinese discourse style. When asked to appraise the effectiveness of the presentations, they said that the Chinese arguments lacked sufficient aggressive and persuasive power. Discussing the construction of the discourse, they argued that the absence of a preview statement and the mere item-by-item listing of justifications blocked development of a "positive tone" in the Chinese arguments and, by inference, projected a "passive" image. As a matter of fact, the listeners sensed a reluctance on the part of the Chinese to have to make a request, that they had to slide inevitably into it as a result of a convergence of forces. Likewise, they pointed out that, instead of stating their propositions somewhere in the beginning and then proceeding to build their case, the Chinese first established a shared context within which to judge their requests. Only after carefully prefacing the request with an avalanche of relevant details, as if to nullify any opposition, did Chinese present their requests. On the whole, the requests seemed to Western respondents to be incongruously cloaked as expressions of a regretted inability: "Nobody seems to be arguing positively for the money, 'I think it's a good idea if we do X for reasons 1, 2, and 3.' [The Chinese style] seems to be a less positive argument, addressing themselves as to why they wouldn't need the money *except* for 1, 2, and 3."

Correspondences between linguistic behavior and social evaluation (Giles and Powesland 1975) led some Americans to suggest that the Chinese were employing a deference tactic so as to avoid pressing their claim too forcefully upon another. The framework provided by Brown and Levinson (1987) would lead one to conclude that the user of such a discourse strategy was minimizing his particular imposition by operating on the basis of "negative politeness."

What has been said so far coincides with Western writings on Chinese ethos. As a matter of fact, it obliquely lends support to Western impressions that Chinese prize harmony in social relationships. The question arises: is the deferential display genuine, or simply the consequence of American perceptions of an unfamiliar discourse style? If genuine, what other Chinese attitudes and aims come into play? And how do they relate to the features noted above?

Preliminary inquiries with several native Chinese speakers asked to enact a similar budget meeting proved revealing. Significantly, they all began by providing the rationale behind their requests, a procedure exactly identical to that of the Chinese in the budget request meeting. Over and over, their responses reflected a conscious choice to state their request or main point last, after first articulating the reasons for it. When pressed further about the reasons for this, they justified their actions by outlining the kinds of consequences that can develop when the opening line of the discourse indicates their position. One person flatly stated that he would not listen beyond the first sentence as he already would have heard what was wanted; in other words, the ability to retain the listener's attention would have been placed in jeopardy. Two other individuals maintained that it would be rude: it would sound as though the person was demanding something; it would also make the person seem immodest, pushy, and inconsiderate for wanting things. Another person elaborated on this issue: giving an impression that you were demanding something, you would lose face for acting aggressively. He added that the use of such a discourse strategy might suggest that you were not considering the other members of the group and, moreover, that you would be hurting people by claiming something for yourself. Accordingly, it borders on naked self-interest and makes one appear self-serving. Furthermore, he observed that if you started out with a statement that strongly hinted at a request for something, despite your eventual elaboration of the rationale behind it, and, furthermore, if the chairman did not grant it, you would lose the respect of the others. One person claimed that it would be a foolhardy approach to hint about or mention your desires at the outset, because you are not aware of what the chairman is prepared to give you and what the others are planning to ask. In such a situation, it is considered a smart strategy if you carefully delineate the justifications that will naturally lead to your request.

Generalizing from their responses then, Chinese attempt to refrain from making prestige or "face"-damaging statements when there might be an open recognition by others that the request may not be granted. Also, Chinese resist any appearance of presumptuousness, overeagerness, and selfishness. By clarifying the circumstances behind a request, they avoid appearing rigid; they also avoid disagreements about the justness of their request. Altogether, their responses and the data suggest that Chinese and Westerners hold significantly divergent assumptions about the appropriate linguistic behavior for a given communicative task; different ways of structuring information receive different valuation in English-speaking and Chinese-speaking cultures. Viewed callously, Chinese discourse appears imprecise, unwieldy and downright inept. Seen charitably, it emphasizes cooperation, prudence and clear-headed caution.

To give the Chinese responses their full due, however, we would also need to reflect more deeply on a Chinese social order that contrasts with an American counterpart in which persons are regarded as more atomistic or autonomous. In the Chinese view, persons are defined by their links and obligations to others – it is a world that coheres through human bonds – and these links are constantly nurtured and communicated, sometimes in ways too subtle for Americans to appreciate.

A good way to look into this world would be to start with Chinese notions of causality and order and then consider Chinese views of deference and harmony. Once this becomes clear, we can go on to clarify why Americans perceive an oblique thrust, subdued stance, reluctance, passivity, and not-so-positive tone in Chinese discourse. We must, then, return to the because . . . so . . . construction mentioned earlier.

The notion of causality that attends the Chinese because . . . so . . . construction is importantly different from English usage and intent. In English, causality identifies a specific, dominant factor – agency. By contrast, Chinese emphasize surrounding circum-

stances and contingent conditions and accommodation to them.
In other words, the former is concerned with establishing an
isolatable cause for a given event while the latter attempts to take
into account a field of conditions that sponsor a given event.
The differences will become clearer if we take an excursion into
Chinese etymology.

Recall that in modern Chinese, "because" is generally translated as *yinwei* 因為 and "so" is translated as *suoyi* 所以 , and
both appear in the construction "because...so..." (*yinwei...
suoyi...*) as an established convention. *Yin* is glossed in the Han
dynasty *Shuowen* lexicon as *jiu* 就 or 'to accommodate,' 'to adapt.'
Yin, moreover, is a concept that philosophers associate with the
writings of the classical thinker Shen Dao, who lived about two
centuries after Confucius (see Thompson, n.d.). In Shen Dao's
writings, *yin* is defined specifically as "accommodation."

Taking into account classical meanings for each element in this
modern construction, we might describe it as follows:

yinwei: 'accommodating' or taking into account those contingent
            conditions which are 'for the sake of' or are productive of a
            particular result
suoyi: 'thereby' a particular 'place' or 'position' is configured as a
            center of these *yin* conditions

Simply put, there is a field of contingent conditions that must
be taken into account in explaining whatever emerges as the
product of the construction. The *yinwei* may be said to establish a
range or field of conditions which form the context out of which
the "so" part of the discussion emerges. The *yinwei...suoyi...*
construction suggests a peculiarly Chinese sense of causality in
which a full range of conditions must be elaborated and considered as causes for a particular event. The need to consider
all relevant contributing factors frustrates the clarity possible
when applying a more linear sense of causality. This ambiguity,
however, is not equivocation but is rather an honest reflexion of
the complexity of any particular situation.

These causal notions reflect the view deeply embedded in Chinese
thinking that things are inevitably connected to one another and
that if you seek to understand and explain any one thing, you
must look at all the other things that are immediately connected to

it. Conversely, since any one thing is linked to many other things, looking at one thing gives you the opportunity to look at everything else connected to it. A "thing" is a particular focus in a network of conditions; part holographically "presents" whole and whole "presents" part. Familiar notions of disjunction, separateness, and discreteness – or efforts to introduce or induce such distinctions – are less evident in Chinese thinking. Similarly, the idea of a discrete self – read "a self-defining, autonomous individual" – is almost insignificant in Chinese thinking. Instead, self is construed more broadly as a corporate self – a self that is always contextualized by and so interdependent with others, a self stretched out to embrace others within one's sphere of influence and so a self that actively seeks to promote collective interest as a way to advance one's own interest. In this conception, to separate a self from significant others is nearly as difficult as to extract a wave from an ocean. In classical times, in fact, "I" and "we" had not been distinguished; both were written with the same character 我. And, until recently, Chinese lacked a special word for "privacy" without pejorative meaning. This is not to say that Chinese do not recognize personal selves nor to suggest that Chinese selves are less fully developed than selves elsewhere but only to say that Chinese selves are most fully developed in interconnection with other selves.

We can note in passing that Chinese grammar facilitates this view of self in communication since it affords interlocutors the opportunity to minimize individual prominence and to promote bonds instead of boundaries. For example, in extended discourse, a speaker can dispense with pronouns such as "I" or "you," "we" or "they" when the referent is understood. This feature differs from the contrastive self-as-against-other distinction prominent in English discourse that is encouraged by a grammatical system requiring explicit subjects. Then again, the choice between retaining or deleting subject pronouns creates opportunities to distinguish self from other, "we" from "they" when so desired. It should also be pointed out that dispensing with subject pronouns allows one to focus on the situation rather than the agent. This, of course, contrasts with the causal/agent-action focus prominent in English discourse.

Looked at differently, a Chinese "I" is immersed in a web of

relationships and interdependencies. Unlike an English "I" that
tends to assert personal autonomy and presence, it is an "I" of
attachment that can claim, for example, that "I am my relationships." It is an "I" that "responds" to or is "responsive" to a
significant connection between self and others. Its variant in a kin-
based society where kinfolks traditionally operated as political
and economic units might not just be "one for all" and "all
for one" but also "one is all" and "all is one." Accordingly,
"obligations" and "responsibilities" (what is owed to others) start
to replace the boundary vocabulary of "rights" and "duties"
(what is owed to one's self) here. Likewise, obligations and responsibilities are shared; shared obligations and responsibilities in
turn entail a shared consciousness. Everyone is nested in some
complex pattern of interrelated and overlapping roles that, in
different foci, constitute social groups and institutions. This sense
of relatedness is evident when two Chinese, upon meeting for the
first time, try to reach out for each other by searching in their
overlapping backgrounds for a common kin, surname, school,
district, village, region and so on as a precondition for later
dealings. (The process also works in reverse: Chinese will actively
avoid deepening the bonds that incur unwanted obligations,
responsibilities, and, inevitably, accountability. The situation is
especially acute for higher-status persons or for people manipulated
– often through deference – into a higher status position and
relationship, for they are then obligated to confer their beneficence
and protection upon the lower-status supplicants.)

The human world is a field of relationships, or, if you will, a
network of links and bonds or a range of social ties; face, *guanxi*
'particularistic ties,' *renqing* 'affective considerations,' and go-
betweens or third-party brokers thus become important. Within
this field, moreover, depending on who you choose to emphasize
or what perspective you assume, each person can be construed as
a condition or cause (*yin*) or as the locus of an effect (*suo*). In just
such a situation, the distinction between cause and effect dissolves.
Each effect has many causes; no single cause is an adequate
explanation in the reticular Chinese view of causality.

Now, if we consider the *yinwei* portion of discourse to represent the field or whole network of conditions and the *suoyi*
portion of discourse to represent the focus or particular part of the

field, then we may comprehend the holistic tendencies commonly attributed to Chinese by Westerners. Even the arrangement of the *yinwei...suoyi...* construction itself suggests a holistic disposition in the movement of foci from big to small.

As for *yin*, the sense of movement described in the *Shuowen* lexicon as "to respond to" suggests a "back and forth movement" or a "movement towards," as might be associated with the sense of adjustment or adaptation in Shen Dao's use of "accommodation." It is also a movement that importantly contrasts with a Western sense of movement as that instigated by a causative agent, that is, something or someone that starts the ball rolling. This latter sense of movement relies on a catalyst for change or some propelling force and is best captured by the imagery of something "springing from" rather than something "emerging from" more characteristic of Chinese thought. More immediately relevant to our inquiry, in human relations *yin*'s sense of movement ultimately aims towards an accommodating conciliation, a kind of bidirectional responsiveness in which each party "moves toward" the other.

Since tradition attributes the development of *yin* as a philosophical category to Shen Dao, let us look more closely at how he used it. In one instance, he writes:

天道因則大，化則細；
因也者因人之情也

It is the Way of Heaven that the results of an accommodation [*yin* 因] are great and that the results of alteration are small. By "accommodation" is meant accommodating to human reality.

And in another instance, he says:

故用人之自為，不用人之為我
則莫不可得而用矣此之謂因

Thus if one makes use of men's self-interest and not of what men do to serve one's own interest, then there will be no man that one cannot use. This is what is meant by "accommodation" [*yin* 因].

In the first instance, "accommodation" is valued over "alteration." The valuation is keyed to the fact that alteration is unequivocally unidirectional and also requires force while accommodation is optimally bidirectional and so voluntary. Alteration involves a subject imposing force upon an object to control and manipulate it. Accommodating to human circumstances, on the other hand, means less concern for objectification and coercive force than for an attitude of tolerance and negotiability that will allow goals and actions to change and modify smoothly. The operative notion is mutuality.

The second instance of *yin* as "accommodation" in human relations means that to get someone to do what you want, you look for what serves that person's best interest in relation to your own; self and other attain personal fulfillment together. The efficacy lies with the person who can manipulate the situation to mutual advantage; both emerge as winners. Accommodation in this sense requires that the participants be conciliatory and open to mutual adaptation and adjustment. From a given set of circumstances, persons negotiate the best possible accommodation for their mutual welfare.

Here we are not talking about a trade-off. Neither are we talking about a situation in which something becomes a means to an end nor a situation in which there is some sort of loss incurred on one side as well as an element of coercion that results in the concession. "Accommodation" as used by Shen Dao involves mutual advantage; each stands to benefit from the arrangement; each adjusts only to personal advantage. There is no force, no loss but only profit for the participants. And, like cause and effect, so with means and ends; the distinction is dissolved. Coupled with *yin*'s sense of bidirectional responsiveness, the negotiable flexibility creates an invisible resonance of mutuality between participants.

Significantly, where there is negotiation, there is always deference. Deference is generally characterized by humility and a recognition of the other's importance. Alternatively, in traditional Chinese thinking, we might say that deference in communication signifies a willingness to yield or reshape one's authority for the communication's decision. It humbles one's "author"-ship and postpones one's proprietary rights over the communication. More than that, it tries to redirect the communication's authorship to involve others; it bids to honor as well as invite others to participate; it builds bonds and resolves the communication so that the larger interest of all can be accommodated. Such being the case, an idea or communication is held in joint custody.

Ideally, what is honored is harmony and not agreement, con-cordance and not conformity, sharedness and not sameness, and most importantly, a comely pliancy and not a blind compliance. The active pursuit of harmony ultimately aims toward a unity of differences, a synthesis of divergences, a confluence of contrasts. It is an attempt to engross all while offending none. It is a unity in diversity that is both dynamic and complex, one that works by way of mutual accommodation and adjustment. To achieve this ideal requires finding ways to creatively integrate differences while keeping intact the integrity of each participating element. Con-fucius himself made repeated references to the fact that "A quality person pursues harmony rather than agreement; the uncultivated person is the opposite" (*junzi he er bu tong xiaoren tong er bu he* 君子和而不同小人同而不和 *Analects* 13/23).

As a way to describe the harmony envisioned by Confucius, later Chinese commentators invoked the image of the stewpot in which different ingredients are brought together to simmer in a rich, savory mix — imagine, if you will, chunks of beef, carrots, and turnip delicately braised in soy sauce spiced with star anise— each ingredient bringing out and enhancing the flavor of the others. The underlying idea is to maximize all key ingredients and reach for the best possible combination under the circumstances. At the same time, the combination sought should not submerge the individual identities and qualities of the ingredients. For this reason, the stewpot image suffers from the fact that some stews can congeal into a gelatinous, lumpy mass of sodden bits. More important is the possibility of an untoward association with the misleading "melting pot" image formerly used to describe the pluralistic makeup of American society — that is, minority groups were expected and encouraged to assimilate — some say, become homogenized — into mainstream society. Perhaps a more appro-priate and familiar image is the fried-rice plate in which a variety of vegetables, meats, nuts, seasonings and anything else at hand is stir-fried together with rice in a memorable medley; yet each item keeps intact its own texture and taste while contributing to the overall tastiness. It is an image that immediately extends to many other sorts of Chinese dishes as well, such as "beef broccoli with oyster sauce," "sweet-and-sour crisped pork," or "fish-flavored eggplant" in which fresh combinations of texture, flavor and crunch achieve a delicious harmony.

Gustatory delights and images aside, one appealing explanation of the difference between *he* 和 'harmony' and *tong* 同 'agreement' describes the former as an activity of "attuning" and the latter as "tuning": "Attuning is the combining and blending of two or more ingredients in a harmonious whole with benefit and enhancement that maximizes the possibilities of all without sacrificing their separate and particular identities. 'Tuning' is finding agreement by bringing one ingredient into conformity and concurrence with an existing standard such that one ingredient is enhanced possibly at the expense of others" (Hall and Ames 1987: 166). Commensurate with what was said above, we may view the difference described as one between an accommodation and a tradeoff.

When Confucius rethought his cultural legacy and the conduct of human relations, he upheld the superiority of subtle influence and voluntary transformations over coercive insistence and aggressive moves. In Confucian thinking, a well-wrought argument opens the way for reflective thought – it allows the other to think feelingly and respond resonantly. It requires finesse, not force, and engages the other's empathetic attention. Engaging the other's empathetic attention in turn stimulates participation and ensures involvement in an emerging order of harmonic mutuality.

When engaged in formal discourse, Chinese have a distinctive sense of how to combine and configure ideas to generate meaning. This relates in large part to a philosophical tradition that, varied though it was, nevertheless stressed resonating connections over static abstractions, contextual particulars over transcendental imperatives. And here we come to the deeper intrigue, one that underlies the essential cultural clash between Chinese- and English-speaking cultures.

Perhaps the most promising explanation for the contrast comes from philosophers David Hall and Roger Ames (1987). In interpreting classical Chinese culture, they make a distinction between two orders, one characterized by causal thinking and a "logical" (univocal, universal) or "rational" (structured, discursive) language and the other characterized by correlative thinking and an "aesthetic" (evocative, imagistic, metaphorical, allusive) language. The dominant assumption in the former favors external ordering principles and formal patterns or univocity over the uniqueness of concrete particulars (i.e., order is conceived: someone or something is "on top" of the details); the dominant assumption in the latter favors the uniqueness of concrete particulars that interact with other concrete particulars to constitute an order (i.e., order is achieved: the particular interaction and configuration of the details make up the order). They caution that the two orders are not mutually exclusive, yet argue for their different importances in Confucius' thinking.

More specifically, as Hall and Ames see it, the logical sensibility dominating Western thinking turns on various transcendental references with roots in philosophical speculation and revelatory religion. In a nutshell, it presumes some unifying or originating principle or cause that stands independent of the world yet regulates and shapes it – i.e., natural laws and eternal forms, God Almighty and preordained Truths, objective reality and ultimate groundings.

This outlook suggests a "two-tiered" world or dual worlds, one the unchanging world of reality and the other the transitory world of appearance, one a world inhabited by a Creator and the other a world inhabited by the creatures of ITS creation. It promotes a sense of permanence or stasis – consider the curious verb "is" and its synonyms (see Graham 1959 for its metaphysical implications and cross-linguistic complications) – and engenders a sense of linearity, a direction, a purpose deriving from teleological assumptions of Divine Providence or from an underlying first principle or cause. It allows, for example, a woman nicknamed Robin HUD by the media – who was convicted of diverting $5.6 million from a federal program to charity – to claim that "I follow a higher law" (*Newsweek*, August 7, 1989, p. 22). It also promotes notions of separateness and disjunction and justifies dualistic bifurcations of the good–evil, mind–body, reason–emotion, reality–appearance variety in which the first member of each pair transcends the importance of the second. The disparity established is often expressed by the deference, awe, and even fear of a "God-fearing" man ("holy," according to *Webster's*, means "to set apart"). The boundary-setting dualistic bifurcations distance interactants. (Interestingly, "satan" comes from Hebrew and means "adversary.")

This transcendental worldview generates a host of rhetorical characteristics that conflict with Chinese views of harmonious relatedness and mutual interdependence. For one thing, it fosters fixed notions of discrete agency and tries to identify particular causes for particular events; even the dummy subject "it" in English discourse figures in the causal/agent-based need to put some subject before the main verb. For another, it presumes that rhetoric is coercive and divisive rather than negotiable and integrative; one argues for one's case as against another's case, thereby intensifying the distinctions between self and other. Moreover, it appeals to principles of rationality and uses reason as the universal knife to cut through issues; no matter how impassioned the oratory, it favors logical appeal over empathetic appeal, intellectual argument over sympathetic understanding. The etymological roots of the Germanic "man" come from an Indo-European verb that means "to think"; evidently, the ability to reason proves the person. Correspondingly, the human capacity for reason ought to make each person equally competent to analyze, criticize, argue, and mutually construct new knowledge in a public arena (ultimately, giving democracy its felicitous beginnings whereby each person is allowed his – and later on, her – "say" in a free exchange of ideas).

Reason opens up arguments for critical inspection; discussants ought to be ready to justify all assertions. Reason also forces closure on individual arguments; facts must be lined up in linear sequences that move one from premise to conclusion in rapid order. Ideas must be fully and clearly spelled out for rational discussion and reasoned understanding; information must be neatly assembled, wrapped up, and packaged for speedy, efficient delivery. In this connection, assertion and closure work to reinforce the boundary between self and others; so, too, does the general requirement for explicitness and definitiveness. Ideas are self-contained, just like individual selves. Participants distance themselves from each other, just like they distance themselves from the subject of the discussion.

Reason is ratio, ratio is to speak; rationality operates by intelligibility, discursive explanation, convincing talk, and, sometimes, proselytization and capitulation. The rest of the world has to be told and the job is not to gain consensus but to convince. Further, rational argumentation of the sort found in the legal, ecclesiastical, diplomatic, academic, and business realms is grounded in the metaphor of war and combat. No matter how refined the language used, how noble the purpose, at bottom, positions and arguments are established, defended, challenged, attacked, destroyed or surrendered (see Lakoff and Johnson 1980). To wit, Person A "argues," Person B "counters," Person A "challenges," Person B "shoots back," Person A "submits" and so on. Wyoming attorney Gerry Spence, who successfully defended former Philippines' first lady Imelda Marcos on federal corruption charges, puts it bluntly: "When I go to the courtroom, I come to do battle. I'm not there to do a minuet" (*Honolulu Star Bulletin*, February 17, 1990, p. A-4).

Notably, Western rhetoric grew out of classical educational ideals that sought to produce public speakers and, at the same time, to invigorate thought through public oral disputation. Western rhetoric was essentially a ritual combat through words, a one-on-one affair that was predominantly male and highlighted verbal prowess and public display. (Its modern, watered-down equivalent can be seen in the "chattering classes" and "talking-heads" populating such American television programs as *Crossfire*.) Yet, in its heyday, rhetoric was instruction as much as combat; through argument, one could sharpen and test ideas, check weaknesses and misconceptions, and ultimately teach others or advance knowledge. In Judeo-Christian thinking, argument not only helped one connect, one-on-one, with a personal God, but it also helped unveil hidden Christian truths; sometimes, it even helped to prove God's existence.

From rhetoric grew formal logic. Rhetoric combined with writing to facilitate a kind of highly abstract, sequential, classificatory thinking that, in scholarly and scientific endeavors, called for sparse linearity and analytic precision (Ong 1982). As art and formal discipline, rhetoric's two-thousand year dominance over Western academic training eventually abated. As persuasion and verbal display, however, rhetoric persists in various guises at all levels of educational practices and sensibilities. For Americans, in particular, their commitment to verbal display starts in the home. Researchers note, for example, that American parents encourage greater vocal interaction in their infants (Caudill and Weinstein 1969) and around the dinner table than do Japanese – and, I would add, Chinese and Hawaiian – parents. Cocktail parties and "conversation pieces" (bric-à-brac displayed in living rooms) alike serve to facilitate polite chitchat and testify to a cultural investment in verbal skills.

For Chinese, on the other hand, rhetoric takes on different contours; participants engage each other with a different cast of mind and under a different cast of circumstances. In contrast to a transcendental worldview, the Chinese immanental worldview is marked by large indifference to the autonomy and authority of transcendental references removed and remote from human actions. Instead, it begins with the assumption that all things are infused with the same psychophysical energy, albeit in different densities and consistencies. Things are not defined by their essences but by their resemblances and relationships; meanings emerge not in the things themselves but in their interplay, their intersections, their juxtapositions, what lies between them; understanding occurs not through analysis or abstraction, but through a tracing out or mapping of the patterns of relatedness that constitutes a "thing."

Stated another way, it is a single-ordered or "one-tiered" worldview in which things are not discrete entities, whole and complete within themselves, but, rather, related to and defined by other things. Things are not made up of static "stuffs" but, rather, are ephemeral and relative, in constant flux and transformation. Accordingly, things are not fixed, named, or labelled into essentialistic kinds or definitive categories – the abstract containers filled with things that belong or don't belong – nor are they put into linear sequences of discrete units governed by cause and effect.

Within this worldview, moreover, people are not disposed to separate themselves and their actions from each other or the cosmos, for that matter. Instead of setting up boundaries, they are more likely to seek common ground and nurture the bonds that link them to one another. While recognizing diverse views, people strive to prevent diversity from turning into disunity and instead seek a fine-tuned, mutual adjustment and accommodation. Even Xunzi, regarded by Westerners as the most rational of Confucian philosophers, stressed accommodation in his arguments (Cua 1985) while Mencius, another great Confucian philosopher, did not try to set himself apart from another or seek out logical flaws in another's argument, but, rather, ignored their differences and used the other's argument – along with a slew of concrete examples – to argue his own point (Richards 1932). As for Confucius, he made shrewd observations and pointed comments by using the concrete examples of everyday experience or by various appeals to collective memory.

For the most part, Chinese refrain from assertive talk and public spectacles of debate and debunk. Oratorical prowess has a less privileged status in Chinese culture than in many Western cultures; Chinese did not develop the art of rhetoric as did Western thinkers. The reasons for this have much to do with the traditional stress on harmony, hierarchy, and cooperation and all that they entail – i.e., conflict threatens social stability; the expression of contrary opinions risks face, potentially disgracing all involved; openly speaking one's mind appears distasteful, even unseemly and downright dangerous in a hierarchical world of tangled ties. For these and many other reasons, persuasive discourse is ideally calibrated to short-circuit open conflict (usually through behind-the-scenes maneuvering or third party intermediaries). This contrasts with the positive value Westerners assign to an open discussion of conflicting views – "laying the cards on the table" and "clearing the air" – which optimally brings disagreements to the surface so that people can build bridges for more fruitful discussion. Failure to appreciate the extent to which Chinese will go to avoid potential public disagreements can lead to embarassment. Thus, a Westerner converted to Communism and appointed temporary head of a university administrative unit in post-Liberation China recounted his own blunders:

I remember a meeting that was to be held involving all the teachers in the department. And one of the party members came to me a day or two in advance and said, "Now what do you think about the questions we're going to discuss?" So I said, "Well, we're going to have a meeting to discuss it. Let's not waste time doing it now." See, this was totally divorced from a Chinese traditional practice in which you have prior consultations and sound out people, and then by the time you get to the meeting, you stand a better chance of having some degree of unity and equal understanding. Another time we were discussing something, and I finished announcing a certain decision and then I said, "Well any questions or suggestions?" So, I waited about half a minute, saw there were none, and called the meeting over. Very un-Chinese, you

see. If you want people to talk, you've got to draw them out.   (Porter
1990: 61)

All this is not to say that Chinese are not skilled debaters and
able conversationalists; the early Jesuits and missionaries in China
already felt their formidable reasoning powers. Chinese history
itself is studded with accounts of heated political and intellectual
exchanges; and, from time to time, pockets of literary men would
privately assemble for enthusiastic argument (Henricks 1981).
But, on the whole, the Chinese version of rhetoric opts for suasion
rather than argumentation; conducted privately rather than publicly, it seeks to engage rather than estrange, to attract rather than
antagonize. It nurtures a tacit and nuanced understanding and
defers to the listener's ability to realize its full significance. It
values not just intellectual insight but a moving experience, not
just solid reasons but an empathetic reasonableness. It places an
aesthetic premium on oblique approaches in which reason takes a
circuitous route and all themes are expected to converge. It relies
on analogy and concrete images or examples to map out patterns
of resemblances or to generate directly apprehended experiences.
It attempts to unravel the links and relationships in an intricately
connected matrix rather than put together the parts and pieces
of a jigsaw-like puzzle. It represents, in particular, a conscious
attempt to array details and present a fair picture of the field
of conditions impinging on a matter. Such being the case, their
discourse can appear meandering and messy to English-speaking
natives; recall, for instance, their specific criticism of example (1)'s
"description of the various odds and ends, the technical matter
that filled up the first half of this..." Often, Chinese speech seeks
to convey a noncommittal neutrality or a negotiable flexibility;
we can see this, for example, in the polite Chinese choice-type
questions which drop the Chinese question particle *ma* 嗎 and
replace it with a choice of positive or negative *Ni qu bu qu*
你去不去 "Are you going or not going?" in contrast to the loaded
assumptions carried in *Ni qu ma* 你去嗎 "Are you going?".

Above all, in polite discourse, Chinese emphasize a willingness
to seek out and create shareable views; they try to draw a circle
around a "we" rather than a line between self and other. Their
style and strategy of discourse reflect a keen awareness of others

that figures importantly in Chinese humanistic values. What strikes Americans as vague, indirect, or noncommittal in Chinese responses are, when put in a favorable light, different strategies for soliciting and enhancing engagement and cooperation between diverse persons. (Put under a less favorable light, the communicative strategy described encourages a portrayal of the speaker as a victim of circumstances rather than as a decisive agent; the same dimensions of Chinese discourse allow the speaker to sidestep or escape accountability.)

Thus, as we saw in our discourse examples above, foregrounding background information makes people aware of the circumstances behind one's request. The wealth – or welter, depending on what side of the cultural divide one stands – of background information provides a perspective, a point of orientation. This lets a listener become gradually oriented to the reasonableness – and inevitability – of a speaker's position. Laying out information also expresses respect for a listener by revealing the manner of one's thinking. It ensures that all participants share a full understanding of the matter. Speaker and listener become bonded in a cooperative endeavor.

Likewise, hints of a regretted inability and the note of reluctance – things that might sound apologetic and justificatory to Western ears – also express deferential intent and negotiable flexibility. They indicate an unwillingness to impinge or at least a cooperative avoidance of possible disagreement and leave room for face-saving options and independent judgments. Intentions and positions become open-ended rather than fixed and assure the other person maneuvering room for reflective, independent thought. In short, the buildup and layout of ideas appeal to the other's dignity and ability to co-participate in the communication's decision. Flexuousness edges out decisiveness.

What appears as passivity – the speaker's subdued expression of self – actually makes it possible to draw the other into active collaboration. Accordingly, the boundaries between persons become effaced and the bonds between them emphasized. What seems self-effacing is merely a subduing of the speaker's impositional role, not an abnegation of the speaker's self.

This helps explain why the direction of Chinese arguments might often appear so slight as to be practically invisible. The means of persuasion are subtle and the advantages for a Chinese speaker are many. It is a sort of soft sell rather than a hard sell; it evokes rather than provokes; it gives a hint rather than a direct hit; it works by invitation rather than imposition. Its selling point – a very important one in Asian cultures – is that it is neither intrusive nor overbearing; the listener feels that one's thinking and judgment-making are one's own.

As we shall discuss in chapter 4, such a discourse style derives from an aesthetic of indeterminacy and open-endedness that makes particularly deep demands on a person. This Chinese aesthetic often produces faint stimuli that require dynamic attention on the part of a listener. In this way, a listener is not at all babied or spoonfed information. Instead, a listener has to slow down and make a commitment to listen long and hard enough for the words to begin to resonate. As a result, a listener becomes convinced by his (or her) own understanding rather than have another's understanding foisted onto him (or her). Sinologist Derk Bodde puts the point this way when writing in a different, though related, context about the ambiguity in Chinese poetry: "The Chinese poet's attitude to the reader is: 'This is the situation, it's up to you to react to it,' not 'Here I am, see how strongly I feel'" (1991: 286). From a different perspective, Shanghai-born American novelist Betty Bao Lord muses: "Conversing in Chinese is . . . like fishing: whether or not a single carp is caught, there is ample pleasure in drifting hour after hour about the lake" whereas "Conversing in English is like playing tennis, my Chinese side agrees; there is no point in the exercise without keeping score" (1990: 214).

Especially in the more intense, emphatic American style of argumentative communication, each participant acts as an independent, unfettered agent and argues unambiguously for his or her position with solid facts, hard evidence, and sound logic. Talk is used to clear the air, purify opinions, clarify differences, sound each other out, or bounce ideas off each other as participants mutually seek to test their validity. In this style of aggressive talking, the speaker assumes the burden of successful communication. As initiating agent compelling change, the speaker is required to express his or her message with purpose, power, and persuasion. Hence the many advertised courses and workshops teaching those less skilled how to speak assertively and with authority. This communicative style emphasizes the speaker's expertise in putting ideas across, in selling an image, and in winning over an audience. That "selling" underpins their argumentative style is prominently reflected in the oft-heard reply: "I don't buy your argument."

In this communicative style, moreover, the focus and task are noticeably more one-sided. As sole author and potent catalyst of the communication, the individual self assumes dramatic importance in striking contrast to the Chinese emphasis on bidirectionality in which individual selves are co-participants in a communication and share responsibility for its success. Furthermore, to speak with a confident and commanding air often creates distance rather than bonds; it sets one's self above others and denigrates the other. More critically, to strike out on one's own reinforces the independence of agents; one not only tries to call the tune but also marches to one's own tune. Better yet if one can make others dance to one's own tune.

From a Chinese perspective, this style of discourse can convey a sense of rigidity rather than receptivity, definitiveness rather than evocativeness, dissonance rather than resonance, and, ultimately, duality rather than mutuality. That participants seem to argue from an unyielding rigidity is evident in the routine of bouncing ideas off each other: in order to bounce well, a hard surface is required. More pertinently, since like attracts like – the notion of "sympathetic resonance" in ancient Chinese thinking – the rigidity can inspire similar intractability in others, thus preventing the binding and joining of bonds or, worse, abruptly cutting one off from the other. A discourse style that starts off straightaway with a frank statement of opinion or intent, for example, "I think it's a good idea that my unit be allotted twenty-thousand pounds because of this and that reason," appears to Chinese as a fixed stance that might also encourage untimely disagreement or discord. Like plucking a too taut string, it has the potential of breaking instead of resonating.

Our discussion so far has drawn attention to traditional Chinese cultural ideals of mutuality and harmony – specifically, that Chinese value acts which generate greater harmony among diverse particulars. In Chinese thinking, ritual and harmony are the means through which people come together and attain their goals. The thing to remember, however, is that harmony is achieved, not imposed. Harmony is not fixed for all time nor can it be taken for granted as part of the *status quo*. Quite the contrary, it must be actively pursued and negotiated. Like a fulfilling marriage, it has to be worked at constantly by both partners. Similarly, interactants ought to dispose themselves so as to arrive at a frictionless communication. But persons don't just fall into an encounter; they actively engage as participants. Ideally, they "move toward" and "respond to" each other. Each person needs the other to make an engagement, each meeting provides new opportunities for creative engagement, and each engagement represents not just getting along, but rather the negotiated achievement of the greater cultural ideals of social cooperation and harmony.

To be sure, the Hong Kong Chinese participants on the tape conduct their budget meeting in a business environment that is unarguably dynamic, aggressive, and competitive; they make no secret of their interest in personal wealth and material advantage. Further, Chinese negotiators everywhere are renowned for their bargaining shrewdness. On top of that, Chinese often treat those outside their trusted circles with wariness and even callousness; among intimates, they can be feisty, mean-spirited, and utterly intransigent. Nevertheless, face-to-face interactions in Hong Kong and other thriving Chinese communities such as Taiwan and Singapore, continue to be variously modelled on significant acts of cooperation that publicly resist dysfunctional appearances of self-interested, self-intentioned, or self-aggrandizing behavior. With those that count, Chinese traditionally strive for interconnection and so encourage acts that optimally forward the mutual welfare of all concerned rather than acts that get one noticed.

It is worth stressing that Chinese actively discourage selfishness and egocentricity, not competition or ambition. Note, however, that Chinese attitudes regarding competition stand in striking contrast to the Western presumption that sameness or equality exists among participants and so makes competition fair. Instead, competition in the Chinese sensibility is qualified by an acute awareness of differences and by a shared consciousness that all participants are enmeshed in relationships of mutuality and interdependence. Thus, for example, Chinese managers in Taiwan are traditionally expected to spread the credit for personal success among family members, work colleagues, and, at the extreme, the entire society, in contrast to American managers who typically attribute success to individual effort or ability (Chang 1985).

Certainly, Americans also have a team effort ethos, but most of the glory goes to a star player; in the US, to "stand out from" or "get ahead of" others is an acceptable part of the competitive spirit. Chinese, on the other hand, are quick to quote old sayings that call attention to the dangers of individual prominence, for example, "the tallest tree in the forest is the one that gets struck by lightning," and "the stone that is furthest out from shore, the river washes away." For them to claim individual success or individual satisfaction for a job well done is to risk charges of "egocentricity" or, more specifically, "selfishness" and "immodesty" (Chang 1985). True, each participant holds responsibility to look out for his or her particular interests, but, at the same time, each must outwardly cooperate with others and look out for the best interest of those enmeshed in their network of obligations. Since every Chinese is anchored in a knot of multiple loyalties, any degradation of one's interpersonal environment ultimately results in personal degradation. Chinese can be fiercely competitive, but they are also intensely reciprocal.

It is true too, however, that our discussion has drawn partly from the world of abstract ideas promulgated by and more familiar to monks and mandarins than to ordinary folks. Nonetheless, we note that the behavior which these ideas and ideals advocate are widely and variously circulated and influential in their respective societies. Whatever people's personal dispositions, the point is that in our inquiry concerning the perceptions Chinese and Americans develop of each other, it is the culturally idealized version that is often served up for public display, and it is more often the culturally idealized version that is put forth in cross-cultural engagements and (mis)assessments.

Analyzing budget requests in real life is complicated by the frictions and factions endemic to any organization. A full explanation requires access to individual speakers which, in our simulation, we did not have. We also need to consider the Chairman's presence, as few Chinese speak without making a statement about their positions in relation to their social superiors. (We deal with this in chapter 5). Nonetheless, I suggest that the Chinese middle managers on the tape draw on their personal experience to do what is natural and necessary – and that is to forestall conflict and foster an atmosphere of cooperation and collaboration. This is part of the cultural ideal of harmony that stresses the merits of joint decision and participation and that sees collective interests ultimately coinciding with personal interests. Even when putting their own opinion or request upfront, Chinese express negotiable flexibility and conciliatory intent. Such being the case, the construction of their requests reflects the incipient beginnings of a harmony-in-the-making. It is incipient because the process, as described here, is only just under way. Most of the details are yet to be worked out. The point, however, is that Chinese cultural ideals run so deep that they are stabilized and strengthened at the outset of the meeting in the very way requests are framed. Proceeding indirectly to convey deference helps to get the participants into harmonic sync. Optimally, by the time a decision emerges, a well-balanced transaction should have been assured and a strong sense of participatory togetherness and bondedness will have been developed.

Judging from the responses of our Chinese informants, they indicate a highly honed sensitivity – some might say an anxious vulnerability – to the surrounding human network. Their statements suggest that one should avoid acts that stir up jealousy, affront authority or incur ill-will – things that can ultimately damage face. To be obvious and forthright in one's intentions would be boorish and ultimately self-defeating.

What about urban Chinese youths from the People's Republic of China? Certainly, they are increasingly and more conspicuously assertive, egotistic, and self-absorbed than those more traditional. Nevertheless, I note that my informants from China are readily able to recognize and respond to the communicative signals and social ends of the discourse examples examined here. Thus, I maintain that strategies in our discourse examples constitute culturally significant symbols and intentions that both inform and distinguish a cultural population. Whether or not the Chinese from the People's Republic or elsewhere choose to use them in their own communications is a different matter.

At bottom, what really matters in the Chinese way of communicating and relating is to nurture the subtle, fragile bonds and links in human relations. Continuity, connections, and conduct entwine in Chinese thinking; if you don't conduct yourself well, you will soon be out of tune with others. Chinese resist foregrounding themselves. Instead, they try to elicit and show cooperation and conciliation, to spread responsibility for communication and decision, and most of all, to nurture harmonious bonds between persons. Chinese are not disinterested in communicative efficiency, and, in fact, have actively promoted it in the last few decades. But they do not appreciate efficiency as they do courtesy, cordiality, and harmony in their exchanges. These cultural ideals are portrayed in subtle nuances that Americans miss altogether. It is a communication style that, on the surface, may appear similar to the American style – just like they seem to be using the same language – but in actual fact, their strategies and goals are very different.

Significantly, the aim of Chinese to nurture bonds through talk bears a striking similarity to some of the goals pursued by American women when conversing with American men. Like Chinese, American women are consistently described as more disposed towards bonds of attachment, favoring connections to others over autonomy and independence (see Gilligan 1982). This creates some parallels in the way they engage in talk and in their communication difficulties with American men. For, without realizing it, American men and women, like Chinese and Americans, are operating on different wave-lengths due to their different dispositions. Although they may appear to be using the same language, they continue talking at cross-purposes. According to the literature on male and female miscommunication, for example, when American girlfriends or wives continue to ask questions in a conversation with an American boyfriend or husband, often they are not only asking questions to get answers, they are asking questions to keep the conversation going. By contrast, American men see questions as requests for information. As another example, when grappling with marital conflict, many American women feel that their marriage is going well so long as the spouses can discuss it whereas American men feel that the marriage is not going well if they must continue discussing it (Maltz and Borker 1982). Notably, to solicit the listener's participation and to demonstrate an amiable flexibility as well, American women are more likely

than men to include numerous tag endings in their discourse, such
as "isn't it" and "don't you think" (see Lakoff 1975). As a
variant, they may also end a response in a questioning tone as, for
example, "E. T.?" when answering someone's query about which
movie they should attend. The questioning tone is intended to
signal to the querier or listener the following message: "E. T. is
only a suggestion on my part and I am open to whatever you, the
listener and fellow movie-goer, might want to see." Unfortunately,
males' different communicative strategy makes them view a solici-
tous female as maddeningly indecisive or as an approval seeker
rather than as a person reaching out to engage the listener in
joint participation (Tannen 1990). The communicative intent of
American women, like much of polite Chinese discourse, seeks to
nurture and affirm the other's existence and presence rather than
assert and express one's own distinctiveness. According to one
account, assertive and expressive behavior primarily distinguishes
and rewards a robust American masculinity which "desires to be
witnessed, seen, known, in the world" in contrast to the nurturing
behavior more characteristic of women's interactions which
"validates, authenticates, receives what another is expressing"
(Obenchain 1989).

Thus, it is not surprising that many previous descriptions of
Chinese in the popular literature – often by men – find them to
have a woman-like sensitivity and dependency on others. Many,
like the American informants in our discussion, characterize the
Chinese way of communicating and relating as passive and feminine rather than active and masculine. In an interview reported
by Rey Chow (1991: 5), for instance, Italian director Bernardo
Bertolucci compared the Japanese and Chinese members of his
film crew for The Last Emperor, observing that "They are very
different... The Chinese are... more feminine. A bit passive."
These characterizations correlate with Dutch researcher Geert
Hofstede's (1984) account about Chinese managers and workers
in Hong Kong, Taiwan, and Singapore as somewhat less "masculine" – masculinity being described as less concerned about
nurturing human relations in the overall quality of life – than
North Americans (and Japanese) in his multi-country, 116,000
questionnaire survey of an American-owned multinational
corporation.

As a cautionary note, the analogy posited between Chinese and American women cannot be pursued much further to presume, for example, that American women will make better international managers or consultants than their male counterparts. For most intents and purposes, to compare the two groups is to compare mangoes and papayas. If we believe the scholarly and popular writings, American women hold a high regard for the verbal means of communication. By contrast, Chinese interactants see the verbal medium as just one symbolic means to affirm relationships. Besides, for more than two thousand years in their history, one of the grounds for the rare divorce – apart from barrenness, theft, incurable disease, jealousy and filial disobedience to in-laws – was a woman's talkativeness.

Nonetheless, while American women and Chinese people are not the same, they are not entirely different. In one essential respect, they are alike in seeing themselves functioning within a network of relationships. This may help explain business writings about American women managers who generally resist the traditional top-down, command-and-control style of management and tend to value shared responsibility, consensus-building, and mutual influence (Rosener 1990). It may also account for American writings that distinguish a female mode of argumentation which seems "eidetic, methetic, open-ended, and generative" – i.e., characteristically indirect, implicit, suggestive, and inclusive – from a male mode of argumentation which seems "framed, contained, more pre-selected, and packaged" – i.e., characteristically assertive, differentiating, antagonistic, and "in the know" (Farrell 1979). Like Chinese, American women are described as pursuing a logic different from American men.

Some final points ought to be underscored. For one thing, not all Chinese usages of "because" and "so" represent a wholesale transfer of native discourse patterns into a new language. Sometimes, it is simply difficult to tell; each case has to be analyzed separately. In a news broadcast at the height of the June 1989 pro-democracy movement in China, for example, ABCs *Nightline* anchor Ted Koppel interviewed a student leader, Jing Huang, studying at Harvard University. Huang used a "because" construction three times in a row, including this answer to Koppel's question: "What made you decide to leave China?" "Yes. Because

I think my life has been in danger. I mentioned I've been followed and my friends suggest that I use public phone because my phone may be (tapped???). That's why I move my scheduled return. So I move up my schedule and return in 7th of this week."

To native English speakers, the response beginning with "Because I think my life has been in danger..." seems to follow naturally from the query. Yet, its Chinese characteristics, including the "yes" acknowledgment at the outset and its grammatical irregularities, not to mention the appearances of "because" and "so" are also undeniable. In this example, whether because... so... has been Anglicized or Sinicized is unclear. However, in many other instances, the because...so...construction is not at all Englished; often, as we have seen, it retains its Chinese spirit. Consider the next example from a discussion period following a public talk given at the University of California, Berkeley. The Chinese speaker was a visiting professor of nutrition from Beijing. He also used the because...so... construction three times in a row responding to questions from the American audience. Note, however, that for many native English speakers, his response is unusual as it does not directly address the American's question:

(7) AMERICAN   How does the Nutritional Institute decide what topics to study? How do you decide what topics to do research on?

CHINESE   BECAUSE, NOW, PERIOD GET CHANGE. IT'S DIFFERENT FROM PAST TIME. IN PAST TIME, WE EMPHASIZE HOW TO SOLVE PRACTICAL PROBLEMS. NUTRITION MUST KNOW HOW TO SOLVE SOME DEFICIENCY DISEASES. IN OUR COUNTRY, WE HAVE SOME NUTRITIONAL DISEASES, SUCH X, Y, Z. BUT, NOW, IT IS IMPORTANT THAT WE MUST DO SOME BASIC RESEARCH. *So, we must take into account fundamental problems. We must concentrate our research to study some fundamental research.*

Alternatively, we might conjecture that the use of "because" and "so" in our discourse examples may simply be a Chinese response to what Chinese perceive as the logical ordering required in English discourse. This is a possibility that perhaps contributes to or coincides with the other explanations offered. Or, their use might be attributable to an interesting hybrid of Chinese and English discourse functions, the latter taking on aspects of what Deborah Schiffrin (1987) has described about the discourse marking features of "because" (marking orienting, supporting information) and "so" (marking upcoming main information) in explanatory or narrative discourse, as perhaps in our example (2). This only adds to the deepening mystery surrounding the ways, features and use of second language acquisition. Note, however, that unlike English, the positioning of Chinese *yinwei . . . suoyi . . .* is constrained by the features of clause combining in Chinese and the general tendency that "dependent" phenomena go before that upon which they depend. Furthermore, as we shall soon see, Chinese thought and expression customarily proceed from the general to the particular, as they do from far to near and from past to present. This in turn contributes to the appearance of indirection in their discourse.

We have one other point to consider. Initially, American informants' assessment of our discourse examples reflected only a vague sense that there was something incongruous about Chinese communicative practices. Only through detailed analysis and reflection and much coaxing on my part did some of the previously opaque incongruities become apparent. The point is that when people are immersed in conversation, so much happens outside of their awareness that the linguistic and cultural roots of these incongruities are hard for them to recognize. Unless people interact intensively over time or are poked and prodded by outside interpreters such as myself, the incongruities may escape conscious notice. Indeed, they may be relegated to judgments about behavior that can lapse into damaging stereotypes. A business communications' consultant made the following observation after repeatedly listening to the budget-meeting tape:

I would probably not have seen the [Chinese] pattern consciously . . . I might sense the patterns. I might say to myself there are differences. But, being able to precisely see it, visualize it, talk about it as we've done here, I'll probably not be able to do that . . . About the most I think I would get in this area is the sense that there are differences in communication. I couldn't say why 'cause I don't think I would have been as aware of the pattern but I might have a ( ) these people seem a little cautious or these people seem to talk about everything. In other words, I could be symptomatically hitting around it. I don't think I would see the pattern.

Conversely, some Chinese are simply unaware that subtle cultural differences in communicative requirements exist. That they seriously conflict is often even less apparent and appreciated. Such was the case with a gentleman in his late sixties who had emigrated to America from China's Guangdong province several decades ago and who had, upon initial interview, immediately scoffed at the above possibility and dismissed it as hardly worthy of attention. Later, I discovered that he had failed his English classes after having transferred from a prestigious Chinese university some forty years earlier. He had, however, performed well in his chosen field of mathematics. I mention this because his facility with mathematics and his problems with English are not uncommon experiences for Asians in general. Moreover, his explanation is typical of the way many Chinese describe their difficulty with English discourse: specifically, they treat their difficulty as simply one of insufficient linguistic knowledge and vocabulary. His explanation is an example of inaccurate, clichéd accounts about language, in particular, and communication, in general. I would argue that the elderly gentleman, and other Chinese, too, fail to recognize significant Chinese and American differences in their approach to discourse. Often, they are lulled into the false belief that a formal competence and familiarity with English words and grammar assure them competence in communicating their social purposes as well. However, one can be talking in one tongue but actually be relating in another.

To sum up, deciphering an unfamiliar communicative strategy is more treacherous than commonly thought. Americans' understanding of Chinese responses can be subtly complicated by cultural differences in the strategies and expectations of discourse, from the linguistic signals of cohesion to highlighting points of emphasis to the very organizational principles themselves. Their understanding gets even trickier when it is undermined from the start by a deceptively similar linguistic code. As we saw, the apparent causality of "because . . . so . . ." really does not coincide with its English counterpart and a strictly English rendition of its meaning and intent violates its Chinese spirit. That their very ways of communicating and relating are also so very different to begin with makes understanding that much harder. Together, the obscured differences and hidden presuppositions work to create faulty

inferences and give especial encouragement to American perceptions of Chinese inscrutability.

A rose is a rose is a rose. "Because" is sometimes "cause" as it
is sometimes "cuz." But one culture's "because" is not always
another culture's "because" and still less a distant derivative of
First Cause as it is, sometimes, a cross-linguistic incidence of
deceptive cause.

3

Missing links

Starting with this chapter, we intensify our focus on one critical part of the puzzle making up perceptions of Chinese inscrutability. In the last chapter, we discussed the different sense of causality underlying the modern Chinese because...so...construction. We saw that, insofar as discourse is concerned, a consideration of the full range of contingent factors obscures the clarity possible for Americans who apply a linear sense of causality.

Yet another area of confusion arises from the way English-speaking Chinese use "because/as" and "so/therefore" to signal the transition between phases or stages of argument. Specifically, I refer to the choice of "because/as" to mark the introduction of their case and "so/therefore" to indicate a shift to the main point. Again and again, one finds this pattern in the examples of discourse I have examined in chapter 2. As noted there, the consistency is even more striking in view of the fact that they were gathered from a variety of formal speech situations such as business meetings, oral histories, and public conferences, and where the Chinese speakers come from different Chinese dialect backgrounds, namely, Mandarin and Cantonese.

In this chapter, I will suggest that the confusion can be clarified if we take into account some fundamental typological differences between Chinese and English. I will further suggest that the selection of "because/as" and "so/therefore" is deliberate and not accidental. That is, these usages seem to derive from Chinese antecedents and to have been transformed into conventional features of discourse among English-speaking Chinese. My immediate purpose, however, will be to suggest that the principles guiding the organization of information at the level of discourse parallel those governing the organization of clauses at the sentence level. Our discussion will proceed against the background of a constant theme called the whole-before-part principle which appears in writings about the Chinese language.

A special thrust of this chapter will be to marshall arguments from the linguistics literature that will best document the points I wish to make. Conversely, I shall forgo the varied, substantial issues regarding the structural features of Chinese and, with the exception of the aforementioned whole–part phenomena, defer till the next chapter other discussions that relate Chinese thought to the Chinese language. In this chapter only, a word enclosed by parenthesis in the numbered examples is a linguistic convention; it indicates that the word's appearance is optional. Also, in this chapter, I make greater use of insights from other people's analyses about other Asian languages – in particular, Japanese – to clarify my own points about Chinese.

What sorts of explanations are available to us for analyzing the recurrent use of "because" and "so" as transition signals in our examples of Chinese discourse? How can we show that they are systematic and conventional Chinese ways of generating information rather than bad English or idiosyncratic examples? Assuming they are systematic, what linguistic principles, if any, guide the organization and production of information? To answer, let us concentrate on what I consider a few crucial variables suggested by the linguistics literature and pursue their significance wherever they lead us. To keep the discussion to a manageable size, I shall condense, simplify, and blend a good deal of material, drawing together strands of research from Chinese linguistics, teaching Chinese as a second language, studies in second language acquisition, as well as recent work on spoken narrative discourse and philosophical writings on Chinese conceptual structure. Quite often, I shall venture generalizations and speculations for which there may be slender evidence.

We can best balance limited evidence and my sense of regularities by attending to the topic–comment relationship in Mandarin Chinese. (Mandarin Chinese, rather than other Chinese dialects, is the unit of reference and study in many linguistic works on Chinese.) This relationship is important because topic–comment constructions form one distinguishing characteristic of

Chinese that contrasts it with English. Take the following, for example:

(1) *Huoshan   de   dianying Xiaweiyi*
     volcano   subordinating particle   film   Hawaii

     zui   hao   paide
     most   good   filming

     Volcano movies [topic], Hawaii is best for filming [comment].

This construction differs from English which has nothing really comparable to describe the relationship between the constituents of *huoshan de dianying* and *Xiaweiyi*. In other words, the relationship of *huoshan de dianying* to *Xiaweiyi zui hao paide* is neither subject to object nor is it subject to verb. It is altogether another kind of relationship and one that is commonly referred to as topic–comment.

The topic–comment construction figures more prominently in Chinese than does the subject–verb construction, although the latter is certainly present in Chinese as well. On the other hand, the topic–comment construction itself is not unknown in English. It functions least like:

(2) As for the kelp on the shore, they're hardly edible.

where a contrastive relationship may be presumed. It is more in tune with the following:

(3) You know the blue surfboard, a giant squid chewed it up.

Since I don't want to stray too far into the details of the Chinese language at this point in the discussion, let me just indicate that the lexicalized "you know," "it," "a," and "the" parts of a sentence like (3) can be eliminated in Chinese since they are understood from the context in accordance with the principles of Chinese syntax, i.e., grammatical word order and the pragmatic role of definiteness, and their appearance would consequently be redundant. (The matter of topic–comment in Chinese is covered more extensively in Li and Thompson's 1981 reference grammar of Mandarin Chinese.) And since Chinese grammar also eschews tense markers, the sentence would then appear as:

(4) Blue surfboard, giant squid chew(ed it) up.

In this case, "blue surfboard" is the topic. In other instances, a variety of topic complements are used to set off the topic. An English-speaking Chinese might say, for example:

(5) As concerns (the) blue surfboard, (a) giant squid chew(ed it) up.
(6) So far as (the) blue surfboard (is) concern(ed), (a) giant squid chew(ed it) up.
(7) Speaking of (the) blue surfboard, (a) giant squid chew(ed it) up.

Li and Thompson (1976) argue that the topic–comment construction is a basic sentence type and point out some of the differences between subject-prominent and topic-prominent languages: the topic is definite, selectionally independent of the verb, sets the framework for the predication, and occurs in sentence–initial position. Chafe (1976) also suggests that the topic sets the spatial, temporal, or individual framework for the main predication; in his thinking, it is "the frame within which the sentence holds" rather than "what the sentence is about." Chao (1968) states that the topic carries old information whereas new or significant information is found in the comment. In other words, the topic imparts "old," "given," or "shared" information while the remainder of the sentence comments on that acknowledged information with new information. That topic and comment share a weak syntactic linkage is supported by an additional fact: a noticeable pause often separates the two components in speech, and a comma is frequently used in modern writing to indicate this.

In short, topic in topic-prominent languages seems to bear a syntactically loose relationship with the other parts of an utterance. This situation contrasts with what happens in subject-dominated languages such as English where the subject is syntactically linked to the rest of the utterance. We should emphasize that topic in topic-prominent languages is better viewed as a discourse level phenomenon. This is an essential point and one that we shall discuss in detail in subsequent discussion. We should also emphasize that the European conception of a sentence has no close Chinese or Japanese counterpart; prior to Western contact and the introduction of Western theories of grammar, Chinese and Japanese divided writing into *ju* and *ku* (*bun* is the modern Japanese word for sentence), respectively, which were lines of verse or else short phrases marked by pauses or breath-groups. These phrases often corresponded to syntactical divisions – but not always, because sometimes, a *ju* (or *ku*) did not make a full sentence and sometimes, more rarely, a *ju* comprised what looks like two sentences. This is one reason why Chinese and Japanese have traditionally regarded the text, rather than the sentence, as basic. This fact will become significant in later discussion.

For now, let me just state that an important difference between subject-prominent and topic-prominent languages is that the topic–comment pattern signals particular relationships of coherence between the subparts of an utterance within an overall frame. For many Americans, the way in which Chinese signal such relationships is just not clear. In fact, it is this characteristic way of knitting together connections and inferring linkages between ideas which often makes the understanding of so much of Chinese discourse such a struggle for Americans.

Perhaps, then, given the prominence of the topic–comment construction in Chinese, we might say that the discourse level phenomenon that we have discussed in chapter 2 mirrors the sentence-level topic–comment relationship and, furthermore, the connective pairs "because" and "so," for example, serve to signal that relationship. To be more specific, connective pairs such as "because/as" and "so/therefore" signal a topic–comment relationship between the parts of the ideas or information that they tie together. In fact, there is a large variety of these constructions in Chinese (see Li and Thompson 1981, ch. 23), of which the following are a representative sample. We will be focusing on the ones listed below primarily because they appear in the data and are thus pertinent to the analysis. Both clauses appear in a fixed order and both contain pairs of specific morphological markers which signal the relationship between the two clauses. In this subset, the markers occur in clause-initial position, either before or after the subject or topic, and can be optionally deleted in either clause.

CAUSAL/REASON
because . . . . therefore, so . . .
yinwei   *suoyi*

CONDITIONAL

if .... then...

$\begin{Bmatrix} ruguo \\ jiaru \\ jiashi \\ yaoshi \end{Bmatrix}$ jiu

CONCESSIVE

although .... yet, but...

suiran $\begin{Bmatrix} dao \\ keshi \\ hai(shi) \end{Bmatrix}$

The picture, however, is more complex. What seems to have happened as well is that the connective pairs "because" and "so" appear to be overgeneralized uses of native discourse conventions. Let me briefly expand on this point. Typically, in many cases of language transfer, not all the lexical varieties and forms from the native language are transferred to the new language. Instead, the native varieties are reduced so that just a few expressions become overgeneralized or overworked in the new environment. The novel and ubiquitous Chinese use of the connective pair "because" and "so" seems to be an example of this phenomenon of overgeneralization. Furthermore, the relationship which they signal survives the transition from Chinese into English.

In this regard, let me also mention that there is some question whether the juxtaposed clauses making up Chinese causal/reason (i.e., because...so...) and conditional (i.e., if...then...) utterances are in a coordinate or in a subordinate–main relationship to each other. Li and Thompson (1978: 262) take the position that "these constructions are syntactically parallel to each other, though semantically they may express relationships which other languages express with subordinate clauses." (Note, however, that later work by Thompson, together with John Haiman [1984] and Christian Matthiessen [1988], questions the usefulness of labelling a clause "subordinate.") What Li and Thompson may mean here is that Chinese tend to signal subordination by inference. (We have already noted that the morphological markers for causative or reason clauses, for example, can be omitted in Chinese, and the clauses are then simply juxtaposed to each other with no overt markings to indicate their relationship.) That is, connections in Chinese must be inferred from position, context, or certain connectives in the same way that causality, for example, in the English utterance "They didn't like each other, and they fought a lot" can be inferred from the English proposition "and." In this utterance, the use of "and" acts more like a causative. Thus, we may construe the English utterance as "Because they didn't like each other, so they fought a lot."

We can more readily apprehend this syntactic difference between Chinese and English if we consider the translation process. To render Chinese sentences into English, conjunctions must be added for clarification. To translate English sentences into Chinese, however, certain conjunctions must be eliminated. The regularity of this procedure compels a Chinese professor of translation at China's Huazhong Normal University to observe that "An English sentence is like a tree with a trunk and some branches attached to it, the trunk being the main clause and the branches being the subordinate clauses and dependent phrases. A Chinese sentence is like a clump of bamboo, each shoot growing independently" (Chen 1986: 437). In the same way, from a native English-speaker's vantage point, links between Chinese clauses, just as links between Chinese sentences are obscured. The missing-link difference, coupled with missing grammatical marking elements mentioned earlier, i.e., "He like eat now" v. "He'd like to eat now," partially accounts for the greater syntactic density and compactness of Chinese texts. It is also one way to explain the fact that the English text of bilingual publications, such as the *Chinese Reader's Digest*, is generally sixty to seventy percent longer than the equivalent Chinese text (Hoosain 1986: 43). From an English-speaker's perspective, then, obscured links in Chinese discourse inhibit full expression of ideas and so introduce a problematic ambiguity.

Before we move into the analysis, however, we must consider other explanations of topic and comment we alluded to earlier.

First, Li and Thompson suggest that, from the standpoints of speech and conversation, topic should be reconceptualized as a discourse level phenomenon in Chinese. One aspect of their discussion revolves around the issue of zero-pronominalization, i.e., "an understood noun phrase referent," in Chinese discourse. They observe that zero-pronominalization is frequently topic controlled in that a topic is followed by a series of comments which are in themselves independent clauses. Once a topic has been established, one can continue to comment on it several times without the necessity of repeating it. In other words, the scope of a topic can extend across sentence boundaries. The effect of this gives you a referent which can continue over several clauses, a phenomenon which they have labelled "topic-chaining." Their discussion implies a high degree of interplay between comment and topic in discourse – an interplay, that is, between the sentence level and the discourse level in Chinese.

To illustrate, I include examples given by Jiang (1983) which show some essential differences between English and Chinese and the conceptual separation between subject and topic in Chinese as well. Thus, example (8a) can be combined through relative clauses and conjunctions for discourse purposes into (8b) in English. That is, to turn (8a) into (8b), the subjects become "I," "she," and "others" in their respective sentences; the relative marker "who" indicates the head noun as its subject.

(8a)   1. I have a sister.
        2. My sister is very tall.
        3. She plays volleyball quite well.
        4. Others call her Athlete.
(8b)   I have a sister who is very tall.
        She plays volleyball quite well,
        and others call her Athlete.

He demonstrates next how Chinese would organize the several clauses or sentences of (8a) and (8b) in discourse. According to his interpretation, the result is an obvious topic–comment relationship.

(9)   TOPIC   COMMENT 1
       wo you   yige meimei   *hen gao,*
       I   have a   sister   very tall
       I have a sister   (She is) very tall

                                      COMMENT 2
                                      paiqiu   da   de   hen hao,
                                      volleyball play asp. very well
                                      (She) plays volleyball quite well

COMMENT 3
bieren dou jiao ta
others all   call her
yundongyuan.
Athlete
Others all call her Athlete.

Jiang states that the topic is "sister"; that is, in the topic clause *wo you yige meimei* "I have a sister," only *meimei* 'sister' is the actual topic whereas *wo* 'I' and *you* 'exist/have' are topic complements attached to the topic. The initial subject has changed from *wo* 'I' to *meimei* 'sister' in comment 1, and then to *paiqiu* 'volleyball' in comment 2, and finally to *bieren* 'others' in comment 3. According to his explanation, the construction of the subject transformations reflects the topic–comment features of Chinese discourse.

What interests us here is that the pattern of zero-anaphora or the lack of an explicit referent in Chinese discourse requires one to make connections or infer linkages in a way unfamiliar to (and so problematic for) many Americans. To understand this point, let me reiterate that noun phrases or pronouns are typically used in English discourse in places where zero-pronominalization is widespread in Chinese. The native English speaker would thus have difficulty seeing what the connections are between utterances if the relationship was not implicit from the words used. The situation becomes acute in instances where the lexical choices do not suggest that there is a connection between the utterances. Suppose that, instead of saying "I have a sister" as in (9), we have "My sister has a pet kangaroo" and, instead of "(She is) very tall" and "(She) plays volleyball quite well," we have "(She's) quite a character" and "(She'd) rather play than eat." Since subjects do not have to be lexicalized in Chinese speech, it is possible for the native English speaker to become confused as to whether the pet kangaroo (which might be female) or the sister is being characterized in the comments. The situation worsens when we consider that Chinese make no lexical distinctions between third person pronouns and so the English use of "she" in comments 1 and 2 very often appears as "he" in their speech. To complicate matters further, it is just as likely in the speech of English-speaking Chinese that "he" might appear in comment 1 whereas "she" would appear in comment 2. In this instance, both the "he" and the "she" are referring to the same entity.

On the other hand, Chinese speakers run into a different set of problems when they try to transfer characteristics of topic-prominence into English. Findings from studies in second-language acquisition show that the carryover is not as easily reflected in a one-to-one correspondence from one grammatical system to another as traditional notions of language transfer would suggest. Instead, the resulting constructions must be viewed as unique creations that represent the ways in which non-native English speakers package their native discourse functions into the framework of English syntax (Schachter and Rutherford 1979). Yet, when the investigators presented the constructions (listed below) to English language teachers for evaluation, the teachers consistently assumed that the unique constructions were "malformed passives" and, moreover, that a reading of (10a), for example, should take the form "most of the food which is served in such restaurants *has been cooked* already." In other words, the points made by the English teachers reflect the fact that they had been operating under the constraints of English syntax where a subject, for example, "most of the food," and verb agreement, for example, "has been cooked," are required. But in fact the errors are examples of the non-native English speakers' struggle to bridge gaps between the grammatical word order of Chinese and the subject-prominence of English.

Schachter and Rutherford have grouped Chinese and Japanese (which contains characteristics of both topic-prominence and subject-prominence) together in the following examples since Chinese and Japanese speakers created similar constructions in English. I take it that (C) represents Chinese and (J) represents Japanese in their analysis.

(10a)   *Most of food* which is served in such restaurants/*have cooked already* (J).

(10b)   Irrational emotions are bad but *rational emotions/must use for judging* (J).

(10c)   *Chiang's food/must make in the kitchen of the restaurant* but *Marty's food/could make in his house* (C).

(10d) If I have finished these four jobs, I am confident that *my company/can list* in the biggest 100 companies in the world (C).

In their analysis, Schachter and Rutherford maintain that the English teachers' misperceptions are traceable to the topic-prominent characteristics of Chinese and Japanese:

Bilingual English-Chinese and English-Japanese speakers inform us that it is far more plausible to interpret the initial noun phrases in each example as a topic, unrelated grammatically to the following verb, whose actual subject and often object are simply not required by the native language discourse conventions.   (1979: 8)

Thus, the appropriate interpretations for examples (10a)–(10d) might be:

(11a) Most of the food which is served in such restaurants (they) have cooked (it) already.
(11b) Irrational emotions are bad, but rational emotions, (one) must use (them) for judging.
(11c) Chiang's food (he) must make (it) in the kitchen of the restaurant, but Marty's food (he) could make (it) in his house.
(11d) If I have finished these four jobs, I am confident that my company (they) can list (it) in the biggest 100 companies in the world.

If we turn our attention elsewhere, we find the "whole-before-part" principle as a regular feature in writings by linguists and Chinese language teachers about the Chinese language. The principle states that the larger unit generally goes before the smaller unit. The Chinese sense of causality in which a field of contributing factors must be considered as causes for a particular event – that is, a movement of foci from big to small – is one instance of this phenomenon. Linguist Timothy Light claims for Chinese whole-part noun phrases that "In noun phrases, when the relationship of whole and part is at issue, whole will precede part" (1979: 155). (We must remember, however, that while whole may precede part, whole does not *transcend* part in Chinese explanations. If we follow Hall and Ames' (1991) argument, the Chinese philosophical view excludes final unity in which the order of the whole prevails over the order of the parts and neutralizes the distinctiveness of constituent particulars.)

Chad Hansen (1985a) gives an insightful explanation about the whole-before-part phenomenon. In his writings on the conceptual structure of Chinese philosophy, he argues that Chinese theories of language adopt a whole-part (holistic) way of dividing things whereas Western models often presume a many-one (individual-istic) dichotomy. According to Hansen, Chinese explanations thus typically focus on comprehending a range or scope of things as set against what is excluded in that range. What matters then is the ability to divide and discriminate things rather than to abstract and categorize them. British philosopher and Sinologist Angus Graham comments about Hansen's insight that "the tendency of Chinese thought is to divide down rather than to add up, to think in terms of whole/part rather than class/member" (1989: 401). This recalls our discussion of a "one-tiered" or single-ordered world as opposed to a "two-tiered" world or dual worlds.

Of special interest to us is the fact that the whole-before-part principle occurs throughout Chinese. In fact, the principle is seen as a powerful tool for the teaching of Chinese as a second language:

Viewed in terms of communicative dynamism, the rule of "whole before the part" is one more manifestation of the general tendency of Chinese to arrange the elements in order of increasing informational weight, the thematic or given elements preceding the more rhematic or new elements. When explained in these terms, "whole before the part" can be taught as the equivalent on the phrase level of Topic-Comment on the sentence level. (Li 1977: 133)

According to Li, it describes the pattern for "quantified expres-sions" (12a), for "partitives" (12b) and (12c), and for the sequence of "hierarchically listed units" (12d). The following examples come from Li's analysis; I have provided the glosses. Note, for instance, that in (12a), the initial noun phrase *xuesheng* 'student' is the topic and the Chinese way of representing the fractions "two-thirds" and "one-third" actually reverses Western practices, i.e., "three" encapsulates the smaller units of "two" or "one". This sort of telescoping encapsulation is again evident in (12d) where the date is expressed in a contracting order, i.e., year precedes month and month precedes day. In all cases, the larger unit goes before the smaller unit.

(12a)   *Womende xuesheng, sanfenzhier   shi*
        We plural student   three-parts-genitive-two be
        nande, sanfenzhiyi   shi nüde.
        male   three-parts-genitive-one   be   female.

        Two-thirds of our students are male, one-third are female.

(12b)   *Sige ren,   yige shengbingle, liangge fangjia,*
        four person one sick   two   vacation

        jiu   sheng   wo yige ren   gongzuo.
        then remain   I   one person work

        Out of four people, one is sick and two are on vacation,
        leaving only me to work.

(12c)   *Riben zhaoxiangji, youde hen hao, youde*
        Japan camera   some very good some

        busuan   zenme   hao.
        not consider particularly good.

        Some Japanese cameras are very good, some aren't parti-
        cularly good.

(12d)   *Ta shi 1920 nian, liuyue   bahao   shengde.*
        He be 1920 year six month eight date born.

        He was born on June 8, 1920.

Likewise, Hsiung (1969: 48) points out other common expressions in Chinese where whole must precede part as, for example,
in:

(13)   *jintian zaoshang jiudian*
       today   morning nine o'clock

Hsiung insists that "morning" here must be identified with the
bigger unit "today" to which it belongs. In other words, the bigger
unit "today" encapsulates a smaller unit "morning," which, in
turn, encapsulates an even smaller unit "nine o'clock."

Still more examples of the whole-before-part principle materi-
alize in the way Chinese construct personal names and addresses.
For instance, in (14a) the surname precedes the generational
name, which generally precedes the individual's name; this reflects
the traditional Chinese emphasis on the kinship aggregate over the
individual person. (In Chinese, the surname appears before the

generational name, which is shared by one's same-sex siblings and represents one's generational standing among kinfolks, and which, in turn, is usually – not always – followed by the personal name, which is sometimes used in familiar address.) In (14b), the country "China" encapsulates the municipality "Panda" which then encapsulates the street "Pigtail" which, in turn, encapsulates the dwelling "36."

(14a) *Yang   Hui   Ling*
       surname generational name individual name

       Hui-ling Yang

(14b) *Zhongguo Xiongmao Shi   Bianzi Jie*
       China   Panda   Municipality Pigtail Street

       sanshiliu hao.
       36   number

       36 Pigtail Street; Panda, China

Some of the preceding points have also been noted by Light (1979). Whether the order of these components is unique to Chinese or not, these components have an invariant pattern whose contracting order – a movement from general to particular – contrasts directly with English's expanding order.

Armed with these explanations, we can now move into our analysis. We have noted that "because" and "so" appear as transitional signals in phases of arguments in Chinese discourse and that they signal a topic–comment relationship between parts of ideas that they link together in Chinese utterances. A closer scrutiny of the discourse examples shows, moreover, that information between the transition markers "because" and "so" is often packed into strings of clauses connected by the conjunction "and." This phenomenon has already been mentioned in chapter 2. Note further that many of these clauses are topic-like constructions. As English sentences, however, they seem incomplete in that the second clause is conspicuously absent; that is, the speaker's message is incomplete until the "so" portion of the discourse is reached.

We know from our earlier discussion that the "because" subset of Chinese constructions is topic-like as these clauses occur in sentence–initial position and set up the context for the following assertion. We also know that topics share a weak syntactic relationship with their comments. That English morphological markers such as "if" or "although" don't always appear is due to their optional omission in Chinese. In light of such considerations, it appears to be an acceptable feature in the discourse of English-speaking Chinese to simply string together topic-like clauses, much as they string together comment clauses in their native Chinese. This feature may explain the mere listing of reasons as noted by our American informants in chapter 2. The fact that they are independent clauses is indicated by the use of the conjunctions "and" or "but" to separate them. The sequential order of this topic-chaining effect (not to be confused with Li and Thompson's topic-chaining discussed earlier) in our data is:

$$\text{BECAUSE} + \begin{Bmatrix} \text{if} \\ \text{although} \\ \text{because/as/since} \\ \text{whenever} \end{Bmatrix} + \text{SO}$$

Take (2), (5), and (6) from the previous chapter as examples. In English, we might say "if... and if..., thus/so..." or "since/because/as... and since/because/as... therefore..." as in (2) and (6). In this respect, the pattern noted in the discourse examples is hardly unique. Another look at the examples, however, reveals something else that does not correspond to conventional English discourse practices. Consider the second half of (5) – reproduced in a different format below – where we find the mixture of "whenever... and although... but... so..." which are unlikely combinations in English:

a. And, AS YOU KNOW,
b. WHENEVER THERE'S A SHORTAGE OF COMPONENTS ON THE ( ) AMOUNT OF TIME, AND, AH,
c. ALTHOUGH WE HAVE ARRANGED DELIVERY OF NORMAL SUPPLIES FOR FOR FOR AT LEAST SIX MONTHS,
d. BUT WE STILL NEED AH AN EXTRA MONEY TO BUY AH THE REPLACEMENT, WHICH COST US five HUNDRED MORE.
e. *So, in other words, I need at least six hundred thousand, sorry, six hundred thousand pounds for an extra uh extra money for the for the new ah budget for for our component.*

In short, it appears that the principles underlying the appearance of these clauses are identical to those underlying their occurrence on the sentence-level description of topic–comment constructions. For the most part, background information is packaged into topic-like structures that form a pattern completed only with the appearance of "so." Moreover, those complete utterances, some of which take on topic-comment properties, between the transitional markers "because" and "so" also serve to set the scene for the main message to follow. In fact, what I have discussed so far provides a basis for understanding why Chinese discourse conveys a circular or spiral effect to English-speaking natives. What I have described is a sort of Chinese puzzle box where a topic-(comment)-like construction connects to another topic-(comment)-like phenomenon, all of which is boxed within an overall topic-comment-like frame.

This configuration has also been described for Japanese in different ways. Speaking about Japanese texts, for instance, Ikegami Yoshihiko (1989) reports Tokieda Motoki's observation about their "Chinese-box-pattern-structure" or *irekogata-kozo-keishiki*. Tokieda explains that coherence does not progress in simple linear fashion in this structure, but, rather, emerges from the gradual accumulation of successive segments of a text. Each successive segment – i.e., a sentence or paragraph – serves as conceptual head and is followed by a connecting word or phrase – i.e., a conjunction or pronoun. This entire combination then serves as a new conceptual head for the next set of segments and connectors. The process then repeats itself, eventually generating a "complete whole." Speaking more generally, anthropologist Joy Hendry (1990) points to a "wrapping" phenomenon that cuts across the ritual, spatial, and linguistic realms of Japanese life and thought. Notice, however, that in talking about a Chinese or Japanese puzzle box, the configuration is not strictly an isolation within another isolation. Rather, the configuration resembles Henry Kissinger's account given in chapter 1 of his conversations with Mao Zedong: "it was like the courtyards in the Forbidden City, each leading to a deeper recess . . ."

Let us now return to the curious coincidence in Chinese discourse and Chinese topic–comment utterances and ask: what does this imply for the analytic separation between the sentence level and the discourse level in spoken Chinese? First, recall that Li and Thompson's analysis suggests a breakdown in the conceptual distinction between the sentence level and the discourse level. Likewise, recent investigations into stylistic differences between written and spoken English narratives show that sentence boundaries tend to disappear in the spoken versions. For a variety of reasons, information is produced in spurts which can be understood as one long, multi-clausal sentence. According to Wallace Chafe (1980), the speaker clings to a "center of interest" or "mental image" of what he or she wants to communicate, while delivering the information making up this mental image in connected sequences of "idea units" (i.e., the linguistic expression of speakers' focuses of consciousness as their thoughts move forward in time [Chafe 1985: 121]) to form a unified, extended sentence. This sentence, however, bears little resemblance to the typical sentence of traditional grammar since it sometimes extends over an entire narrative. Instead, what emerges is a series of connected syntactic units that sometimes blurs the analytic distinction between the sentence level and the discourse level. Accepting this line of reasoning, we might view the examples of Chinese discourse as gigantic sentences, their unique configuration and internal connections conforming in certain vital respects to the topic–comment construction prominent in Chinese. From a different vantage point, the situation resembles what Alton Becker (1979: 246) has described about classical Malay – specifically, a sentence in classical Malay is "more like a paragraph." For Chinese, this vantage point may be more appropriate, given the traditional disposition towards texts rather than sentences.

To be more specific, it seems that the topic–comment relationship informs our discourse examples in three ways: first, Chinese tend to order the whole or larger framework to precede the parts or elements; second, the appearance of "because" and "so" to signal phases in argument bears a remarkable resemblance to the topic–comment configuration; third, pieces of information in our data appear as a series of linked topic-like structures (with or without morphological markers and connected by a variety of conjunctions) to provide a steady progression in argument. These three features demonstrate how Chinese arrange information to cohere sensibly and predictably.

The idea that our discourse examples are not idiosyncratic constructions or lucky coincidences but rather are systematic ways of organizing information draws sustenance from other works in spoken English discourse cited by Chafe. These studies indicate that the typical sentence should be analyzed as a multi-clausal unit where the clauses are quite often linked by coordinate conjunctions such as "and" and less often by subordinate conjunctions such as "if," "when," and "because" in English, the inverse in fact of what occurs in our discourse examples. Apparently, the use of subordinate conjunctions requires a great deal more forethought and preparation in that the speaker must take into account the tighter semantic relationship between the two clauses (see, for example, Longacre 1985). In other words, the cognitive task and the subsequent verbalization process are somewhat weightier when connecting subordinate clauses than when connecting co-ordinate clauses. It is in this sense that we might argue that Chinese deliberately conceive and deliver information as one gigantic unit, which, in turn, is packaged into the framework of the topic–comment construction.

The psychological reality of the "gigantic sentence" hypothesis takes on heightened significance when we examine examples (5) and (6) in chapter 2. Not only is each argument and its qualifying points compressed into a topic–comment mold, we see immediately that the topic–comment construction is juxtaposed to another topic–comment-like construction. As stated in chapter 2, I have indicated this spoken phenomenon in writing by separating the arguments into paragraph-like statements.

In sum, as we sort out the range of explanations available to us, a fairly systematic picture emerges. The fundamental premise organizing information in the topic–comment relationship is reflected on the level of discourse; the relationship of main point to the rest of the discourse mirrors the order of comment to topic. Information is packed into clausal units which are linked together by various syntactic devices to form a coherent, recognizable whole. Furthermore, the use of "because/as" and "so/therefore" to mark phases of argument in Chinese discourse can be viewed as the reproduction or extension of familiar modes of organizing information. And, in their new contexts, they may mean something different from that assumed by native English speakers.

We see that the different levels of linguistic analysis are reconciled in an integral manner. Just what other discourse or social
functions underlie these forms of linguistic behavior remains an
open question. In this respect, we might remember that nearly all
the speakers in our discourse examples confronted communicative
requirements of face-to-face interaction; these in turn are culturally
defined. Here we might draw on one line of explanation from
work by Patricia Clancy (1982). Her Japanese informants had
been asked to recall the contents of a soundless film in the presence of a listener. As it turned out, they also dispensed with
the intermediate units of sentence boundaries in their discourse.
Instead, they produced information in fragments analogous to
the "idea units" explicated by Chafe and somehow pulled them
together into one long Japanese sentence to provide a summary
effect rather than a narrative account. Clancy attributes the
phenomenon to many factors, including the requirement for greater
conversational involvement in Japanese social intercourse. That is,
delivering their narratives in spurts or clausal fragments lets the
listener gradually process the information and also lets the speaker
check on the listener's comprehension. The greater frequency
of listener's response signals – otherwise known as *aizuchi* in
Japanese, those mandatory mutterings showing listener's encouragement and attentiveness and which essentially blurs the boundary between speaker and listener – and the speaker's use of pauses
and final sentence particles (what traditional Chinese grammar
calls "mood particles" or *yuqi ci* to convey a speaker's feeling,
state, or intention) ensure a more intense cooperative interaction
between Japanese participants than between English-speaking
natives. It may be said that these rapport-building and rapport-
monitoring devices turn discourse into an earnest sort of co-
production; they reflect an exquisite sensitivity to others that is an
important part of Asian cultural assumptions about personhood,
personal dignity and human intercourse. Much like our Chinese
speakers, Clancy's Japanese speakers aspire to generate greater
possibilities for mutual engagement and participatory meaning-
making.

Further, following Schachter and Rutherford, we might also
ask to what extent the systematic use and attributes of "because"
and "so" as transition markers are reflections of a similar kind of

discourse strategy carried over from Chinese into English. While such an examination goes beyond the scope of this inquiry, nevertheless, we have access to one bit of evidence which emerged from my experience while gathering example (3) in chapter 2. Recall that since the speaker was bilingual, I had asked him to bear in mind that he would be addressing different linguistic audiences, one being Chinese/Cantonese and the other being native English speakers. As it turned out, the exercise resulted in identical appearances and positions of *yinwei* 'because' and *suoyi* 'therefore' as transition signals in their respective presentations. Again, the evidence is slender but tantalizing, and, given what I have already discussed, I venture to guess that further inquiry might well establish that this is not an isolated incident. In terms of what "because" and "so" actually mean to Chinese as "transition markers" in their discourse, Chinese and English, is another matter that might profit from further scrutiny (see, for example, p. 140).

Speculations aside, our analysis has begun to explain how aspects of Chinese syntax contribute to the puzzle of Chinese inscrutability. Our analysis also exposes the drawbacks of relying on a sentence-level approach when seeking important linguistic insights about communication and about cross-linguistic differences and difficulties. Enlarging our focus beyond the sentence boundary enables us to avoid some parochializing constraints and to probe more deeply into the reciprocal relationship between grammar and discourse and their mutual influence on linguistic behavior. Eliminating this sentence-focused bias also enables us to consider whether appearances of incoherence or illogicity in one language might be traced to cultural differences in the signalling of information at different levels of language.

Our discussion also suggests a link between discourse processes, syntax, and culture. However, the link is not a straightforward one; it is a relationship decidedly more complex and more opaque than previously assumed. The issue needs mentioning in part because of the many arguments made about the parallels and intersections among language, thought, and culture. Without denying their relevance (and my own occasional indulgences in such matters), the past discussions seem to focus more on the static, mental planes of language structure (where things are conveniently isolated and, given the traditional links between Western linguists and logicians, analyzed for their literal meaning, propositional or referential truths, or the ways they encode or represent reality) and less on the dynamic, interactive dimensions of language use (where things are messier and difficult to untangle from their context). As our discussion indicates, Chinese – and Japanese – structure their discourse to generate greater conversational involvement between speaker and listener; their linguistic behavior and repertoire of communicative signs and conventions are geared to social functions that are very much culturally based. Attending to the communicative ends of speech and discourse allows us to put an interactive spin on the parallels and intersections among language, thought, and culture; it enables us to put the focus back on people as interacting persons and on language as a social instrument with a variety of communicative functions. (What actually happens to such parallels and intersections in the case of bi/multi-linguals with all their gradations and degrees of fluency and bi/multi-culturalism complicates matters considerably. The complications increase when we also consider whether their languages come from a linguistic/cultural area or are geographically – and radically – distant. And what can one say about such parallels and intersections when we confront code-switching or Pidgin and Creole languages?) To a certain degree, it also enables us to make inroads into the mutual influence of spoken interaction and grammatical features – that is, why grammatical systems in different cultures have the features they have and how they affect communication and vice versa. At the least, attending to the communicative ends of speech and discourse allows for a shift in emphasis from, say, the tabulation of linguistic and cultural differences to the examination of miscalculated and misunderstood signals by which cultural differences emerge in the first place.

At bottom, Chinese and Americans operate within fundamentally different social universes. Culturally, they are persuaded by their languages in ways still mysterious; their languages help to promote thought and action in different ways and vice versa. But what actually contributes to the cultural impasse in Sino-American interactions is how and whether they successfully convey their messages and intentions to one another. As we have seen, Chinese have a distinctive way of linking together ideas and utterances within an overall framework; often enough, Americans flounder in their efforts to grasp what these connections are and what they signify. Understanding is slippery stuff, even more so when one's loose links leave the other at loose ends.

4

Backforwardly speaking

We turn now to another vital part in the puzzle of Chinese inscrutability. In chapter 2, I began to explain some serious contradictions and unmet expectations in the discourse strategies of Chinese and Americans. We saw in chapter 3 that one source of their misunderstandings stems from typological differences in the ways that they link, highlight, and signal ideas. Another source grows out of some deep-seated cultural differences in generating meaning and eliciting response. Chinese rhetoric emphasizes an aesthetic and evocative open-endedness. The Chinese aesthetic sees communication as inherently negotiable and collaborative; the communicant's responsibility for fleshing out meaning is just as essential as the communicator's role in evoking meaning. This aesthetic draws a good part of its sense and rhetorical force from the exigencies of a participatory ritual order and from a keen awareness of the imbalance of power and status in a hierarchical world.

To go further into the underlying forces influencing Chinese rhetoric requires that we examine stylistic ideals that Westerners might see as circular starts, tangential views, and subdued stances – what might otherwise be described as non-beginnings, multiple views, and non-endings. We use Westerners' accounts of the Chinese "eight-legged essay," along with a brief description about its features, to begin our discussion of the social and cosmic resonances of these ideals and of an evocative and participatory thrust in Chinese rhetoric.

The topic is so broad that our discussion will have to be highly selective and limited to points of relevance for this chapter. This means that our discussion will be too simplified and condensed to fully reflect the rich variety that actually existed in classical times and thereafter. On the other hand, we will stress a remarkably uniform Chinese mode of apprehension and presentation as well as a culturally learned sense of how things should combine to generate meaning and elicit response.

Throughout, we assume that oral and written forms, notwithstanding important differences between them, follow parallel strategies in communicating ideas and in meaning-making (see Li and Thompson 1982 for some differences between spoken Mandarin and written Chinese). Strategies formerly distinguished as distinctly oral or as distinctly literate have mingled in written communication. Conversely, strategies usually falling within the literate tradition, in Western societies at least, have spilled over to oral use in public settings. As for the latter, a Chinese was startled into remarking, upon listening to a Harvard man's learned response to a minor question at a party, "Why, he talks like a book!"

To begin this chapter, as we might, with a discussion of ancient Chinese rhetorical practices could take us too far afield too soon. Better that we anchor our discussion, as I have indicated, by first describing what Westerners and others have to say about the forces influencing Chinese rhetoric, or, more specifically, Chinese ways of constructing and generating meaning, and from there press on with our examination of Chinese communicative aims and see how they might relate to ancient rhetorical practices. Such is the route I take below.

As it happens, contemporary Western attempts to isolate essential characteristics of Chinese rhetoric have led many straightaway to the "eight-legged essay" (see, for example, Kaplan 1968, Cheng 1982, Matalene 1985). Otherwise known as the *bagu wen*, it persisted through many evolutions for nearly five centuries and only began to yield its influence in the early decades of the twentieth century. Made up of eight carefully specified parts or "legs" and compressed into several hundred Chinese characters in stylized language, it was the chief torment in the Chinese "examination hell" (Miyazaki 1981) – essentially, a literary gauntlet through which survivors could hope to pass on their steep path to position and power in official life. According to one account about the eight-legged essay:

The Octopartite Composition, or Eight-legged Essay, was the core of the Chinese educational curriculum and the most important subject in the official examination for nearly five hundred years. Until it was abolished in 1898, every student had to devote a disproportionate amount of energy to mastering its structure and stylistic intricacies. He would be given a *Thema* from either the Four Books or the Five Classics, and had to proceed from one "leg" to the next of his treatment according to a definite sequence, using the appropriate formulae and rhetorical devices. (John Minford in Cao 1982: 389)

The Classics included the *Book of Changes*, the *Book of Songs*, the *Book of Rites*, the *Book of History*, and the *Spring and Autumn Annals*. Some Confucius reputedly edited as a core curriculum. Others he frequently cited. To the Five Classics, Neo-Confucians added the Four Books – the *Great Learning*, the *Doctrine of the Mean*, the *Confucian Analects*, and the *Sayings of Mencius* – all variously related to the teachings of Confucius and still being learned by heart by Chinese schoolchildren in Taiwan, Hong Kong, and Singapore. Together, they counseled restraint, urged moderation, commended sincerity, and privileged traditional wisdoms and historical understandings.

Rigid and rigorous, the eight-legged essay's form and content differed greatly from Western ones. It was, moreover, based on cooperative principles and assumptions very difficult for Westerners to uncover. Instead of extended arguments that brought things to a tight close, a succession of related images was balanced and counterbalanced to converge into an integrated whole. A theme was elucidated, followed by a "turn" or differently angled perspective in the argument, and next came the "eight legs" of the last four paragraphs, themselves setting forth a carefully balanced conclusion with contrasting examples patterned in alternating, contiguous lines, thus elegantly satisfying the formal demands of antithesis and parallelism. Throughout, the topic – perhaps a quotation by Confucius set as theme by the examiners – was repeated, its premise constantly implied rather than explicated. At the essay's end, the author's ideas emerged in just a few lines, often merely to affirm conventional wisdom. Just as links between Chinese words, clauses, and utterances could be obscured, the links between contrasting, concrete examples were tenuously secured and more often left to the reader. As Willard Peterson observes:

The idea of "legs" derived from a complicated interplay of opposites in the composition of each essay – negatives with affirmatives, abstract statements with concrete ones, simplicities with profundities ... (t)he essay, then, emphasized the play of words and sentences against each other, with negation or counterbalancing of statements impeding the formulation of what we might consider an argument. (1979: 50–51)

From this brief explanation, it is evident that the Chinese way of joining disparate elements to convey a point can pose serious problems for native English speakers accustomed to definitive statements, supporting evidence, and the finality of closure. It is especially the case when the point is driven home from a direction contrary to what they expect. It gets even worse when the point is not so much driven home but allowed to emerge gradually using the very different joining and expanding techniques of analogy, parallelism, and complementary opposition. Consequently, their appreciation of the demanding task of correlating all parts coherently and consistently around a persistent central theme can also recede in kind. As a case in point, consider the following translated final paragraphs of an essay written by Wang Ao (1450–1524), considered a master of the *bagu wen*. Its topic – "If the people enjoy sufficiency how could the ruler suffer from insufficiency?" – is so differently approached and put together that many native English speakers would no doubt mistake this example as a series of themes rather than the central theme:

If the people are enjoying sufficiency, for what conceivable reason should the ruler be left alone in poverty? I know that what was kept in the common households would all be available to the ruler, without its being hoarded in the treasury to enable the ruler to claim, "This is my wealth"; what is stored in the farm and fields would all be accessible to the ruler, without its being accumulated in the vaults to enable the ruler to claim, "These are my possessions." With inexhaustible availability, what worry is there for failure to respond to demand? With inexhaustible supplies, what anxiety is there for lack of preparedness in emergency?

The sacrificial animals and ritual cereals are plentiful to be used in religious offerings; and the jades and silks are abundant to be used as tributes and diplomatic gifts. Even if these were insufficient, the people will naturally supply them in full. Wherein will there be a shortage? Food and delicacies, beefs and drinks are abundant for entertainment of state guests; carriages and horses, arms and equipment are enough for the preparation of wars and defense. Even if these were insufficient, the people will take care of the needs. Wherein again will there be insufficiency?

Oh! The establishment of the tithe was originally for the good of the people, but in this very usage lies the sufficiency of national expenditure. Where then is there any need to increase taxation to attain national wealth? (in Tu 1974–75: 401–402)

Contemporary Western efforts to identify essential elements in Chinese rhetoric have also been accompanied by stereotypical characterizations of Chinese rhetorical style that generally call attention to its indirection, notably the presence of circularity, multi-angled views and the absence of a topic statement. Here, for instance, is an analysis of some six hundred foreign student compositions, Chinese speakers being prominent among them. By "Oriental" below, the American author is referring to Chinese and Koreans (see footnote 13 in Kaplan 1966: 10, also Kaplan 1987; why he did not include Japanese is curious):

Some Oriental writing... is marked by what may be called an approach by indirection. In this kind of writing, the development of the paragraph may be said to be "turning and turning in a widening gyre." The circles or gyres turn around the subject and show it from a variety of tangential views, but the subject is never looked at directly. Things are developed in terms of what they are not, rather than in terms of what they are. Again, such a development in a modern English paragraph would strike the English reader as awkward and unnecessarily indirect. (Kaplan 1966: 10)

He goes on to scrutinize an Oriental's composition: "The concluding paragraph-sentence presents, in the guise of a summary logically derived from previously posited ideas, a conclusion which is in fact partially a topic sentence... The paper arrives where it should have started" (11). Groping for images that best reflect the reversed rhetorical priorities of American and Oriental discourse, he paints the following:

AMERICAN   ORIENTAL/CHINESE

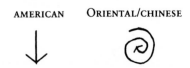

The sames images predominate in the spontaneous expressions of Americans and Chinese alike. Thus, whereas Americans readily cite the "adage of the old preacher" to me as a rule of thumb in formal discourse:

Say what you're going to say
Say it
Then say what you've said

some Chinese, by contrast, offer the following proverb:

Hua   lung   dian   jing
paint   dragon draw   eye

which translates into: "When you draw a dragon, you paint in the eyes last."

One Chinese explained, "It's not a dragon if the eyes are not painted in; it is the eyes which give it life" and then went on to phrase his explanation in terms which evoke an image of circularity:

If that dot you don't put down – only one dot you don't put down, it's not a dragon. As long as you spend so much time turning a circle, then what's your point? Put it down – that's the point! The eye distinguishes the dragon. And that is the last step . . . Maybe there's a story in ancient time when a person draw a dragon and then when he paint the eyes, and then the dragon become alive.

Like Westerners, Chinese also consider the eight-legged essay to be influential in present-day discourse. Some assert that Chinese writing is like their thinking; it moves in circular patterns:

the structure of the once popular "eight-legged essay" style of writing is a classic example of thinking and writing in circles and ellipses. The cardinal rules for writing a Chinese composition, *ch'i* (topical statement; literally "opening the door"), *ch'eng* (lateral elaboration), *chuan* (twists and turns in the arguments, or excursions into tangential and oblique dimensions), and *ho* (convergence), are the epitome of cyclical thinking. (Hsiung 1969: 50)

Still commanding a loyal following in China and in Taiwan, the cardinal rules referred to above – subsequently adopted by Japanese as *ki-shoo-ten-ketsu* (Hinds 1983) and by Koreans as *ki-sung-chon-kyul* (Eggington 1987) – had been given to me earlier in Chinese and Pinyin with an English translation by a middle-aged gentleman from China who laughingly recalled their significance on what his American colleagues described as his "inscrutable" speech habits:

qi	起	to start, begin, open
cheng	承	to carry on, sustain, follow-up
zhuan	轉	to turn, look at the problem from another angle
he	合	to conclude, whereby the author's opinion is established or hinted

And, by another's reckoning: "This format is very old yet it is still very popular among the intellectuals, especially in Taiwan. Whenever you want to write a very formal article or formal governmental official memo, you have to follow this way. My M.A. thesis in Taiwan follows in gross outline this style rather than the American style."

The foregoing accounts from Chinese and Westerners alike give credence to the view that subtle elements in the eight-legged essay continue to influence present-day discourse. This is true as far as it goes but there is more to it than that. In point of fact, the eight-legged essay is just one prominent example of longheld ideals about generating meaning to which most literary genres subscribe and which, ultimately, go back to the traditional Chinese worldview.

To understand modern Chinese we must scrutinize its past. I propose as a first step that we turn our attention to classical Chinese poetry. The reasons for this are twofold. In the first place, poetry holds a powerful and prestigious position in Chinese literary life and therefore in Chinese conceptions of meaning-making. Confucius himself extolled its merits and saw in poetry's images and metaphors a means to enrich political and diplomatic discourse as well as serve as a practical guide for speech and communication. "Unless you study the Odes," he advised his son, "you will be ill-equipped to speak" (*Analects* 16/13). In the second place, the aesthetics of poetry influenced the eight-legged essay: *qi cheng zhuan he* 起承轉合 is an old structural scheme used in classical poetry, predating its use in the *bagu* by several centuries. Despite important differences between them, both poetry and essay favor evocative imagery and nuanced description; both share similar methods of forging links and generating meaning; both hold to the dominant Chinese view that "words inspire and one intuits."

Before launching into poetry, we need to understand better the worldview which informs it and which, in many respects, constitutes a common ground for the classic formulations of Confucian and Daoist philosophies. As we began to explain in chapter 2, the ancients believed that the cosmos (and humans too) has no external creator or ultimate primal cause. Rather, the cosmos is seen as spontaneously self-generating and made up of perpetually transforming, complementary bipolar elements, with humans actively participating in the creative process. All parts are interrelated, interdependent, and mutually responsive. Events are construed in dynamic patterns of juxtapositions, oppositions and contrasts. *Qi* 氣, psychophysical, moving energy, itself sometimes visible, sometimes invisible, assumes different forms and consistencies and permeates all things. Cyclic processes prevail in this world picture, an interest in rhythms, resonances, and reverberations predominates, context, contingency, and conjunction assume keen significance, and all existences are characterized by their transforming power and capability. Multiple directions and multi-layered correspondences are emphasized over beginnings and endings; continuities and bonds over sharp breaks and disparity; movement and action over rest and stillness; process and function over essence and attribute; aspect and phase over fixity and stasis; complex balances and complementaries over abstraction and causality; internal spontaneity and diversity over external imposition and uniformity. Things and events fluctuate between dynamic change and integration, paired and interacting particulars empower each other, and disparate elements are merged into a new synthesis. Given this understanding, words like "parts," "elements," and "things," such as I have used (reluctantly), do a deep disservice to Chinese ways of thinking.

Westerners have commented variously on the pervasiveness of this worldview in Chinese habits of thought and expression. Joseph Needham, author of the multi-volume series *Science and Civilization in China*, for instance, writes about a Chinese "co-ordinative" or "associative" mindset that contrasts with a dominant Western "subordinative" mind-set:

the universe itself is a vast organism, with now one and now another component taking the lead – spontaneous and uncreated it is, with all the parts of it cooperating in a mutual service which is perfect freedom, the larger and the smaller playing their parts according to their degree, "neither afore nor after the other" ... The conviction that the universe and each of the wholes composing it have a cyclical nature, undergoing alternations, so dominated (Chinese) thought that the idea of succession was always subordinated to that of interdependence. (1956: 288–289)

Accordingly, Chinese literature scholar Andrew Plaks argues that attempts to fit the cosmic dynamisms and interdependencies resonant throughout Chinese narratives into the confines of Western cultural patterns are completely misguided:

Since in Chinese narrative, as in Chinese philosophy, existence is conceived of in terms of overlapping patterns of ceaseless alternation and cyclical recurrence, it follows that any attempt to mimetically reduce that experience to discrete models – mythic or geometric plots such as lend themselves to the aesthetic sense of unified narrative shape – would appear erroneous from the very start. (1977: 335)

Alternatively, French Sinologist Jacques Gernet points to the contrast between Western philosophical preoccupations with universal categories and stable abstractions and Chinese concerns with functional complementaries and phasic potentialities:

Our own philosophical traditions, which owe so much to "the suggestions stemming from certain grammatical functions" are founded upon categories considered to be universal and are concerned with abstractions and ideas that are stable. Chinese thought, in contrast, recognises only functional classifications and oppositions. It is concerned not with "yes" or "no," being or non-being, but with contraries which succeed, combine with and complement one another; not with eternal realities but with potentialities and tendencies, phases of flowering or decline. In the place of the idea of law as an immutable rule, it favors that of a model or schema for development. (1985: 242)

He looks to the Chinese language to account for these differences:

Given that Chinese is an uninflected language, all that helps to guide one through a phrase, with the aid of a very limited number of particles, are the links between terms of similar meaning, the oppositions between terms of opposite meaning, the rhythms and parallelisms, the position of "words" or semantic unities and the types of relationship between them; and yet the infinite possible combinations of two semantic units are the source of an inexhaustible fund of meanings. At every level, meaning stems from the way terms are combined. No doubt this is what accounts for the predominant role played by complementary pairs of opposites and correspondences in Chinese thought and above all for its fundamental relativism. Nothing has meaning except through opposition to its contrary. Everything depends upon position (*wei*) and timing (*shi*). (Ibid)

When he then assesses the difficulties Christian missionaries faced upon translating Western ideas into Chinese, his specification several paragraphs later of "being" and "substance" in Western thought to "becoming" and "sensory perception" in Chinese thought is consistent with the distinction between a logical as opposed to an aesthetic order discussed in chapter 2:

In the history of Western thought, the opposition of substance to accident ... encompassed that of the noun to the adjective which is so fundamental to Indo-European languages. Here, too, the language no doubt helped to produce the concept of the existence of permanent and ideal realities, independent of the unstable diversity of what can be observed through the senses. But for the Chinese, whose language lacked inflections, the abstract concept of substance could not have the same logical necessity as it did for the European missionaries. (1985: 243)

Note also that within this worldview, all parts theoretically have the possibility to be "in focus." And, as each element runs into or grows out of another, their relationship becomes ultimately circular. With multiple entry points and open-ended beginnings and endings, Chinese discourse sometimes takes on the appearance of those patterns of dots in children's comic books; once traced together, they all connect in a pattern, with neither one nor another dot paramount. And, this, in fact, is precisely how an astonished American friend describes her conversational encounters with a Chinese friend: "I know that if I keep listening, somehow the topics will link up, just like those dots in comic books!"

Perhaps the most resonant expression of cosmic dynamisms, correspondences, and interdependencies appears in traditional Chinese poetry. This poetry has features and assumptions that contrast strikingly with Western ones. On the one hand, the uninflected nature of the Chinese language gives it an "ambiguous," "impersonal," and "universal" air; dispensing with conjunctions, tense, pronouns, and so on makes Chinese poetry somehow more "compact," "timeless," and "egoless" (Liu 1962). A Chinese poet's use of clever parallelisms, complementary pairings, and subtle but sophisticated allusions and analogies may be unfathomable to most Westerners, yet they are a constant source of fascination to a Chinese reader whose culture stresses the delight and stimulation of "meaning beyond words" (*yan wai zhi yi* 言外之意) and "inexhaustible meaning" (*wu qiong zhi yi* 無窮之意). That Chinese poets saw themselves as co-participants with the cosmos only accentuates their disposition towards an aesthetic restraint and a muted presence (although some poets, such as Li Bai, can be wildly outspoken and unrestrained). Alternatively, since ancient Chinese believed that everything in the cosmos was interconnected, their poetry often sought to describe their sentiments and perceptions about the "sympathetic resonances" between cosmic phenomena and human phenomena.

On the other hand, a Chinese poem is intimate and interpersonal, its themes often accessible and arresting even to naive Western readers. This is due to the fact that a Chinese poem has long been viewed as an authentic expression of a poet's emotions and experience, typically written at a specific time and a specific place for specific individuals and occasions. By way of contrast, a Western poet often has in mind a generalized, abstract audience; he or she tries to reach beyond the occasion for some universal truth. In particular, a Chinese poem aims to establish a dialogue with its reader and, in turn, expects its reader to approach it much like a good friend who is interested in the poet and takes the time and trouble to intuit, discover, or reconstruct the nuances behind – or more likely between or beyond – the words. A friend is someone who has a good ear, one who *zhi yin* 'knows tone' (Owen 1990) – that is, someone who can read the tone of a message that, more often than not, is obliquely referenced and put into words imbued with multiple meanings.

From this, we might gather that Chinese attach great cultural importance to auditory skills as opposed to, say, articulatory skills, and, in fact, Chinese have traditionally emphasized good-listening as well as good-speaking. A "keen-eared" sensitivity and understanding of the faintest stimuli is much prized in all Chinese wordarts. Indeed, *wen dao* 聞道 'hearing (the) way' is the dominant type in ancient Chinese texts. By the same token, ancient performance ideals and musical peaks rest in the "silent sounds," for example, of a stringless zither or an effortless whistle, both of which reveal a cultural fascination with the aesthetic possibilities of a refined restraint, remote resonances, and the minimalization of sound and effort. Kenneth DeWoskin (1982) points out too that, for the ancient Chinese, an astute mind developed in tandem with auditory perspicacity; long, pendulous ears identified a sage and acute hearing described his superior intellect. Writes DeWoskin: "In the *Huai-nan-tzu* and the *Spring and Autumn Annals of Mr. Lü*, there are numerous comments on the sage, his hearing, and his music, most of which speak to the great sensitivity of the sage's ear, his ability to hear the faintest music, even soundless music, and his skill in interpreting the nature of things by hearing their sounds" (1982: 37).

From this, we might also gather that Chinese expectations between reader and writer differ somewhat from Western ones. To a greater extent than Westerners, Chinese rely on a reader's ability to think through a thought rather than the writer's ability to spell it out completely. Concurrently, the bonds between reader and writer also differ. Expectations that a reader has the personal imagination and resourcefulness to work out a thought translates into respect for the reader's receptivity and participatory ability in fleshing out meaning. (Participatory here does double duty; as we shall later see in our discussion of Confucius' thoughts, it includes both participating with others in effecting and enhancing communication and participating in the cultural tradition as well. As for receptivity, I refer to a capacity to be moved or inspired by one's environment – in effect, to develop a broader and deeper capacity to become co-participants with the cosmos.) The reader is expected to grasp an understanding from the writer's skilled accretion of detailed imagery. In this way, reader and writer collaborate in the invisible resonances of meaning-making. As part of an aesthetic of indeterminacy and open-endedness, one evocatively suggests and stimulates and the other works out meaning personally.

Poetry's claim to reflect a person's genuine emotions and experience gives it an influential and interesting role in Chinese civilization. For one thing, poetry served as a subdivision of rhetoric, its ambiguity and indirection enabling veiled criticisms or upright remonstrances concerning specific political or social issues. Given that a ruler's integrity and leadership qualities in ancient times were thought inseparable and so a public matter, a Chinese poet's literary energies were often directed towards influencing central government. Consequently, sometimes poetry was the voice of reason(ableness), other times, it veered close to becoming a voice of treason. That poetry continues its role in Chinese political affairs as the people's voice of protest, indignation and criticism can be seen in the flood of political poetry following China's Cultural Revolution (Yu 1983) and the June 1989, pro-democracy movement. Alternatively, since Chinese believed that poetic emotion was rooted in authentic personal feelings, poems, like songs, were employed in ancient times to gauge popular opinions about government. Tradition maintained that music, in particular, came under the administration of a government department, the Bureau of Music, which regularly dispatched emissaries to distant provinces to collect popular songs and so enabled a ruler to assess his people's moods. Poetic description not only revealed the tone of a sociopolitical order, it also revealed a person's character, intelligence and level of self-cultivation; accordingly, poems came to be used in the civil service examinations and served as letters of introduction.

Much of this view of poetry's use and power can be traced to Confucius' alleged compilation and praise of the *Book of Songs* (*c.* 1100–600 B.C.) the earliest surviving collection of "song-words" or poems meant to be sung. Poetic sociopolitical rhetoric began with the *Songs*, filled as they were with melodies of joy and celebration as well as sour notes about political and social malfeasance. Confucius and his followers regarded these songs as authentic expressions of historical moments and advocated their study so that people could enter and experience the world of its creators; just as a sociopolitical order was knowable by its poetic/musical tone, so too personal feelings were knowable by the poetic/musical tones of a sociopolitical order. Confucius also believed that the *Songs* offered people unparalleled opportunities for self-expression and decorous conduct. For instance, committing them to memory enabled people to use them to sound out others' intentions, to make oblique rhetorical points and to engage in polite discourse. Doubtless, this will appear odd to a modern Western reader unless it is pointed out that Confucius was largely referring to court exchanges; in this connection, the Western reader will recall that, until modern times, European nobles also had to manage courtly niceties and innuendoes in numerous languages, including English, German, French, or Italian, in contrast to the single language dominant in most Chinese courts. All in all, Confucius' admiration of the *Book of Songs* reveals his predilection for the delicate conveyance of meaning through veiled messages and discrete mediums and the development of a well-spoken, refined manner. Here is what he said in the *Analects*:

The Master said, "Be stimulated by the *Odes*, take your stand on the rites and be perfected by music." (8/8)

The Master said, "If a man who knows the three hundred *Odes* by heart fails when given administrative responsibilities and proves incapable of exercising his own initiative when sent to foreign states, then what use are the *Odes* to him, however many he may have learned?" (13/5)

The Master said, "Why is it none of you, my young friends, study the *Odes*? An apt quotation from the *Odes* may serve to stimulate the imagination, to show one's breeding, to smooth over difficulties in a group and to give expression to complaints." (17/9)

Most Chinese poets express their sensitivities and creativities through a series of juxtaposed images, filled with hidden significances and tantalizing implications. Readers, on the other hand, face the challenge and stimulation of apprehending the relations that lie hidden between connections and intuitively or reflectively realizing the meaning beyond the words. As a result, Chinese readers become alert to the use of understatement and nuance; things concealed become as provocative as things revealed. As in hearing sounds, so also in reading poetry, one learns to grasp at links and pick up trifles to eke out meaning. The dynamic collaboration between writer and reader is possible due to their shared conception of an innate parallelism in the natural order which language, as a human artifice, mirrors; the parallelism, being assumed, is sought out by writer and reader as an active principle by which to join and apprehend adjacent lines (Owen 1985).

Since Chinese poets tended to leave connections implicit rather than asserted, their opening images were often suggestive and helped slip the reader into the real subject matter of a work. Chinese saw oblique referentiality as evocative but regarded direct entry into a matter as devoid of emotional evocativeness – that is "short on feeling" and not "alive" (Yu 1987). Accordingly, when the ancients wanted to sway people, they slid into their argument with a suggestive analogy rather than a direct statement. Through a succession of related images and with the classical guidelines of *qi cheng zhuan he* 起承轉合 noted earlier, poetry traditionally

shared with the eight-legged essay and other literary genres a
participatory thrust towards an aesthetic and evocative open-
endedness as well as a pervasive sense of social and cosmological
concordance.

How in fact do Chinese juxtapose words and images to generate meaning? Recall that in the Chinese worldview, many objects
and events tend to be structured in bipolar pairings: yang goes
with yin, heaven with earth, the sun with the moon. Each of these
pairings is assymetrically empowered. Thus, despite – or, perhaps,
because of – their interdependency, yang, heaven, and sun are
somehow more dominant than yin, earth, and moon, just as ruler,
husband, and elder brother traditionally prevailed over subject,
wife, and younger brother (see Fox 1988 for similar asymmetrical
pairings and parallelisms in East Indonesia). Other more common
pairings include taking complementary extremes to develop approximations: *shang xia* 上下 'up' and 'down' and *zuo you* 左右
'left' and 'right', or abstractions and relativizations of amount or
degree: *da xiao* 大小 'big' and 'small' (size); *gao ai* 高矮 'tall'
and 'low' (height); *chang duan* 長短 'long' and 'short' (length).
Mutually dependent rather than conflicting and irreconcilable,
these paired interactants permeate Chinese discourse; the eight-
legged essay's "negation and counterbalancing of statements"
merely amplifies the conceptual operations of these complementary
opposites.

Aside from these bipolar pairs and complementary opposites,
there are other two-character paired compounds which make up
many conceptual categories in literary Chinese. Stephen Owen
explains how these paired concepts are contiguously aligned in
parallel couplets. From his explanation, we also get a better
glimpse of the way Chinese words and statements play against and
counterbalance each other:

each line of a parallel couplet can often be seen as the expansion of one
term of a common compound. A frequent example occurs in couplets
describing landscapes – in Chinese, *shan–shui* 山水, "mountain-and-
water." The general category through which a poet conceives of his topic
is not a unitary idea, a "landscape"; rather, the category is a *pair* of
terms, and those terms dispose themselves each into one line of the
couplet. The resulting couplet consists of one line on a "mountain" scene
set in parallel to a line on a "water" scene.   (1985: 88)

In other words, an experience or perception was often broken down into its component parts and set in parallel segments. Thus, in the following portrayal of a return journey home through the mountains, an entire experience – the travel by day and rest by night, the crossing of valleys/streams and mountains, the going towards and the arrival, movement and rest – is captured in a parallel couplet (Owen 1985: 92):

水	宿	隨	漁	火
water	spend night	follow	fisherman	fire
山	行	到	竹	扉
mountain	travel	arrive	bamboo	gate

For night's lodging on waters, follow the fisherman's fires
Travel through mountains to reach your bamboo gate

Read together, they provide a sense of a completed whole. The intricately interlocked components of couplets energize each other, each taking its sense from the other, each giving the other enriched meaning. And, since each word simultaneously occupies a position within a line and between the lines and so acquires a dual significance, translation can become enormously difficult. In François Cheng's (1986: 42–43, translation by David McCraw) analysis of the poet Wang Wei's description of an excursion through nature, for example:

行	到	水	窮	處
walk	reach	water	be exhausted	place
坐	看	雲	起	時
sit	look at	clouds	rise	moment

Walk to where the water ends
Sit watching when clouds arise

he argues:

If one goes back to the word-for-word translation and reads the two lines simultaneously, one will see that in each case the combination of words in parallel construction gives rise to a hidden significance. Thus "walk–sit" signifies movement and rest; "reach–look" signifies action and contemplation; "water–cloud' signifies universal transformation; "exhausted–rise" signifies death and rebirth; "place–moment" signifies space and time. Rich in this series of significations, the two lines represent in fact the two essential dimensions of life.

and, more deeply:

Rather than holding exclusively to one or the other, the true manner
of life suggested by these lines may be perhaps to comply with the
Emptiness which is found between the two that alone permits man to
avoid separating himself from action and contemplation, or from space and
time, and to participate internally in the true universal transformation.

Chang Kang-i Sun (1983: 222) additionally reinforces the suggestion that parallelism's force derives from a symbolic attempt
to express the balance, totality, and interrelations of *Dao* itself,
which, as she explains, is made up of numerous bipolar qualities
combining in constant rhythm. Parallelism thus confers a sense of
process; each segment feeds off the other and their meanings
unfold interactively and reciprocally. More prosaically, as Angus
Graham (1989) reminds us, parallel statements in a language
structured by word order – where nouns can take verb positions
and verbs can take noun positions – aids syntax by clarifying
ambiguous structures; parallelism also informs the construction of
longer, more complicated sequences.

How else might Chinese words and statements play against and
counterbalance each other? For one answer, consider that two
couplets, like the lines of a single couplet, can lie in dynamic
juxtaposition. Owen explains that, although each couplet is a
complete unit of perception and thought and can hold its own
under critical scrutiny, it also interlocks with other couplets to
form a complete poem. As a result of the Chinese technique of
conjoining interdependent yet independently organized couplets,
ideas interweave and converge. Sometimes, thoughts appear nested
within each other. And, sometimes, different perspectives are offered. Consider, for example, the poem "Gazing on the Peak"
by Du Fu whose topic is gazing and which appears in Owen's
discussion of parallel balance in Chinese poetic structure (1985:
101–103):

What is it like – Mount Tai, the Great Peak?
岱宗夫如何
Across Ch'i and Lu a green unceasing.
齊魯青末了
Here Nature concentrated unearthly glory,
造化鍾神秀

Dark north slope, the sunlit south divide dusk and dawn.
陰陽割昏曉
Sweeping past breast growing layered cloud;
盪胸生層雲
Eye-pupils split, moving in with homing birds.
決眥入歸鳥
The time will surely come when I pass to its very summit
會當凌絕頂
And see in one encompassing vision how tiny all other mountains are.
一覽群山小

The great Qing dynasty commentator Qiu Zhao-ao summarizes the poem's structure:

Written when gazing on the Eastern Peak [Mount T'ai], the poem's meaning can be sketched in four layers. The first couplet is of its color when gazing from afar; the second couplet is its stance seen from up close. The third couplet is the scene when gazing intently and minutely; the last couplet is the subjective response when his gaze reaches its limit.

Elaborating on Qiu Zhao-ao's comments, Owen acknowledges the possibility of a Western-style linear reading, i.e., "a continuous approach to the mountain, first present and physical, then speculative and anticipated," but suggests the greater profitability of a Chinese-style parallel reading. Owen's analysis below, moreover, strikes a matching chord with our discussion in chapter 3 about the Chinese topic–comment puzzle box. Recall that one such construction was locked into another such construction within an overall topic–comment framework:

The seventeenth-century commentator is telling his readers how to understand the relation between couplets – not as linear argument or narrative sequence, but as a pair of quatrains, each constituted of a balanced pair of couplets, which in turn are made up of a balanced pair of lines. The structure of the whole is formed of equal pairs within equal pairs.

As Owen explains it, the first half of the poem is written in an impersonal voice as the scene is being described: "A 'far' couplet followed by a 'near' couplet implicates a viewer to measure out the perspective." The second half of the poem illuminates the poet's subjective response to the scene: "intent gazing toward is matched by attaining the object of the gaze." The inner couplets balance personal with impersonal voice; the outer couplets balance a view from a distance with an anticipated view from the peak.

And with that gaze from the peak, the poet circles back to answer the poem's initial question. The poem's structure presents a unique balancing of question and answer; perception is matched by reflection. Completeness, balance, and convergence, achieved through multiple juxtaposition and parallelism, interplay on different levels.

As in Du Fu's poem above, parallelism in most Chinese verse can disappear in the end. In fact, most Chinese poetry does not exhibit strict parallelism throughout. Rather, parallelism usually occurs in the middle and occasionally at the beginning of a poem; in some forms, it is not required at all. A non-parallel ending can generate a dynamic, outward movement that is suggestive and lets the mood or thought linger on. Or, as James Hart explains, "it ... may be ... a deliberate attempt to go from the obvious parallels to the more subtle, in order to encourage the reader or listener to develop his acuity in discerning the pattern where it is not clearly visible" (1984: 58). This implies respect for what is invisible as well as visible, for what is said as well as unsaid. It also implies respect for a participant's ability and self-reliance in thinking through a thought. As Chinese see it, writer–reader and speaker–listener work together; one suggests and entices and the other actively engages in filling out meaning, and between them, a bond of cooperation emerges.

Of course, it is a bond also encouraged in the writings and poetry of Western and other cultures. But there is a real difference in the underlying cultural dispositions and in how one fills in the details. For one thing, the bonds between Chinese writer–reader or speaker–listener imply a deep and dynamic mutuality between participants that reflects belief in the interconnectedness and interdependence of existence. Chinese put ideas together to draw others into a collaborative effort, to make people partners in mutual meaning-making. Persons reach out to co-respond with and energize each other; aiming to generate a greater harmony of sharable views, they broaden a communication's focus to accommodate all parties involved.

Furthermore, communication by its very nature is ritual-based and so, for Chinese, takes on aims and means conspicuously different from Western expectations and experience. In particular, Chinese are disposed to use words to present rather than

"re"present meaning, to transmit and evoke rather than to establish and articulate. Persuasion takes on different dimensions too,
since Chinese believe that reason and emotion are integrated rather
than separated. Optimally, persuasive discourse is scored in the
dulcet keys of human connectedness and frictionless communion.

Notably, the ancient Chinese saw music as a metaphor for
ritual action. They regarded ritual action and music to be prime
civilizing influences that refined individual emotion yet integrated
participants into the social and cosmic orders. Music united
persons in bonds of cooperation and pleasurable engagement
whereas ritual kept them distant through forms of restraint; in
short, ritual action and music helped to bring persons together to
bind and join in harmonious attunement. Both ritual action and
music were refined ways of communicating and enhancing rapport
without relying entirely on words alone. This, in turn, is congruent with a worldview that cherishes the bringing together of
particulars in poetic synthesis. Persuasion in this conception tries
to hold sour notes and dissonance in check; it aims to engage a
kindred concern and compassion while steering others one's way.
These aims stand in striking contrast to the Western perspective of
rhetoric in which reason, logic, and intellectual rigor are emphasized and in which persuasion takes for granted – indeed,
relishes – the prospect of verbal confrontation between autonomous agents as they mutually seek to clarify, develop, or validate
ideas and new knowledge.

Confucius was a key figure in articulating and evoking ancient
Chinese concerns. It is worth examining some of his views as the
next step in our scrutiny of longheld Chinese ideals about generating meaning. Our discussion, however, is not intended to
discuss Confucianism in all its complexities or to denigrate other
major contributors in the Chinese milieu but only to point to Confucius' influence since he has been interpreted and reinterpreted
over the years to form a corporate Confucianism. Despite the
diversity and richness of change, it cannot be denied that Confucius is a major player in the definition of Chinese culture.

Confucius envisioned a society of people in a hierarchy of
relationships and reciprocal obligations, living a life of respect and
respectful virtues, and willing to participate in the making of
communal harmony. His was a secular, human-centered view, a

great part of which rested on a vigorous optimism about the possibilities of human action and self-effort and on a belief in the power of culture to transform and engage people in human(e) relations.

We should remember that Confucius formulated his ideas in times of exceptional and prolonged turmoil. Against this backdrop, he plumbed the resources of China's cultural legacy, synthesizing and reformulating ancient notions and seeking in tradition a thread of continuity to perpetuate social coherence and stability. He called for a series of reforms from the bottom up, ranging from the development of quality, cultivated persons to enlightened statecraft. He urged quality persons to take charge of developing their humanity through vigilant self-cultivation, insisting that righting a society begins by righting one's person and one's family. He championed a personal commitment to *li*, the rituals of propriety or civilized conduct, as the means by which one's humanity can felicitously develop and flourish. He argued for a society governed by cultivated men with deepened humanity and learned ability, in effect setting the groundwork for the Han dynasty's later establishment of the world's first civil bureaucracy with socially mobile candidates selected by competitive examination.

More specifically, as Herbert Fingarette (1972) makes clear, Confucius perceived humanity through the imagery of ceremony and therefore of tradition; he turned a commitment to humanity and human(e) social relations into something close to a religion. Humanity flowers in community and communal acts; communal acts are anchored in the inherited forms of conduct and relationships. No matter what one's status or station, active participation in the cultural heritage through *li* or ritual action secures human dignity and social unity; all else – the discipline, refinement, realization, and cultivation of self or its "cutting, filing, polishing, and chiseling" – feeds into the full expression of one's humanity and the ceremonial harmony of civilized intercourse.

Viewed this way, the achievement of personhood is inseparable from ritual action; both are eminently social in Confucius' vision of a participatory ritual order. By the same token, ritual action is not intended to mask the self, but, rather, is revelatory of its qualities and maturity. Much like poetry, ritual action best steers prosocial, human(e) dispositions into culturally meaningful modes.

For those who claim that ritual action is simply "a ritual" or not meaningful is thus to miss the very point that person-making and ritual action are reciprocally related in Confucian thinking.

The core of Confucius' vision is the comprehensive virtue of *ren* (Chan 1955). Variously glossed as 'goodness,' 'benevolence,' or 'human-heartedness,' *ren* is perhaps best encapsulated in Peter Boodberg's (1953) 'co-humanity.' *Ren* signifies a sensitivity to others (Elvin 1985) and a personal growth that is fundamentally relational and contributory to the broader good (Hall and Ames 1987). *Ren* materializes in different relations as filial piety, marital devotion, sibling deference, hierarchical loyalty, trustworthy friendship, and, minimally, concern toward those one knows. A sense of mutuality and support, even of reverence, underlies many of these relations.

Originally, *ren* meant 'the distinctive quality of a man,' 'manliness,' 'manhood' (Lin 1974–1975). In Confucius' reformulation, however, *ren* signifies a lifelong process of transformation and refinement. *Ren* is latent in each person and must be constantly nurtured and nourished. Continuous personal change, in turn, implies a personal pliability and malleability. And, in fact, the etymological roots of *ren* connote among other things, "gentility," "softness," "mildness," "lenity, comity, tenerity, mansuetude, forbearance," "graceful, complaisant, patient and tender, tolerant, yielding" (Boodberg 1953: 328).

As Confucius saw it, the way to express and cultivate *ren* is to participate in human relationships with others through *li* or ritual action. Upon closer scrutiny, this suggests that the very starting point in developing and refining one's self entails a deep personal transformation *in* interaction; one is expected to integrate with rather than isolate one's self from others. This suggests too that *ren*-cultivation is grounded and authenticated in social experience rather than in metaphysical speculation; one ought to be fully engaged in social living. In short, to achieve first-class human status, one turns outward rather than inward in Confucian thinking.

Note, however, that the process is selective: one's co-humanity develops and unfolds in continuous relations with those capable of buttressing and enhancing one's efforts. And, as later Confucians point out, despite the fact that one is necessarily embedded in networks of assorted structural constraints, what counts is that

one applies oneself to advance through *ren*-cultivation. The procedure is ultimately circular: one advances by helping others to
advance. Confucius puts it this way: "Wishing to establish himself,
he establishes others" (*Analects* 6/30). The point here is not that
one is selfless, but, quite the contrary, one inevitably enhances and
advances oneself in the process. We can see this philosophy put
into action by an Overseas Chinese manager: "I think I have an
obligation to look after my men. But I know that if I look after
them eventually I look after myself" (in Redding 1990: 157).

Conversely, Chinese see a willingness to labor and sacrifice for
significant others as the proper medium through which deeply
private feelings of love and affection are expressed: "We Chinese
show our feelings for one another in our work, not with words"
(in Potter and Potter 1990: 194). (Indeed, to utter their feelings is
to sully them. On a similar note, utterances of praise or expressions like "thank you," "please" or "excuse me" work to create
distance, subtly subverting the mutual support and consideration
taken for granted among family intimates.) Following Fingarette's
lead, if we allow for a milieu that honors the secular world as a
sacred domain, work might assume a sacred aura as well. For
Chinese, hard work and mutual aid signify a commitment to human relatedness and social belongingness; work is good, especially
when it contributes to others' welfare. The same attitude prevails
in anthropologist Dorinne Kondo's (1990) account about the
meaning of work for part-time, female confectionary workers
in a Tokyo ward. Unlike their middle-class counterparts, their
precarious economic existence compelled them to seek petty wage
labor, not just to augment the family income but also as a symbol
of their deep commitment and loyalty to their families.

Correspondingly, self is identified by and thrives in the relational links established in social living. And, since self is extended
to incorporate others, then there is created a sense that intentions
and aims must remain open and negotiable to accommodate the
concerns of others as well. Flexibility and open-mindedness are
parts of the extension of self, whether for self-cultivation or for
developing a corporate self; in Confucian thinking, these are two
parts of the same activity.

To be sure, an open-minded and pliable person can end up
remaining simply impressionable and moldable, just as bonds can

turn into bondage or obligations can become entanglements. The potential for human failings and human abuse has been and continues to be real. Just as real, however, is a longstanding cultural conviction that quality people are responsible for advancing their life directions and circumstances in a social matrix. Conversely, a shared commitment implies sturdy personal effort and coincides with a willingness to contribute that effort to others. For these reasons, Chinese have assumed that a quality person is both resonant and supple, one capable of translating inner resolve into tireless action and one able to bring order and harmony to self and others.

In Confucius' time, *li* had not yet ossified into a rigid set of codes and rules; the fundamental social patterns were obvious but specific guidelines for conduct were not always spelled out. Accordingly, he expected people to exercise personal judgment (Creel 1979). This being the case, *yi* – what is 'appropriate' or 'right' – became another significant element in Confucius' vision of a participatory ritual order. *Yi* entails making discerning judgments and taking appropriate action in light of particular circumstances and with respect to traditional emphases. What is right or appropriate is constantly being negotiated; what is important is the larger picture and the (long-term) result felicitously gained rather than the application of specific rules and principles. Although not specifically addressing *yi*, one Chinese woman's perceptions (during a recent discussion I attended) about the differences between Chinese and Americans illustrate *yi* in practice rather nicely:

When growing up, my Western friends got 1001 rules to do this or that but, myself, I always learn to think of result I want. The basic idea of the result you want – some result you wish for – is harmony and so in everything try to figure out what to do. In my upbringing, no rule, but fashion from the circumstances the result you want.

Yi then is not simply a matter of knowing right from wrong or choosing one or another course of action. Far from it. *Yi*, as her remarks suggest, is the ability to judge each unique situation so as to occasion greater harmony. *Yi* might also be understood as an ability to draw from and reflect well on the store of insights and past *yi* judgments that uphold the cultural tradition (Hall and

Ames 1984). In its first aspect, *yi* is individuating and requires a
personal sense of appropriateness in order to respond judiciously
to different situations. In its second aspect, *yi*, like good taste, is
communally anchored – that is, socially acceptable and intelligible.
And, in fact, the character *yi* 義 is made up of two parts that
portray a communal sense and a note of sacrifice as well: the top
half represents the sheep radical which, when found in *xi* 犧
contributes to the meaning of 'sacrificial offering' or when found
in *xiang* 祥 contributes to the meaning of 'offering received with
favor,' and the bottom half has the radical 我, which, as stated in
chapter 2, in classical times often meant '"I" writ large,' the
corporate body, the collective, as in *wo guo* 我國 'our country.'
(Only in recent times has 我 come to denote exclusively the singular 'I' and the pluralizer *men* 們 added to *wo* 我 to render it 'we'
women 我們.) Understood this way, *yi* denotes doing what is appropriate in concrete instances for the sake of the group, even if it
entails some sacrifice on one's part. Consider the phrase *yi er* 義兒
'a child adopted for the public welfare' in contemporary Taiwan.
This phrase goes hand in hand with another widely used expression there: *xisheng xiao wo wancheng da wo* 犧牲小我完成大我
'sacrifice the little me to complete the big me.' Such phrases, in
turn, accord with the original meaning of *li* 禮 as 'sacrifice.' They
reflect and reinforce a communal sense of participating in something greater than oneself. Hence, the traditional reference to
China as "the land of *li* and *yi*" (*liyi zhi bang* 禮義之邦).

What makes it all hang together is *shu* 恕, explained in the
Analects (15/24) as "Do not impose on others what you yourself
do not desire." *Shu* is commonly glossed as 'mutuality' or 'reciprocal action.' Others describe *shu* more elaborately as 'using
yourself as a measure to gauge the wishes of others' (Lau 1979) or
just simply as 'likening-to-oneself' (Graham 1989). *Shu* shares
with *ren* a connotation of 'compassion.' When paired with *zhong*
'loyalty' (especially that owed to one's superior), as it has been
traditionally, *shu* carries a sense of deferential regard and respect.
With *shu*, one learns to make distinctions and yet resonate with
others; this means that one must reckon on or have foresight into
what is intrusive or inconsiderate toward others. On the other
hand, *shu* plays a key role in extending and enhancing one's
self. Knowing one's self, one can know others since it is pre-

sumed that everyone shares basic human(e) capacities and dispositions.

Ultimately, *li*, *ren*, *yi*, and *shu* are dynamically relational; together with *zhi* 知 (usually translated 'wisdom' but explained better as the capacity to know and follow appropriate action), they reinforce and enhance each other to shape and solidify Confucius' vision of a participatory ritual order. On the one hand, their conscientious practice points to a person with lots of inner momentum, one who aspires toward sound judgments, humane sensitivities, and life sensibility; what counts is that one tries as best as one can to make something of oneself despite – or perhaps because of – less than optimal conditions. On the other hand, they all imply a keen awareness of others and their importance in one's own development and stature as a worthy human(e) being; what counts is how one treats others as an expression of respect for one's co-humanity. For Chinese to say *ta bu shi ren* 他不是人 'He or she is not a person' (alternately, *ta bu ren* 他不仁 'He or she is not *ren*') is to say that the person in question is guilty of misconduct or inappropriately relating to others and so not fully human.

Interestingly, in the two-part makeup of *ren* 仁, the left represents 'person' and the two horizontal lines represent the number 'two.' Put together, they suggest human relations and engaging oneself with others. However, as we have seen in Confucius' thinking, people engage and relate through ritual action. Yet, relating through ritual action does not just mean that one simply adopts the proper role. For Chinese, roles are not just fixed sets of expectations to which individual persons must tailor their behavior as might be implied in such notions as "role prescriptions" and "role fulfillments" replete in Western social science literature. To be sure, ancient Chinese classics have devoted entire volumes to the minutiae and requisites of ritual action, from the *Yi Li* (*Etiquette and Ritual*) to the *Zhou Li* (*Rites of Zhou*) and the *Li Ji* (*Record of Ritual*). Confucius himself sketched out some of the ways one should comport oneself in a variety of activities. And, certainly, Chinese do demand that people conform to prescribed actions. But, they also stress reciprocal obligations and the collaboration these produce, as implied in the 'two-ness' or Boodberg's 'co-humanity' of *ren*.

Taking a hint from linguists George Lakoff and Mark Johnson's (1980) observation that "container" images and metaphors
permeate Western thinking, and from Chad Hansen's observation
that "Western philosophy of mind dealt with the input, procession,
and storage of content (data, information) . . ." (1985b: 500), we
might say that terms like "role fulfillment" – or even "potential"
as in "fulfilling one's potential" – are like Western conceptions of
"time" or "schedule" in that they call to mind some discrete,
bounded unit that awaits filling. This in turn suggests a substance
rather than process orientation more characteristic of Chinese
thought. ("Case" is another obvious example of the container
metaphor, as in "building an airtight case.") How about "putting
a dent in your argument," or "an argument shot full of holes"?
And, if the container metaphor is mixed with the stative, we have
"fall into a state of despair." Even "privacy," the Anglo-Saxon
assumption that people want to have a little wall around them
sometimes, betrays a container outlook. So too does "text,"
something fixed, isolated, and bounded. Consider also expressions
such as "to be completely *within* your rights" or "*pouring* himself
into his career." A more exaggerated instance of the container
image comes from one writer's account of the controversial
American pop star Madonna: "she invented herself as a mutable
being, a container for a multiplicity of images" (Sante 1990: 26).

Quite apart from this, because one's demeanor expresses inner
cultivated disposition in Confucian thinking, just knowing one's
role cannot be enough. As stated, for the Confucians, one must
sincerely – almost reverentially – seek attunement with others
and try to reciprocate regard and respect through ritual action.
Without this inner sense of reverence, ritual becomes empty
formalism, reflecting, in turn, one's personal shortcomings or
diffidence in cultivating one's humanity. Hence Confucius' vigorous
denunciation of the village worthy – a nice enough person who
deals honestly and pleasantly with others yet lacks the inner
ambition for *ren*-cultivation (*Analects* 17/13). Moreover, if the
rituals of respect are undertaken perfunctorily or halfheartedly,
they can never become personalized (i.e., become invested with
much of one's self). Instead, they sink into the sort of witless
copying that would have made Confucius shudder.

By the same token, words uttered should coincide with actions taken. The character for *xin* 信 , another key Confucian virtue, glossed variously as 'truthfulness,' 'fidelity,' 'good faith' or 'living up to one's words,' is also written in two parts. The left represents 'person' and the right represents 'to speak.' In combination, they indicate a person standing by his or her word. *Xin* is a key virtue because interpersonal credibility becomes necessary if one's growth and circumstances are relationally anchored. What one says ought to be realized, otherwise, the social fallout can be personally devastating. *Xin* is closely associated with another ancient virtue 'sincerity' (*cheng* 誠) which connotes integrity and earnestly realizing or bringing to fruition what one says or intends.

To be *xin* or *cheng*, then, one has to back one's words with action and not promise more than one can deliver. For these and other reasons, Confucius was steadfast in his warning throughout the *Analects* against an excess of words. Some sample statements include the following:

The gentleman desires to be halting in speech but quick in action.   (4/24)

The mark of the benevolent man is that he is loath to speak ... When to act is difficult, is it any wonder that one is loath to speak.   (12/3)

The gentleman is ashamed of his word outstripping his deed.   (14/27)

In short, Confucius promoted the view that a quality person ought to act on what he or she says. For Confucius, then, saying is enacting; it is a call to action.

To be *xin* or *cheng* also suggests that the distinction between speaking and doing is less rigid in Confucian ideology than in Western tradition. In the latter, one can speculate without accountability and play "Devil's Advocate." Both are examples of what Confucius himself specifically disdained: "entertaining conjectures" and "insisting on certainty" (*Analects* 9/4). In a Chinese context, these are considered dysfunctional. As a contemporary instance of this, consider that management technology transfers between the West and China have been continually hampered by a Western insistence on giving theoretical overviews in presentations as opposed to a Chinese preoccupation with various sorts of hands-on experience: "A common request among Chinese trainees is for the trainer to skip the theory and philoso-

phies which accompany management techniques and get straight
to the 'practical' applications" (Cragnin 1986: 338). DeWoskin
clarifies that, "Classical Chinese thinkers of various persuasions
made a distinction between knowing how to do something and
knowing about doing something. The former was always considered superior to the latter. Interest in the latter could, in fact,
impede success with regard to the former" (1982: 177).

Concomitantly, Confucius believed that the richness of life and
thought cannot be fully grasped in words. The *Yijing* attributes
these words to Confucius: "The written words cannot exhaust
speech and speech cannot exhaust thought." As Tu Wei-ming
explains, "words are convenient means to catch the sagely meaning, the intent of which is to direct us to gain personal knowledge
of the Tao [Dao]" (1986: 13). Chinese perceive words as limited,
exhaustible, and unable to fully describe *Dao*'s limitlessness and
inexhaustibility; what lies beyond words ultimately cannot be
expressed by ordinary words.

Looking at the etymology of *Dao* 道 , we see that it is made up
of two parts: the left side indicates movement and the right side is
a head. Combined, they mean 'path,' 'to guide someone along a
path,' 'to head them along a certain direction,' or 'to point out a
way.' Thus *Dao* is dynamically relational, and yet *Dao* is open-
ended as well since each person is different and faces different
circumstances, obstacles, and quandaries; in short *Dao* is neither
fixed nor definite. (Yet note that due to inherent differences in the
Chinese and English languages – and consequent cultural outlooks
– *Dao* is often translated into English prefaced with "the" and less
often with "a" which makes it seem more definite than it is; the
English translation reifies *Dao* and gives it a more unified view
than found in its native Chinese. Even to refer to *Dao* as "it" as I
have done is to reify it more than should be the case. On the other
hand, to translate *Dao* without "the" or "a" would often sound
like broken English. As it happens, the most commonly used word
in the English language "the" is, conversely, one of the most
commonly misused words by English-speaking Chinese.)

How does one guide? One way is to use words and so *Dao* also
carries the meaning 'to speak.' However, since *Dao* is not something out there to be identified or delineated but rather an attitude, a
disposition, a style of living embodied, exemplified, or modelled in

a person's actions, *Dao* is difficult to describe and put into words; words can set up artificial boundaries around things that are otherwise very fluid. Besides, as Herrlee Creel suggests, putting *Dao* into words, talking about it, even pointing it out, is difficult for the simple reason that, "all who would talk, or point, are themselves part of the *tao*, and cannot attain any outside position from which to deal with it objectively" (1983: 315). And so when actually put into words, the words themselves are geared to direct rather than dictate, to stimulate rather than to indoctrinate or proselytize. In short, words point beyond themselves. Linguistic endings become the beginnings of an imaginary journey; "dis-closure" rather than "closure" is emphasized. Such convictions as "meaning beyond words" or "inexhaustible meaning" are part and parcel of a holistic perspective in which words and talk play just one, albeit significant, role in the whole expressive network through which meaning emerges. It should be noted that such convictions are shared by Confucians and Daoists alike.

What, on the other hand, is distinctively Confucian is his view of the communicative and integrative roles of ritual action and music. As he sees it, they are the different levels of social grammar that assure the greatest possibility for self-expression and for facilitating social intercourse. Reflecting on the way Chinese view speech and music, Hall and Ames write: "It is interesting that the character *shuo* 說 in the classical literature which has the meaning 'to speak' and 'to persuade' when pronounced *yüeh*, can mean 'to enjoy' [or, more commonly, 'to delight,' 'to please,' 'enjoyable']. Similarly, the character *yüeh* 樂, which has the meaning 'to play music' can, when pronounced *lo* or *yao*, also mean 'to enjoy.' These two characters for 'enjoyment,' *yüeh* 說 and *lo/yao* 樂, with their attendant associations with speech and music, occur in the first passage of the *Analects* (1/1)" (1987: 277). Here, Hall and Ames stress the "en-," the 'coming about' of "enjoy" – the getting together as social beings for good fellowship rather than for a narcissistic, solitary joy. As in music, so with communication, the point is to enhance rapport and achieve harmonious attunement. Moreover, the fact that 道 and 說 also mean 'to speak' only serves to reinforce our view that Chinese ideas about communicating differ importantly from Western ones.

Meanings aside, the ultimate communicative roles of ritual,

music, and language are evocative; they are geared to integrate
emotions, maximize harmonious relations and nurture productive
engagements between distinctively different persons. Also, by
participating in the creation and pleasure of harmonious relations,
one goes beyond the confines of one's self to live a fuller life – a
truly human life. Thus Tu Wei-ming is convinced that the persuasive power of Chinese dialogic encounters "lies not in the
straightness of a logical sequence devoid of emotion but in its
appeal to common sense, good reasons, and a willingness to
participate in the creation of sharable values" (1981: 46).

By the same token, effective persuasion in a Chinese milieu has
traditionally aimed to sway another's thinking by touching a
responsive chord in his or her heart. Here we might note that the
character for thinking *si* 思 includes the heart radical *xin* 心. Why
the heart? Why should thinking involve feelings? For one thing,
unlike Western tradition which sees humankind's distinctiveness
as derived from the ability to reason, the Confucian school of
thought takes the heart – specifically, its humane impulses – to be
humankind's most distinguishing feature and what separates them
from animals. It is the locus of virtuous conduct, the "organ of
judgement" in Angus Graham's reckoning; it helps make them
become human. The fact that the heart is the seat of thought and
emotion for Chinese and that there is no hard and fast division
between them in ancient and contemporary times can be illustrated
by Chinese placing their hand over their heart when saying "I
think." Another everyday example is the phrase *wo zai xinli
xiang* ... 我在心裏想 "I've been thinking (in my heart) that ..."
As Chinese see it, thoughts spring from the heart; thoughts are felt
in the heart. Noted translator Arthur Waley, in his analysis of the
use of 思 in the *Analects*, writes:

Never is there any suggestion of a long interior process of cogitation or
ratiocination, in which a whole series of thoughts are evolved one out of
the other, producing on the physical plane a headache and on the intellectual, an abstract theory. We must think of *ssu* [思] rather as a fixing of
the attention (located in the middle of the belly), on an impression
recently imbibed from without and destined to be immediately re-
exteriorized in action. (1938: 45)

This in no way implies an emotional rather than intellectual
conviction but only says that Chinese thinking avoids excluding

one in favor of the other. For the ancient Chinese, *si* 思 is a sort of heartfelt thinking that guides a mature human towards appropriate judgment and action. Like a belly laugh or a gut instinct, it comes spontaneously from one's depths.

In discussions with his disciples, Confucius insisted that they progress by thinking for themselves: "When I have pointed out one corner of a square to anyone and he does not come back with the other three, I will not point it out to him a second time" (*Analects* 7/8). The *Yijing* expresses a similar view: "When the wise one observes image and text, then his thoughts have already gone more than halfway"; in other words, you get most of the picture by looking at a part as long as you get the right part. Another old Chinese saying advises that one should just provide broad directional guidelines and let a communicant draw his or her own conclusions: "Draw a bow without shooting; just make the motion." Together, these views subscribe to an aesthetic of indeterminacy and open-endedness that calls for a communicant to meet the communicator more than halfway. A communicant has to work at meaning-making; one takes the initiative to dot the "i"s and cross the "t"s. Just as one is expected to apply oneself to personal realization and self-transformation, one is expected to make real effort to realize meaning on one's own. Understanding thus involves actively using one's heart/mind rather than passively receiving meaning; correspondingly, in making a point, a communicant is thereby relieved from pushing the point to completion. Likewise, a communicator avoids the risk of appearing assertively egotistic or unduly interfering with the natural course of another's understanding; a communicator takes the role of a guide, one who skillfully employs stimuli to suggest and evoke.

Throughout the *Analects*, Confucius tacitly advocated the spontaneity of naturally derived understanding; there was no call for pressure or force from one to another (see Fingarette 1980). Arguments were conducted in the spirit of restraint and conviction and words were designed to convey an implicit understanding or to startle people into thought. Pointing to the "Chineseness" of Confucian and Daoist discourse, for example, historian Frederick Mote writes: "both display the same predilection for concepts by intuition rather than by postulation, for suggestive rather than for explicit language, for similitude rather than syllogism" (1971: 70).

As part of the aesthetic of indeterminacy and open-endedness, Chinese might approach an issue roundaboutly rather than addressing it directly. To bring others around to one's point of view, one might skirt the edges of an issue; going round and round an issue also gives the communicant an opportunity to come up with the answer on his or her own. In this regard, background information might be foregrounded to help the other along. Thus prepared, a communicant can enter into the core ideas on his or her own and make them personally compelling.

The same aesthetic of indeterminacy and open-endedness can work to a speaker's advantage in a hierarchical world of tangled ties where one must often proceed by hints and indirection. On the one hand, putting thoughts vaguely or obliquely helps to mitigate threats to face and person. It creates an ambivalent context, allowing meaning to be read in many ways, and so lets the speaker off the hook; at the very least, it allows for a felt-soled progress to judge another's resistance or gives one a chance to strategically retreat. On the other hand, deferring to another's capacity to realize a communication's full significance essentially shifts its "author"-ship to another. It is a way of showing respect through deference, which, when skillfully used, packs a powerful persuasive punch. As one ethnographer reports about present-day rituals in Taiwan: "in Taiwanese terms, one shows respect (*chieng*) to others by deferring (*niu*) to them...this...can get other beings to behave as one wishes" (Ahern 1981: 33). Her account coincides with the advice given in a major Chinese treatise on persuasion, the *Kuei Ku Tzu*, written by an individual of the same name during the Warring States period (481–221 B.C.): "To persuade is to please. To please is to gain something from the person (under persuasion)" (*Kuei Ku Tzu* 1/1) (Tsao 1985). Treatises on early Chinese rhetoric in fact often advised how to sway the "dragon" (read "emperor") without ruffling his scales.

In this section, I have put Confucius' ideas in the most favorable light so as to get another handle on some of the influential forces behind Chinese ideals of generating meaning. What have we learned? In the first place, from a Confucian perspective, quality Chinese ought to put as much effort into showing one's – or recognizing another's – co-humanity as they put into avoiding a face-off. Moreover, Confucius not only stressed accountability and restraint in one's words and actions but also aspired in his own actions to the view that words ought to stimulate rather than overwhelm, to guide rather than dictate. Confucius also placed great stock in casting thoughts in such a way as to make judgments self-evident. His ideas contribute to a model of persuasion that appeals to a profound sense of social responsibility and harmony from people who aspire to share a kindred humanity. Optimally, in public acts of persuasion, Chinese aim for a meeting of hearts-and-minds rather than a head-to-head confrontation.

The upshot of this is that when fashioning or participating in persuasive discourse, Chinese tend to refrain from overt signs of pressure or imposition and instead try to subtly suggest and obliquely direct. This in turn is wholly congruent with the def-erential regard and respect that characterizes *shu*, the thread that Confucius explicitly declares binds together his thoughts (*Analects* 4/15). In relations that count, Chinese communicative rituals ordinarily tilt towards positive social interaction and interdepend-ence with a focus on the "commonality" (Tu 1976: 154) of human experience. A cultural sense of commonality can perhaps be seen in the constantly revolving Chinese yin–yang figure: the dark patch and light patch are different yet complementary and each contains a smaller patch of the other. People come together to collaborate and create an invisible "sympathetic harmony," the sort of attunement that ought to move in sync with the rhythms and cadences of the natural order.

We have now reached a position where we can return to the stereotypical characterizations that began this chapter and give them fuller treatment. Recall that Chinese rhetorical directions seem backwards to Westerners because they end up where West-erners might start off. As Kaplan describes it, Chinese will back into a topic, stack it with tangential views, and withdraw into vagueness. That is, Chinese discourse might appear to consist of non-beginnings, multiple views, and non-endings. I have suggested throughout that such characterizations often arise because people mistakenly assume that the underlying aims and ends of another culture's discourse will coincide with their own.

Note that Chinese fall victim to the same error as well. For instance, some Chinese informants vehemently denied that the underlying aims and ends of English and Chinese discourse could differ significantly. Then again, as I have argued in chapter 2, many individuals are simply unaware of the communicative requirements and subtleties of their own, much less another, rhetorical tradition unless poked and prodded in very specific ways. What is readily available to them instead are the surface manifestations of language that many insist on taking as valid points of comparison. Such was the case with one Chinese who attempted to use the eight-legged essay as a base to explain apparent similarities with the formal features of English written discourse:

To initiate [*qi*] is something like the statement of the problem. We get into *qi* [and then] the second step [*cheng*]. So far we get this and that, all related to the first one, sort of like a literature review. The alternative [*zhuan*] is to turn into my point – my theory is this and that. To conclude, we present the data; why you think their theories are wrong and yours correct and refer back to the problem [*qi*].

Upon reflection and after some probing on my part, he ruefully conceded that "although the structure is the same, the contents may differ." Admitting this possibility, he then went on to declare that a typical Chinese practice is to resist a firm conclusion and so it sometimes leaves doubt as to where the author stands:

My feeling is that many Chinese scholars in Mainland China and Taiwan don't make clear the conclusion in last part which would stand out sharply as a contrast from the thing he try to criticize against . . . Many [Chinese] academic articles are vague with no definite conclusions. [The writers] try to compromise between different theories, ideologies.

We shall have more to say about indefinite conclusions and vague "compromises." Let us now move on with our discussion and consider how Chinese (and others) might explain the rhetorical features that Westerners might see as non-beginnings, non-endings, and multiple views. Optimally, we can place what they say against what has been discussed so far to get a firmer grip on the ways they coalesce in an image of Chinese inscrutability. At the least, they will give us the purchase to dig deeper into other contrasts between Chinese and American rhetoric and to clarify much that seems opaque. We begin with the following Chinese thoughts about Kaplan's observations:

Kaplan's remark that "Things are developed in terms of what they are not, rather than in terms of what they are" truly describes a stylistic device widely used in Chinese writing, Classical or Modern, creative or expository. This style form is known as 含蓄 the literal translation of which is "reservation" and which is defined by 黃永武 as "the use of devious and evasive words to express an idea indirectly and only partially, so that the full implication is not contained in the words but is left to the conjecture of the reader, and its effects will subsequently be more deeply felt (p. 14)." 張嚴 (1955) similarly defines 含蓄 as a style form in which "only half the meaning is expressed in the words and the other half is to be gathered by the reader using his imagination." (Lee 1973: 54)

As Chinese see it, reserve makes for depth and restraint makes for strength. To retreat from stating a conclusion outright or spelling ideas out bespeaks a cultural delight in non-endings and stimulating the other's imagination. To Chinese, such a discourse style promotes a penetration of insight. To Westerners, it represents a defect of logic. While the consequent vagueness or indefiniteness may be intellectually invigorating for Chinese, Westerners instead view it as incomplete, and, more often than not, feel shortchanged.

Verification on the latter point comes from one of my early interviews with a Chinese- and Burmese-speaking Englishman whose work involves him in intensive reading of contemporary Chinese journal articles:

I notice that even in modern writings, many Chinese prefer other people's opinions in their articles all the time. You don't get opinions – their opinions – you get *other* people's opinions. And a perfectly good article would be to summarize, to collect up a lot of opinions on an issue, but you never actually commit yourself to an opinion . . . I always feel the author must have an opinion and simply hasn't stated it. He's just giving many opinions; he hasn't given us an answer . . . Anyway, what you sometimes end up with is no clear commitment by the author to one of the opinions or to his own. I remember I talked about this with [a Chinese colleague] and he seemed to agree.

Puzzled that Chinese are likely to heap together a multiplicity of views yet fall short of a definite closure, he felt obliged to suggest that they are guided by a strategy which he believed to be based on caution and restraint: "One possibility is the 'some say' approach. One can adroitly bring in a number of other people's opinions, the sheer weight and number of it covers one without definitely committing oneself."

A Japanese observer too notes that Chinese are likely to consider all angles of a subject without requiring decisive final remarks:

I have been struck in conversation with Chinese by the way in which, in evolving a particular idea, they also take into account facts that are at variance with or contradict it. They will examine a case from every angle, but avoid any hasty, definite conclusion, preferring to confine themselves to a statement of a general trend than to commit themselves to any one-sided idea. This gives breadth to their view.   (Shiraishi 1965: 88)

Unlike others, he intuitively grasped the aesthetic and intellectual thrust of Chinese discourse: looking at several sides of an issue signals a many-sided, many-layered understanding. Not content with simply making a point, Chinese play one angle against the other, circumscribing a topic to find or elicit different kinds of understanding. Each angle, while having a particular limited value, thus acquires keen significance when placed in a special relationship with another. When Chinese accomplish this by using contrast, the contrasts co-operate to build a picture, and a communicant grasps meaning by apprehending the particularity of the opposed but complementary aspects. As in art, so with Chinese discourse, "positive space" suggestively points towards "negative space."

A many-sided perspective suggests too that one might look at things obliquely. In looking at things obliquely, one is eventually led to a kind of live whole without the flatness and dullness of a direct angle view. This direct angle view in turn contributes to what linguist Michael Clyne (1981: 65) has described as the obvious lopsidedness of the "Anglo-Celtic" linear orientation.

For Chinese, a many-sided perspective also marks the non-egocentric orientation of a quality person. The ability to see different angles signifies a broadened and deepened non-judgmental capacity to integrate with rather than impose a limited perspective onto the natural order of things. Put another way, a plurality of perspectives diminishes selfish bias whereas asserting a one-sided explanation makes one appear a self-intentional agent, one acting on or pursuing personal interest that is incongruent with global commitments. Thus, the *Analects* (2/14), for example, makes the distinction between a quality person and an uncultivated person: "A gentleman is catholic; he can see a question from all sides without bias. The small man is partisan; he sees a question from only one side."

Seen in this light, we might attribute the "vague compromise" mentioned above by the Chinese informant to the fact that Chinese try to recognize competing claims and soft-pedal differences of opinion by integrating them into a many-sided view. On the other hand, Chinese also take criticism personally. In Chinese thinking, ideas are not something "out there" to be analyzed, validated, or rebutted. Instead, Chinese regard one's ideas as entangled with one's identity or sense of personal worth; an attack on one's ideas is therefore an attack on one's self, or, more specifically, one's face. In this event, Chinese try to minimize threats to face by hedging one's claim while looking for commonality with others. Thus, in response to my question as to why Chinese avoid a strong stance when criticizing another's argument, an American born Chinese gentleman who recently retired as head of an academic institute in China said:

Chinese generally try to avoid direct confrontation, try not to make the other person look bad. So they often look for points on which there might be agreement or similarity, even if the other person is thought to be ninety-nine percent wrong. This might be considered a manifestation of the "live and let live" philosophy. By so doing, you are also protecting yourself because in your own arguments or writings you may not be one hundred percent correct. You would wish these to be pointed out in a non-humiliating face-saving way.

This way of thinking is a natural outgrowth of a societal order that relies less on impersonal rationality than on the personal confidence of others. Chinese are anchored relationally rather than rationally; taking his statement at face value, they search for likemindedness rather than highlight points of divergences. Almost offhandedly, he then said:

In modern times, Chinese expository writing, especially non-academic articles, have tended to follow a formula sometimes described as "concept plus example" [i.e.,] stating some point, concept or idea, then citing an example to illustrate the point, rather than pursue a well-formulated argument with strong evidential support. Solid quantitative data is often noticeably lacking.

Here it seems we are faced with another instance of Chinese non-endings that untutored Westerners might view as lacking assertion, decision, or just plain unconvincing. But pairing an idea with an example is simply a variation of the traditional Chinese reliance on analogy for explanation or illustration; this reliance on analogy squares well with a Chinese sensibility that values the use of discrete mediums and intermediaries to delicately convey meaning or indirectly drive home a point. Part of analogy's traditional appeal is that it offers immediate insight; obscure statements are paired with others more accessible, the similarities in one used to shed light on the other. Meaning is self-derived rather than externally imposed; understanding is purer and the impact that much greater.

Chinese regularly use analogy in conjunction with authority to expand and bolster their arguments. But then so do many other cultures, Western included. What makes the Chinese case unique is the extent to which Chinese rely on analogy and authority rather than convincing argument and logical prowess in their discourse. Far more than Westerners, Chinese regularly regard tradition as *the* source of legitimate authority. Tradition both grounds and focuses the intent and direction of their formal discourse; for Chinese, tradition offers past examples of reasonable explanation and action and one readily defers to its authority.

To be sure, Chinese have also questioned, critiqued, reviled and repudiated the same authoritative sources; symbols of authority, from Confucius to Mao and Deng, have had their ups and downs. Relying on tradition as both source and resource for social action and thought can be hobbling, as some Chinese intellectuals have despaired; it can be backward-looking as some Western observers have argued. Nevertheless, Chinese embrace tradition and in turn are braced by its authority; they have entertained and espoused ideas under its authoritative – and, at times, protective – canopy. More often than not, in fashioning persuasive arguments or seeking richly detailed ideas, Chinese pursue perspectives of time-tested depth or many-sided breadth; they regularly promote continuities or bonds of different sorts. Thus, rhetorician Robert Oliver, for one, is able to write about communicative practices in ancient China that:

the principal sources of proof on which judgment should be based were authority and analogy. Speakers took care to represent ideas as being not their own but an authoritative derivation from ancient precepts or practice . . . Authority and analogy were used almost to the exclusion of both formal logic and citation of specific evidence or supporting facts. (1971: 263)

Similarly, Frederick Mote observes that Confucius' arguments, for example, were constructed as "chains of contingencies, or upon implicit appeals to a self-evident reasonableness, or upon the authority of a manifestly superior ethical system of wide acceptance . . ." (1971: 43). In a present-day corroboration, political scientist Timothy Cheek reports too that Deng Tuo, formerly editor of the People's Daily who had penned a series of newspaper articles lampooning Mao Zedong, "writes in a clipped condensed style relying heavily on cut-and-paste quotations. This, of course, is the traditional Chinese 'proof' – ancient documents carry far more weight than words of the contemporary historian" (1981: 475).

Variations upon this dominant strategy are many. The Russian historian Vitaly Rubin (1976: 100) notes about the Classics that third-person reference in the formulaic "they say . . ." conveniently lets people drape themselves in the authority of others. This is the "some say" approach suggested by the Englishman interviewed above. Another variant appears in the purported editing of the *Spring and Autumn Annals* classic by Confucius: "By allowing the *Annals* to speak rather than by directly delivering his own private judgments, Confucius is basing himself on the objective public judgments of history. He is allowing the public facts to speak for themselves" (Schwartz 1985: 401).

The key word is "public." Intensely conscious of their cultural legacy, ancient thinkers were actively engaged in reinterpreting, refining, or revitalizing its aspirations, commitments, and values. Their challenge was to look forward while thinking back, to grapple with time-tested ideas in novel ways. Since the cultural legacy eventually came to be regarded as a single, shared, public body of venerated knowledge, the construction of philosophical discourse evolved into a collective enterprise as yet another significant instance of participatory meaning-making. Chinese thinkers developed the "philosophy-by-commentary" approach, which was notably non-individualistic, yet camouflaged a surprising array of creative advances, adaptive appropriations, and reformulated insights. In artfully tilling the fertile field of the past, they displayed their capacity to draw meaning from the tradition and extend its concerns. In reviewing the accumulated insights and accomplishments of the past, moreover, they sought explanation, solution, and direction for the challenges of the present and future. In paying homage to traditional wisdom, they signalled a non-egotistic capacity to accept the limits of individual faculty while also achieving a sense of cultural continuity and coherence.

Even in ordinary talk, contemporary Chinese will often display their personal versatility and ingenuity within the tradition, for instance, by wittily evoking an analogy from the past that hits the mark in the present. Their conversation might be laced with symbolic references – maxims, images, and exemplars drawn from the cultural tradition – and delightedly capped with a well-aimed *chengyu* (a four-to-seven character adage) that hits a conversational bull's-eye. Not only does the use of adages tacitly buttress communal values, but their command demonstrates the sensitive appropriation of cultural resources, allowing one to drive home a point indirectly yet incisively.

However, Westerners who encourage consulting one's own opinion as ultimate judge have trouble appreciating the adroit use of a quotation from the past. They are often suspicious of claims that appeal to authority as well:

The attitude which aroused my greatest antipathy was the veneration for authority, rooted in centuries of Confucian unquestioning obedience of superiors and official pronouncements. I remember expressing doubt about some formulation in one of our *Chinese Literature* articles and being told, "But that's how it appeared in the *People's Daily!*" (Shapiro 1979: 78)

What if their cultural tradition also views history as constructed or punctuated by the breakthrough innovations and heroic actions of willful, exceptional agents? What if (at least in the popular consciousness), history takes on obsolete, irrelevant or remote characteristics? Consider, for example, the prevalence of such statements as "'Move and you're history,' snapped the gunman" or "It's history. It's done with, and I don't want to talk about it." Consider, as another example, the following thoughtful observation from a Canadian woman who had taught in China:

When we first attacked the kind of writing [by Chinese students of English] that struck us as cliché-ridden or trite or far-fetched, our students, puzzled, asked us if we had no respect for tradition. The Chinese appreciate the ability to use well-known phrases that echo famous works of literature; this notion is in direct conflict with our attitude, which values self-expression that is "new" or "fresh" or "original." (Hynes 1981: 121)

On one level of analysis, as these observers suggest, such Chinese discourse strategies border on a timid conformity in thought, a lockstep compliance with authority or even a denial of one's individuality. Possibly, they permit the speaker an elegant "out": responsibility for the communication can be conveniently shifted and the speaker safeguarded from making original or committed statements with potential face-threatening consequences. In delicate situations and public occasions, Chinese tend to choose each word carefully for what it implies as well as what it avoids saying. Explanation by way of association is favored as the safest and easiest way to communicate; the speaker is without blame and the hearer is sufficiently informed.

On another level of analysis, as members of a social order that stresses continuous tradition, individual Chinese often adopt a muted force and presence. Rather than pursue the otherwise boundary-setting distinctions of autonomous – read "maverick" – innovators, they have been historically disposed to contribute to the cultural tradition as active participants. Hence Confucius' oft-quoted, demure, non-individuating insistence that he is merely a transmitter rather than an innovator (*shu er bu zuo* 述而不作 *Analects* 7/1). To his mind, he is simply carrying forward the spiritual and unifying values of his culture, albeit giving it imaginative conception and direction; the past continues to resonate in the present as tradition is invested with personal significance. The Chinese students' response to their English language instructor above figures as one important instance of this. Conversely, an interest in spotlighting personal expertise, skills, and talents or in staking a claim to innovative ideas, which is expected in cultures where original creations and actions are of chief importance, is simply curtailed or absent. For Westerners, one can assume the posture of a sort of "God" with a small "g" and create new

worlds for others or bring things to life. For Chinese, to lay claim
to ideas and explanations as one's own property implicitly denies
the communal sense of ideas as they are derived from a variety of
common social experiences and engagements. Indeed, given the
cooperative and participatory dimensions of Chinese discourse
altogether, it can seem dysfunctional.

So far, in this section, we have looked into some of the reasons
behind Western perceptions of non-endings and multiple views in
Chinese discourse. We observed a Chinese disposition for non-
endings that, in turn, conflicts with Western expectations for firm
endings in formal discourse. Let us now look at how Chinese
respond to formal Western requirements for topic statements that
contradict their own cultural disposition towards open-ended
beginnings. Upon initial inquiry, many immediately disclosed their
consternation, lamenting, as one did that:

I didn't have the American custom to give the important statement in the
first paragraph. I am used to developing my idea at the last. That's my
real idea. I explain everything, maybe talking about something not
important, solve the difficulty first, clear the way first. And, then, the last,
I say, this is my idea now. I was trained in the Chinese way.

I think Chinese way more recognize that the important should be put
in the last part – that's my feeling. I did not have the American sense of
opening sentence, opening paragraph. For example, in article, we seldom
use opening paragraph or opening sentence. Chinese way is step-by-step
and then you read until the end and then you understand what I mean.

Further questioning led to additional observations that American
discourse cuts quicker to the core of a message and, moreover, is
organized in such a way as to be eye-catching:

you have to do something important in the beginning. Some things, yes,
like in an article, you have to put the most important in the end. But, you
still have to increasingly give a hint, a clue to the reader that this article is
very important. *That*, you have to read it at the beginning. This is
American way, not Chinese way.

Some Chinese see the formal requirements of American discourse as redundant:

especially in composition class, I never study such a thing – topic sentence.
Because, it seems to me the topic sentence and the conclusion is almost
identical. Why I have to put it this way and sort of shifting words and
actually come out same meaning? I always bothered by that, actually.

Tally up their responses and it is no wonder that Chinese tartly pronounce American discourse to be "backwards, always giving their conclusion first!"

Their consternation is revealing because it draws attention to the diminished importance of an introductory thesis or preview statement in Chinese discourse. Mentioned earlier in chapter 2, this English thesis or preview statement sometimes takes on aspects of a classificatory or labelling device, and, in fact, all are parts of the same Western "two-tier" system of identification, abstraction, and categorization. Alternatively, defined beginnings and endings recall the container metaphor rife in Western thinking. In particular, native English speakers expect labelling, like they expect establishing or isolating a cause, because it allows them to get a firm (read "overarching") grip on a matter; its absence is therefore disconcerting. This expectation occurs in the American's assessment of example (1) in chapter 2 – specifically, that the Chinese businessman should have put a "label" on his message: "The real thesis to this whole comment, the one sentence that *labels* it, that makes it easy to understand and digest, is at the very end."

From a Chinese standpoint, however, abstracting a quality, labelling it beforehand, and imposing one's own preconceptions upon it rather than let the communicant grasp it go against their communicative requirements for unedited or uncoerced understanding. More than that, it seems to assign priorities for the communicant and so, in Chinese eyes, reduces the communicant's task and pleasure in working out meaning personally. Said another way, it "re"presents rather than presents meaning and so is less appreciated. Likewise, forcing contents to align with a preassigned title is viewed as artificial; it blocks the natural flow of feelings and thoughts. For example, some kinds of poetry had been originally written without titles, the title being affixed only later as an identification device; since the title was merely the poem's initial words, it often appeared nonsensical. Similarly, chapters in the *Analects* had been untitled and their titles were only later manufactured from their opening lines. (Then again, Walter Ong [1982: 125] has also commented that Western manuscripts, prior to print culture, went without titles, usually using only the first word of the text instead.)

Perhaps it is in this connection that some Chinese will intuitively reject a thesis (or topic or labelling) statement:

I don't find the American style, where the topic sentence appears first, to be effective. It's not necessarily more persuasive nor convincing than the Chinese style, where the speaker, at the same time as he is speaking, is reasoning with the listener to allow the listener to see whether what he says makes sense or not. This Chinese speech style is more open-minded, less biased, not constrictive as the American style, where it immediately sets you up to a particular frame of mind. You see, with the American style, you can react immediately to what the speaker says without listening to the rest of his explanation.

He can be read as suggesting that such a discourse style encourages selection and highlighting of a sort that involves another's (read "preconceived," "predetermined") interpretation; the discourse may thus appear somewhat "biased," "constricted," and not very "open-minded." At the least, it might leave the speaker open to untimely interruption and misinterpretation. (Recall, if you will, the declaration in chapter 2 by another individual that he would not listen beyond the first sentence as he already would have heard what was wanted.) Rather than risk such unwanted possibilities, it seems that he would rather try to set up a context in which a joint understanding can be nurtured.

It is quite possible that his remarks might strike some thinking Americans as unfair, misguided, and even reductionist. For them, it is obvious that topic statements need not "spill the beans." Often, as another Chinese informant already observed above, they are supposed to fetch the listener's attention, show the topic's importance or orient the listener to what follows next. Alternatively, a thesis might be adumbrated which is then often modified, further refined and investigated or even rejected. But what seems obvious to native speakers from one culture is not always so obvious to native speakers from another culture. Both are liable to respond to one another with their different understandings – that is, misunderstandings – of culturally significant symbols and intentions. As it is, sometimes Americans and Chinese are out of tune with one another; other times, they read each other's music wrong; quite possibly, they are cross-culturally tone-deaf.

In 1903, the unsettling incongruities and vexed experiences drove an Englishman to exclaim: "The Chinese are the opposites of us in every thought and action . . . The end is the beginning and the beginning is the end . . ." (Ball 1903: 717). And, more recently, Brookings Institution political scientist Harry Harding concurred with a Chinese informant's statement above: "I usually find, in reading articles from the Chinese press . . . a massive amount of supporting detail, with the principal conclusion stated for the first time in one of the final paragraphs" (personal communication, July 1986).

But, as we know from our discussion, Chinese priorities and requirements are placed differently. Often enough, the more explicit and assertive style of formal English argumentation clashes with a Chinese preference for mutual engagement and active participation in meaning-making. For one thing, it undermines the aesthetic pleasure of indefinite suggestion. For another, it seems to ignore the existence of the other. Furthermore, not only does it create a gap between speaker and listener but it also reinforces the speaker's isolation and enclosure in a world of his own, rather than communal, meaning-making. Given the way in which Chinese relate language to music, they might object to an explicit style's "flatness of tune and dullness."

Alternatively, Chinese might liken definitive statements and firm conclusions to staccato notes in music; they are registered immediately with maximum impact yet are cut off just as abruptly. They might also consider that such a communicative style reflects badly on a speaker's sense of delicacy; it makes the speaker appear pompous and it also insults the listener's cultural sophistication. More valuable for Chinese are the sounds that linger; the meaning may not be immediately grasped, but, rather, soaks in to make it go deeper and last longer. Consider as an example the famous fishtrap declaration by the fourth century B.C. Daoist philosopher Zhuangzi, which notes that traps and snares are cast aside once fish and rabbits are caught. It ends with "Words exist because of meaning; once you've got the meaning, you can forget the words." That is to say, what should linger in the mind of the communicant are not the words themselves but what they convey.

Joseph Needham (1956: 281) writes about Chinese thinking that things respond to one another not by mechanical causation, but by a kind of resonance. In communication also, Chinese prize remote resonance – the encounter between dynamically responding parts. The vibrant but invisible resonance is reflected in the neutral tone, aptly named mood particles alluded to in the previous chapter that ubiquitously punctuate Chinese (as well as Japanese and Thai) talk and most often appear at the end of an utterance or clause; they serve as conversational monitors and solicitors of the listener's engaged involvement and ensure the bondedness of the interacting parties. Seen in this light, we can appreciate why a key advertising strategy in Asian cultures has been to nurture and stroke the audience's mood. For example, in juggling the markets of Asia and the US, advertising giants Dentsu, Young and Rubicam adopt a hard-sell technique for Americans and a more low-key approach for Japanese. Alexander Brody, president and chief executive officer of Dentsu, Young and Rubicam, the holding company, explains: "In the West I say 'Go out and buy it.' In the East, I talk about the sea and the stars . . . I create a feeling!" (Perlmutter and Heenan 1986: 150).

Together, the circular start, suspended finale, and tangential views form one significant instance of a worldview that encourages open-ended beginnings and endings and a multiplicity of directions. As in dreams, the edges of Chinese communications blur, boundaries merge, impressions enter and exit with ease, gradually fading out as mysteriously as they emerge. Perhaps this is why Zhuangzi could awaken from his sleep and wonder whether he was a butterly dreaming he was a man or a man dreaming he was a butterfly; the boundaries between otherwise different realms are seamlessly joined in Chinese thought.

What, finally, can we say about the traditional Chinese emphasis on sincerity and Chinese skepticism of "clever talkers" (*Analects* 17/18) and "plausible men" (*Analects* 15/11)? To what extent do such attitudes persist among the English-speaking children and grandchildren of transplanted Chinese? One revealing answer comes from Honolulu special prosecutor Darwin Ching in the aftermath of a politically sensitive, traffic ticket-fixing trial. The grandson of native Chinese speakers, he attributed his success in the lengthy trial to the fact that he was "sincere" as contrasted to the "smooth talk" of the (Caucasian) defense attorney (*Honolulu Star Bulletin*, June 16, 1989, p. A–3). The statement had been made in the context of closing arguments to the jury. Interviewed later, he acknowledged that the defense attorney is "a fluid speaker" and "weaves a very good argument." However, he himself was trying to tell the jury to not "get swept away by it" but rather to "look at substance, not form" (personal communication, February 1990). Ching's remarks recall Zhuangzi's mistrust of articulate argumentation: "One does not think well of a dog because it is good at barking nor of a man because he is good at talking" (*Chuang-tzu* 24/71, A. C. Graham translation 1981: 150).

Drawing together the many strands of evidence presented in this chapter is not an easy task. No doubt many aspects of this discussion require further documentation and elaboration. In particular, to analyze and compare discourse by mixing and matching modern styles with classical ones is a tricky business: for one thing, the classical styles may not fit the modern ones very well; for another, the modern styles may have only retained the aesthetic and not the function of the classical ones. In this connection, the formal ideals and strategies described may be remote and possibly irrelevant to younger, urbane Chinese. Alternatively, they may not be able to voice some of them comfortably as everyday operating procedures. Furthermore, the same formal ideals and strategies must be placed against the volubility, directness, and even contrariness of many Chinese in relaxed circumstances. Despite these reservations, we see by a number of indicators that the rhetorical norms which native Chinese and native English speakers must know and recognize are fundamentally different. Certainly, people often overlook the fact that the sociocultural assumptions underlying each other's rhetorical strategies are not the same, that those of the one culture can seem incomprehensible or intolerable to the other.

To sum up, I have suggested that the Chinese worldview stressing integral connectedness and interdependency, multidimensional and continuous change worked its way into rhetorical conventions and strategies of overlayering, of building correspondences, of open-ended beginnings and endings. Subjects are engaged from multiple perspectives; the end is never fixed and much is negotiable. Meanings, intentions, and connections are implicit, inferred, or implied. Understatements, muted thoughts, and subdued stances come partly from a devotion to "transmit" rather than "assert." Chinese tend to present ideas in a round-about, suggestive, or indirect way and to insist on delicate invitation and joint participation as implied by the vocabulary of "beyondness," "inbetweenness," or "inexhaustiveness." The suggestiveness of inbetweenness and non-endings generates a fruitful ambiguity which, in turn, encourages multiple responses and interpretations; suggestiveness becomes both a quality and a challenge. The aesthetic invitation to participate – to "sympathetically harmonize" – underlies Chinese ritual actions and communications and aims to ensure the bondedness between participants. When we combine this aesthetic with a deeply rooted Chinese tradition for obscured links, partially rendered thoughts, deferred theses, and oblique references with no final resolution, we have a situation ripe for the continued Western portrayal of Chinese as "a mysterious and inscrutable people who do things backwards."

5

Effacing talk

We come now to another significant part in the puzzle of Chinese inscrutability. In previous chapters, we saw how subtlety and evocative open-endedness arise out of indeterminate endings. We observed that Chinese communicative rituals cater to a bone-deep sense of social harmony and interdependency that inspires people to seek possibilities for mutual engagement and joint action.

In this chapter, we turn to Chinese concerns about face and form and the cultural expression of hierarchical respect and deference that has alternately charmed and confused Westerners. We proceed by enlisting the help of Chinese-speaking bilinguals to analyze and assess an actual communication of a Chinese subordinate making a suggestion to his superior in Chinese, and supplement our discussion with scattered accounts of superior-subordinate relations in Chinese workplaces. This excerpt will also let us see that the rhetorical ideals and strategies described for traditional Chinese poetry and literature can be generalized to everyday discourse. Indeed, the evocative and participatory thrust in Chinese rhetoric becomes even more pronounced and more definitely formalized when talking to someone of greater power and authority.

By all accounts, Chinese communicative rituals require a constant attendance to hierarchical status and the rituals of social deference: markers of respect must be articulated and meaningful ritual action personalized. These are core values that still permeate Chinese social existence and reveal themselves in the strategems and signals of face-redress. Particularly in Chinese discourse, strategies of face-redress must be put "on record." The note of reluctance baffling Americans in our examples of Chinese budget requests examined in chapter 2 is one aspect of this emphasis. The greater emphasis on overt and elaborate signalling of face-redress is one of the most disarming yet disconcerting elements in Sino-American interactions and one that continues to generate substantial commentary in the literature on US–China relations.

For the most part, Western accounts of Chinese facework concentrate on its performative aspects. Sociologist Erving Goffman (1967) gives much footnoted discussion to Chinese self-presentation rituals and has embellished with considerable insight social historian Kenneth Latourette's observation that "The emphasis on face may be due to the fact that the Chinese, even more than some other peoples, have had the attitude of actors" (1964: 584). Noting the central place of theater and opera in Chinese culture, political psychologist Lucian Pye (1968: 168–169) asserts a strong link between Chinese concerns with face and their distinctive sense of dramatic performance and formalistic behavior permeating everyday life.

But when Westerners treat facework as just masked performance or theatrical flair, they are missing the real point about Chinese conceptions of face and its redress. For one thing, skillful facework among Chinese springs from a sense of propriety together with an attitude of restraint and a deep regard for hierarchy derived from participating in *li* or ritual action; those with only a partial grasp of this understanding can mistake facework's sincere respect for mere craft or even hypocrisy. Further, Chinese conceptions about facework demonstrate an overwhelming sensitivity and responsiveness to the surrounding human network; this is not surprising given their longstanding view of a person and his or her identity as relationally constructed. Outwardly, strategies of face-redress take into account the collective implications of one's actions. Inwardly, failures of face can induce an acute sense of shame if the ritual requirements of facework are absent or breached. Chinese strive with their facework to articulate the eminent virtues of respect and cooperation through repeated acts of deference and yielding or adjusting and accommodating in social situations. Facework is in fact bound to the active pursuit of harmonious attunement. (Another aspect of Chinese facework has to do, of course, with the ardent pursuit of personal gain or favor [Hwang 1987], and this often happens by manipulating or "pulling" *guanxi* [關係] 'social connections' networks – those interpersonal ties based on shared kinship, locality, dialect, or school, etc., in which favors are exchanged or reciprocated. Nonetheless, people engaged in *guanxi* practices remain keen to cultivate and nurture "good human feelings" [Chang and Holt 1991] in the interest of social harmony, especially as they become entangled in *guanxi*'s heavy and carefully calculated obligations [see Yang 1989, King 1991].)

Due to the strict hierarchy and centralized authority in many Chinese work organizations, communicative requirements for signalling relationships of face-redress stiffen. Particularly in strategies of persuasion, assigning a non-face-threatening intention to the communication is essential. Underlings don't just increase the honorific content of their language. In addition, they take advantage of the linguistic resources available to them to be modest in referring to themselves and to efface their own role in the communication. As Brown and Levinson (1987) might put it, they try to strike the right note of deference by maximizing acts of negative politeness. But, in view of the participatory dynamics of Chinese discourse, we should add that underlings also increase their efforts to create an engaged involvement and make their communication a joint enterprise. How Chinese achieve this is the topic for this chapter.

The surest entry into the matter is to look at one significant taped interaction between a Chinese male subordinate and his male superior. In this instance, the subordinate is initiating a suggestion that will benefit the company's operation. The formal features of this situation are compelling in that institutional opportunities for such a direct attempt at influence and persuasion are rare. The reader is advised at the outset that the senior person has signalled his approval, with some qualification, at the end of the subordinate's presentation. What concerns us in the analysis are the communicative constraints imposed by status and power distinctions on Chinese strategies of persuasion. For the subordinate's part, they include subtle displays of hesitant reserve, willing humility, and negotiable openmindedness that signal his reluctance to impose; these subtle displays open the way for his superior to impose his own judgment and intentions. Some of

these communicative devices and conventions have been discussed
in earlier chapters; all of them impart a special Chinese flavor and
so contribute to a performance readily appreciated by other
Chinese. We will discuss their use, why they matter to Chinese,
and how such rhetorical values and performances come to set
Chinese apart from Westerners.

The conversational excerpt to be examined is fairly long and
not a particularly outstanding example at that. Some of my
Chinese informants had balked at its "inelegance" – one stressed,
for instance, that more "deference," hence a sort of elegance,
would be introduced if the subordinate had started off with an
apology, thus bracketing his discourse with apologies fore and aft
– and would have preferred a more eloquent example. Still, it is
significant because the iron hand of restraint continues its rule in
Chinese interactions and communications. As we shall see, the
subordinate is careful to tone down his initiative and enlist the
superior's participation by an optimal mix of deferential demurrals and disclaimers that, in some Western eyes, would appear the
antithesis of eloquence and make the subordinate appear timid
and lacking in self-assurance.

There are other reasons why it makes an exemplary illustration.
For one thing, it is a spontaneous interchange, having come
from a collection of naturally occurring conversations (the tape-
recorders were voice-activated and the tapes themselves were
collected as preliminary steps in a research project on natural
Chinese conversations), and so gives the reader a non-simulated
experience. For another reason, and by happy chance, the
"because . . . so . . ." (*yinwei . . . suoyi . . .*) connective pair turns up
once again to bracket the excerpt's message in various ways. By
happy chance, I mean to say that its presence had escaped my
notice in the initial data-collecting. It was brought to my attention
by one of the Chinese translating the episode. How and why the
translator rendered it is significant. Prior to the analysis, he had
puzzled long and hard over the appropriate English gloss for
yinwei in line 10. To his mind, *yinwei* functions here as a sort of
"affix" and the gloss "because" comes closest to capturing its
operational meaning. His remarks seem to suggest that *yinwei* has
taken on a discourse function which, for want of something
better, has been inadequately translated into English as "because."

Both interactants, a young salesman and his immediate superior, are employed by a television–radio station in Taiwan that also produces audiovisual education materials. The salesman, about twenty-five years old, is of Taiwanese origin whereas his immediate superior is in his mid-fifties and had originally migrated from Shandong province in the People's Republic of China. For purposes of discussion, the age (here I am referring to the traditional Chinese deference shown to their elders), political differences (here I am referring to the history of animosity between the two ethnic groups in Taiwan), and previous interactions (here I am referring to the history of their relationship) are only peripherally important to the interaction. Throughout, the Chinese superior murmurs sublinguistic "hm"s, meaning "I hear you." While these back-channel cues are of course important, they are not relevant for purposes of this discussion and so their appearances will not be marked. Finally, rather than provide an inclusive and exhaustive study of the sociolinguistic and other features contained in this excerpt, we will only enumerate points of major concern.

The excerpt itself occurs in the midst of a run-through of budgetary matters between the subordinate and his superior. Briefly, it appears that both are involved in the publication of a magazine (called "Listener's Comprehension Exercises," as an informant later determined from listening to earlier bits of the tape) that deals with audiovisual teaching materials. They help prepare the magazine's contents before sending them onto another company named "Hoover" for printing. Once the printed matter has been sent back to them, they next attach their subscribers' name labels onto the cover page for the magazine's eventual distribution.

In the excerpt, the subordinate is proposing a plan that will save them some time and money in their production procedures. Apparently, the magazine's contents and cover page are currently printed in separate steps (why, we do not know). The subordinate suggests that it would be less costly and more time efficient to print them together as a whole, and outlines how this procedure might be accomplished. He sets up the situation in lines 6–13, suggesting that since they have already accumulated some 60–70,000 names on their listener response name list, it might be cheaper if they go ahead and print 100,000 copies at a time, instead of printing them in batches of 20,000 one time and then 30,000 another time, as they are currently doing. He goes into the details of his plan in lines 14–31. Noting they have just completed work on the magazine's twenty-second issue, he jumps ahead to use the production of the twenty-fifth issue as an example of how his suggestion would be implemented. First, he states that they will need to get a cover page for it. Then, they will have to wait while its contents are assembled and finalized (by, it seems, other staff members). When this assembling is finalized, he proposes in line 21, that he and his superior can then insert a partial draft (of, as the same informant surmised from listening further to the tape, a feature called "Special Features in Today's Modern American English") into that section of the publication for audiovisual teaching materials. (Line 21 is not particularly clear here.) And, if they can also figure out the approximate number of copies they need to print, they can then rush the material (meaning both the contents and cover page, plus the estimated number of copies they need) over to Hoover and ask them to get it back to them fast, whereupon they will then have the luxury of two weeks in which to bind and distribute the magazine. He adds that they might need to hire part-time workers to help get the job done quickly in the manner he proposes. In lines 32–39, he is reinforcing his proposal, in effect, saying that printing the cover page and the contents separately as they are now doing means that the costs are higher. It would really be more cost effective if they could print the cover page and contents together as a whole, and, if this should be the case, then perhaps they might start getting the cover page ready for the twenty-sixth issue in advance. In lines 40–41, he tries to get some feedback from his boss.

We should note that there are several gray areas and further points of ambiguities in the subordinate's presentation. One has to do with the presentation's lack of referents (or zero-anaphora which we discussed in chapter 3) and tense markers that are normally found in English discourse, but typically absent in Chinese discourse. It should be added that their absence posed initial difficulties for my Chinese-speaking informants, which were later resolved. For example, some of them had first thought that there were two magazines under discussion – i.e., one, a monthly and the other, dealing with audiovisual teaching materials –

whereas, in truth, there was only one. And, due to the absence of tense markers, some of them thought that the subordinate had already talked his plan over with the Hoover boss (line 3) whereas, I believe, he had not done so as yet. This point will become significant in later discussion. Other difficulties have to deal with gaps in our information about the technicalities of the subordinate's proposal. For example: (1) how and why do they need to "find" the cover page – that is, are the cover pages already selected in advance and stored somewhere or do staff members have to design one anew for each issue?; (2) why do they continue printing out copies in sporadic batches since they already have accumulated some 60–70,000 names of their audience? (Listening further to the exchange between superior and subordinate immediately following this excerpt, it seems the superior is anxious to keep costs down, and the audience mailing list does not give a true picture of the number of copies they actually need to print for each issue.) Whatever the situation, these ambiguities are not critical to our analysis.

A number of male and female Chinese-speaking informants aided with the translation and analysis. Of these informants, three came from Taiwan, two others were Hong Kong natives, one was raised in China and later lived in Hong Kong whereas another was born in Beijing and later moved to Taiwan. With the exception of one who was in his early fifties, all were in their twenties or thirties at the time of the interview, all were fluent in Mandarin Chinese, and all could understand the subordinate's communicative signs directly and immediately.

Approximate English glosses and approximate English translations have been provided for the non-Chinese reader. In this connection, the following abbreviation conventions are used: asp indicates aspect; clsf indicates classifier; honf indicates honorific; ptl indicates sentence particle.

1. *Lingwai   wo   zai   xiang   a.*
   In addition   I   asp   think   ptl

   One other thing I have been thinking about.

2. *Women   xianzai ...*
   We   now

   We now ...

3. Wo...*wo*   *gen*   *Haohuade*   *laoban*   *shangliang*   *a*
   I   I   with   Hoover   boss   discuss   ptl

   I $\left\{ \begin{array}{l} \text{am going to discuss} \\ \text{have discussed} \end{array} \right\}$ it with the Hoover boss.

4. *Jiushi*.. *Wo*   *xiang*   *wo*   *bu*   *zhidao*   *shangci*
   That is I   think   I   not   know   last time

   tamende   *jiage*   *shi*   *zenme*   *yang*   *suande.*
   their   price   be   how   way   calculate.

   That is.. I don't really know how they calculated the price
   last time.

5. *Na,*   *wo*   *xianzai*   *xiangyixia*...*wo*   *yao*   *wen*   *ta*
   Ptl   I   now   think   I   want   ask   him

   le.
   ptl

   I've been thinking about it...I'd like to ask him.

6. *Jiushishuo,*   *haoxiang*   *zhei*   *yang*   *yin*   *a*   *bijiao*
   That is   appear   this   way   print   ptl   somewhat

   langfei   *bijiao*   *hua*   *qian*   *duo*   *yidian.*
   wasteful   somewhat   spend   money   much   a little.

   That is, it seems that this method of printing is somewhat
   wasteful, sort of spending a little too much money.

7. *Weishenme*   *ne?*
   Why is that   ptl

   Why is that?

8. *Yici*   *yin*   *sanwan,*   *yici*   *yin*   *liangwan,*
   One time   print   30,000   one time   print   20,000

   yici   *yin*   *ji*   *wan,*   *zheige*   *feichang*
   one time   print   several   10,000   this   very

   fei.
   wasteful.

   Printing 30,000 [copies] at a time, printing 20,000 at a time,
   printing several tens of thousands at a time, this is very
   wasteful.

9. *Suoyi   wo zai xiang you   meiyou bijiao*
   Therefore   I   asp think   have haven't somewhat

   haode   banfa.
   better   procedure

   Therefore, I have been thinking whether there might be a better way.

10. *Pirushuo   ruguo . . . yinwei . . xianzai neige*
    For example   if   because   now   that

    tingzhong   laixinde   mingdan, a,   yijing   you   yi
    listener   letters   name list   ptl   already   have   one

    da   dui   le.
    big   pile   ptl

    For example, if . . . because . . we have now amassed a great many names on the listener's response name list

11. *Na   you   ji   wange   le.*
    Ptl   have   several   10,000s   ptl

    There's several ten-thousand [names]

12. *Jiu   zhishao   you   wu   liu   wan   le.*
    Then   at least   have   five   six   10,000   ptl

    There's at least fifty to sixty thousand [names]

13. *Na   women   zhishao   yao   yinge   liu   qi   wan*
    Ptl   we   at least   want   print   six   seven   10,000

    a   peihe   zai   xia   yi   yuede   neige   liang.
    ptl   match   asp   next   one   month   that   quantity.

    We would have to print at least 60–70,000 [copies] to accommodate next month's volume

14. *Suoyi   women   keyi   niding   yige   jihua.*
    Therefore   we   can   draft   one   plan

    Therefore we can think up a plan.

15. *Pirushuo,   xianzai   shi   ershier   qi   ma.*
    For example   now   be   22   issue   ptl

    For example, we're now done with the 22nd issue

16. *Danshi, women shuo ershiwu qi   chulai.*
    But   we   say   25   issue   produce

    But, let's just say we're going to put out the 25th issue

17. *Na, women xian ba   ershiwu qide   fengmian*
    Ptl we   first take   25   issue cover page

    zhaochulai.
    find

    [In order to do so] we're going to have to get a cover page
    for the 25th issue.

18. *Shuo zheige shi yong zai ershiwu qide.*
    Say   this   be   use   asp 25   issue.

    And say that this [cover page] will be used for the 25th issue

19. *Ranhou   deng deng deng deng deng.*
    Afterward   wait wait wait wait wait

    Afterwards, we'll wait and wait and wait and wait and
    wait [for, apparently, the editorial staff to finalize the con-
    tents/layout of the 25th issue]

20. *Na ershiwu qide   neirong, tamen yijing*
    Ptl 25   issue   content   they   already

    bianchulaide ma.
    assemble   ptl

    Now, [let's just say] they [the editorial staff] will already
    have assembled the 25th issue's contents

21. *Women xian keyi ba   yi   bufen nichulai dao*
    We   first can   take one part   draft   (to)

    neige shiting   jiaocai.
    that   audiovisual   teaching material

    [If the layout is completed] we can draft a portion [of the
    feature they are responsible for preparing] and put it in that
    [section of the contents reserved for] audiovisual teaching
    materials

22. *Ranhou   women zhei yiduan shijian, a,   women*
    Afterward   we   this clsf   interim   ptl   we

    keyi xian ba   ta zhaochulai.
    can   first take it find

Afterwards, during this stretch of time, we can figure out
[the number of copies, given their knowledge of the audience
name list accumulated, to be printed]

23. *Shuo neirong mashang   gei   ni,   ni*
    Say   content   immediately give you   you

    mashang   bang wo   nongchulai.
    immediately   help me   get (it) out

    Let's say that we will get the contents [plus cover page and
    estimated number of copies] to you [Hoover] fast, and you
    [Hoover] get them done fast.

24. *Chulai   yihou   women   jiu   keyi ... zhei ...*
    Produce   afterward   we   then   can   this

    zhishao   you   liangge   libai shijian   women   keyi
    at least   have   two   week   period   we   can

    zhuangding ...   fachuqu.
    bind   distribute

    After [they're] printed, we can ... this ... we'll [effectively]
    have about two weeks in order to bind them ... [and then]
    send them out

25. *Zheige   shijian   dui   women   lai   shuo   jiu   bijiao*
    This   interim   for   us   come   say   then   somewhat

    youli   le.
    advantageous ptl

    This stretch of time will be somewhat advantageous for us.

26. *Na women   keyi .. bu   guan shi   zhao linshi*
    Ptl we   can   not   care be   find part time

    gong   huo   zenme   yang.
    work   or   what   way.

    We can .. Even if it means that we have to hire part-time
    workers [to help us rush it out] or whatever

27. *Ba   ta   quanbu   fawan.*
    Take   it   all   send

    [we can] just send them all out [at once]

28. *Fa   wan   yihou zhishao ...*
    Send   finish after at least

    After they're sent out, at least ...

29. *Yinwei   yici   yinge   shiwan   zhang.*
    Because one time print   100,000   piece

    Because we'll be printing one hundred thousand [copies] at a
    time.

30. *Na dajia   dou   bijiao   pianyi le.*
    Ptl everyone   all   somewhat   cheap   ptl

    Everything will be cheaper

31. *Wo   xiang...wode   xiangfa   shi   zhei   yangde.*
    I   think   my   opinion   be   this   way

    Suoyi...
    Therefore

    I think... My opinion is this way. So...

32. *Yinwei   benlai   kaolü,   lingwai   zhao   yige*
    Because originally   consider   another   find   one

    fengmian   a.
    cover page   ptl

    Because originally another cover page was considered [for
    the twenty-fifth issue, probably]

33. *Lingwai zhao yige fengmian   jiu   bu   suan*
    Another find one   cover page   then   not   regard

    neige   zazhi   le.
    that   magazine   ptl

    To find [print] only the cover page is not calculated into the
    [publication] price of that magazine [in other words, printing
    the cover page separately, as they are currently doing, is
    expensive]

34. *Chengben jiu   gao   le.*
    Cost   then   high ptl

    The cost will be high

35. *Women   haishi   yong zheige zazhi.*
    We   better   use   this   magazine

    It'd be better if we use this [way I've suggested for printing
    cover page and contents as a whole] for this magazine.

36. *Jiu   women   xian she   yige...*
    then   we   first devise   one

    That means we'll first have to devise one...

37. *Yaoburan,   she   yige   ershiliu   qide   fengmian.*
    Otherwise devise   one   26   issue   cover page
    What about we design a cover page for the 26th issue

38. *Na   women   tixian   chulai   fengmian   le.*
    Ptl we   in advance   produce   cover page ptl
    [In that event], we'll have its cover page out in advance.

39. *Ranhou   fachuqu.*
    Afterward   distribute
    Afterwards, we can just send it [all] out

40. *Buxiaode.   Nin   juede   zhei   yangzi   hui*
    Not sure   You (honf)   feel   this   way   know how

    buhui   bijiao . . .
    not know how   somewhat

    I'm not sure. Do you (honf) feel that this way can or cannot
    be somewhat . . .

41. *Wo   bu   zhidao.   Wode   xiangfa   shi   zhei   yangzi.*
    I   not know   My   opinion   be   this   way.
    I don't know. This is my idea.

All the Chinese-speaking informants participating in the examination uniformly recognized the episode to be an interaction
between a superior and his subordinate by what they described as
"the tone of voice" and "a hesitant quality in the speech of the
subordinate." Yet, despite their agreement, some commented that
their expectations of a certain degree of ritual distance were not
entirely met. For example, they observed the presence of the
sentence particles *ne* and *a* in lines 1, 3, 7, and 32, for example,
and the use of *deng, deng, deng, deng, deng,* 'wait, wait, wait,
wait, wait,' in line 19, which impart a startling tone of familiarity,
making the speech more "colorful" and so, in their view, nar-
rowed the customary ritual distance between the interactants.
Significantly, the act of introducing and putting forth a solution
verbally in contradistinction to a Chinese aesthetic preference to
leaving it implicit indicated to them that the speaker must hold
some kind of authority as well. Given these considerations, they
concluded that the speaker had displayed an uncharacteristic
amount of "egalitarianism." That is, not only did he offer an

original suggestion, he moreover "was asserting his solution almost as if he were a partner rather than a subordinate." Altogether, their remarks are significant because they throw into sharp relief Chinese communicative expectations regarding indeterminate endings in polite discourse.

Even more intriguing, some felt it was simply out of a subordinate's province to make a suggestion to someone senior. As one Chinese observed, making his suggestion involves conflicting pulls: "Well, on the one hand, he has to speak; on the other hand, he dare not to speak in front of authority."

Their responses point to a traditional way of thinking about status, authority, and hierarchy that remains robust in various Chinese interactions. The hierarchical–deferential system compels a subordinate to attend to the face-challenging implications of his or her actions, in particular, actions that eschew cooperation, assert individuality, or usurp functions appropriate to another. Anthropologist Robert Silin provides further insight into the sensitivity to face in large-scale Taiwanese organizations. He develops his theme in the context of a "culturally stylized awe" which, along with acts of personal loyalty and judicious propriety, are cultivated by Chinese persons enmeshed in a dominance hierarchy: "To publicly express alternative ideas is to express lack of confidence in the boss. Such expressions are ultimately threatening to his position as chief, and, at least vaguely, disrespectful. Individuals who hold such ideas are assumed to harbor personal, egocentric, anti-group ambitions (ch'i-t'u)" (1976: 65).

Anecdotal evidence affirms how deep these attitudes run. While interviewing a former employee of a large Taiwanese agency, I learned that his first appearance on the job, which he subsequently held for two years, was marred by what he retrospectively regarded as a strategic blunder:

The role of subordinate is pretty set. I had a job that involves translation. At one time, I remember there were some English words which my boss didn't know how to translate into Chinese. He didn't know the meaning, but I know it, so I told him that this meant this. I was very surprised because I thought I helped him. I think he was very offended. I told him in front of other colleagues, lost [his] face. The only explanation I can come up with is that I was too bold, too presumptuous, that [I show] I have better knowledge than him. So, you see, the role [of a Chinese subordinate] is pretty well set.

His superior's swift reaction clearly indicated to this informant that he had breached ritual boundaries, leaving him ruefully to conclude that maintaining a proper footing with one's superior means above all a show of "submissive respect." On the other hand, those expected to defer to the authority of someone more powerful or resource-laden can ask for help when needed. Further, Chinese seniors traditionally are more involved in the personal crises and life cycle events of their underlings (although nowadays this involvement is changing and lessening). In this regard, Samuel Chang reports from his survey comparing American and Taiwanese managers: "The Chinese felt more strongly than Americans that supervisors should help with subordinates' personal problems, that companies should look after the welfare of employees and their families..." (1985: 151). In short, the relationship between Chinese seniors and underlings is reciprocal and interdependent. This falls right into step with the Confucian emphasis on the five relations (*wulun*) – i.e., ruler/subject, father/son, elder brother/younger brother, husband/wife, friend/friend – which, with the latter's exception, are characteristically hierarchical with reciprocal obligations and sentiments – i.e., loyalty, filiality, respect, obedience, respectively, on the subordinate's part – and which, as early Confucians saw them, served as models for all other relationships.

Likewise, a superior assiduously cultivates an aura of authority to which a Chinese subordinate's deferential and respectful actions contribute. Subordinates often show respect by avoiding the appearance of offense or infringement. Not only is this respect by avoidance indicated verbally and non-verbally, it is also institutionally sanctioned by a lack of genuine options and alternatives that would permit subordinates to exercise their ingenuity and initiative. More than that, rewards have traditionally been few and punishments have come easily. Unless opportunities are available and attractive, it is not surprising to find Chinese subordinates wary of stepping out of line and incurring the risk of disfavor. Such acts of avoidance, in turn, reaffirm the superior's power and authority to define what is acceptable. In short, the lines of authority and distinctions of hierarchy become reinforced as a social fact. Thus, in another of my interviews concerning a Chinese manager's relations with Chinese staff subordinates, an informant recalled:

Some of the people [i.e., staff subordinates], they have ideas or suggestions, they dare not say it out because they thought it might offend the superior. They just keep it to themselves; don't want to appear too competent in front of the boss because it challenges his competence, even though you're helping out the company. His own dignity may be offended.

When we return to the excerpt, the delicacy of the subordinate's position becomes clearer. Despite what Chinese informants consider to be some inelegance and assertive overtones – even a certain brashness – in its makeup, it shows a cautious restraint throughout. For one thing, the subordinate sprinkles his talk with subtle and not-so-subtle hints that forestall personal culpability and that also protect against the undesired dissonance of a disrespectful intrusion. Take, for example, his mention of the "Hoover boss" in line 3. This seemingly casual mention may imply that the subordinate had legitimate grounds for broaching the issue and so alleviated a part of the onus from his intrusion. In this instance, he had shown forethought to the issue by having discussed it with someone, that "someone" happening to be a person of some authority. As argued in chapter 4, alluding to authoritative ideas is a conventional strategy in Chinese discourse; the mere mention of certain important individuals can endow a communication with legitimacy and status. As it happens, it was another informant who brought the matter to my attention, thus revealing a remarkable Chinese sensibility to the subordinate's communicative strategy.

Equally important, the strategy of bringing in a third party is also partly a variation of a Chinese aesthetic requirement to "transmit" rather than assert, and partly a reflection of a Chinese communal orientation in which personal culpability or accountability is mitigated by spreading or shifting responsibility for the communication. Just as credit is not an individual matter in Chinese thinking, neither is responsibility. We should note, however, that another informant disagrees with the above informant's claim regarding the significance of the subordinate's mention of the Hoover boss. The source of the disagreement has to do with tense, which, in Chinese, is not specified. That is, it is not altogether clear in the subordinate's discourse whether he had indeed already discussed the matter with the Hoover boss, as the above informant apparently assumed, or, whether, as the second informant argued and which I am inclined to believe, given the use of the imminent action – i.e., *yao* + verb + *le* – in line 5, the subordinate will discuss the matter with Hoover. Whichever the case, I want to stress that the Chinese strategy of bringing in a third party to buttress one's position is not the least at issue.

Perhaps the most concentrated, if not most eloquent, display of cautious restraint appears in lines 40 and 41, where the speaker has shifted from the information task to the formal expression of ritual distance and regard. Here the subordinate's delivery begins to falter despite his otherwise fluid speech and enthusiastic manner. Here, he markedly increases the polite, honorific content of his discourse. He speaks tentatively and drops his voice in striking contrast to his otherwise fluid delivery. This latter feature needs to be stressed because, as we discussed in chapter 2, a shift to a lowered voice is a conventionalized Chinese technique to indicate matters of great seriousness or great feeling. It is therefore culturally significant.

We might say that the subordinate in these two lines has shrewdly deflected hints of challenge and presumptuous assertiveness. With such non-threatening signals, he has underplayed the effrontery of his initiative. Likewise, he has symbolically reinforced the ritual distance of hierarchical respect. We might also argue that his cautious restraint owes its inspiration to and is congruent with the attitude of negotiable flexibility and conciliatory intent – perhaps better rephrased as a "negotiable openmindedness" – mentioned in chapter 2. Negotiable openmindedness here refers to communicative behavior which moves the speaker's discourse closer to an open-ended position. Particularly when faced with the formal demands of rank and authority, a Chinese subordinate is keen to adopt a more supple interactive posture and assert greater accommodation in his (or her) rhetoric to minimize any potential social fallout and highlight his (or her) cooperative capacity as well. In short, he (or she) judiciously yields and conveys to his (or her) superior a firm sense of his (or her!) involvement in the communication, all the while bringing about a symbolic reversal in the "author"-ship of his (or her) communication.

Does this explanation hold up to scrutiny? Here are some Chinese comments about the significance of lines 40 and 41:

An inferior doesn't have any power to make decision; he can just suggest. He's got to have these two sentences here, because up to here [line 39], that's his idea, ok? And, he got to get his boss's idea . . . He does it by saying this [lines 40–41]. This is a very typical way that an inferior or an employee speaks to his boss. They have to obtain the idea from the boss . . . The boss is the person to make the decision, so this guy just couldn't say "and then we will do this, do that, do that." He couldn't stop at that point [line 39] because after he make some suggestions, he got to ask his boss what his boss thinks about his ideas.

The first respondent makes it clear that, given the ritual requirements of superior–subordinate relations, a decisive finality is discouraged in favor of a suggestive indeterminacy. From one perspective, the subordinate is actively seeking to solicit the superior's judgment – i.e., "trying to drawing in the other party to ask his opinion," as another informant concluded; in a manner of speaking, he invites his superior to complement his contribution and to participate in mutual meaning-making. By so doing, he brings the superior into sharp focus; he conspicuously recognizes his presence and power and the hierarchical relationship between them. From another yet related perspective, an indeterminate ending is calculated to shift responsibility for the communication's decision – specifically, the subordinate reshapes his communication and redirects its "author"-ship to his superior. To do otherwise injures the superior's authority and violates ritual boundaries. Furthermore, the subordinate verbally assures the superior of his willingness to accommodate to his superior's wishes. He "gives room to the boss" to sponsor or veto his idea and in so doing repairs his intrusion onto the superior's interactional turf. For a second respondent, then, nurturing an atmosphere of receptivity is far more important than projecting a facade of confidence:

Your idea, you should not be sure your idea is correct. You must get approval from the boss; he can overthrow it, put down your idea. Even though your idea is good, you don't know how the boss will think. Maybe the boss will like it. In this situation, I present this idea, I will calculate the boss like it, right? He will like me, "Oh, you are smart worker, you take care of the company," something like that. Another two points is that maybe he's not confident enough, maybe he present the wrong idea, so he has to use this ending. Even if he is confident enough to present this correct idea, he does not want to hurt the authority of the boss. He still has to give room to the boss to consider, [i.e.,] "anyway, if you like to oppose it, it's all right, too."

In short, the subordinate's dilemma, i.e., "he has to speak, he dare not to speak," is resolved by assuring his superior the opportunity to exercise his prerogative of judgment. By providing him with space for judgment and by yielding responsibility for the communication's decision, the subordinate soothes the superior's face and ends up protecting his own face as well.

To strike a balance between asserting a sensible innovation while honoring the ritual requirements of rank and relation, the subordinate studiously studs his discourse with a highly developed mode of polite circumspection that emphasizes his willing humility. Thus, according to the third informant:

When you're talking to a superior, the speech has to be polite and accurate. You give the introduction first to the problem – maybe longer than Americans – and the reason is to give the boss a good picture. And, then, to the point. The ending is pretty important – makes it more "smooth." That might make the boss concerned with your problems if you say it like this. [You] just give him ideas and he got the power to decide, so he makes the decisions. So, that's why [you] have to make [your]self humble to try to persuade him.

More specifically, humbling oneself through deferential and respectful behavior represents a conscientious effort to make cooperation a basic frame of reference; it signals a willingness for personal accommodation and possibilities of mutual adjustment. For Chinese, a willing humility shows one's sense of propriety and one's level of cultivation and interest in pursuing harmonious attunement; it is an indispensable knack one develops to fully participate as a responsible contributor to social harmony in a milieu traditionally dominated by hierarchy. Especially in persuasive discourse, it becomes a powerful device for engaging others and for bringing others around to one's way of thinking. Viewed this way, humbling oneself in Chinese terms is a far cry from simply expressing what foreign observers might take as "demeaning self-effacement" or "accommodating capitulation."

Together, these three responses indicate that negotiable talk for Chinese involves deference and deference in turn involves a significant interactive capacity for yielding. They point, furthermore, to a distinctive Chinese outlook on the binding and joining power of ritual actions in general and on the yielding and ceding emphasis of dialogic encounters in particular. The strategy of

yielding and ceding not only makes regular patterns of cooperation possible but is also a culturally important mechanism for
nurturing social cohesion in a participatory ritual order in which
social rites – and not individual, much less human, rights – have
traditionally prevailed. Certainly, such a strategy makes a happy
fit with Chinese admonishments to be "round" and "smooth" –
or "accommodating" and "non-intrusive" – in dealings with
people. Such a strategy in fact strikes the Chinese *wuwei* (literally
"no doing" or "doing without doing") posture of non-impositional
and non-coercive action.

Let us look more closely at the array of devices in lines 40 and
41 which helps mitigate what Chinese informants consider to be
aggressive or self-assertive overtones in the suggestion-making. As
we have noted, they indicate the speaker's reserve and discomfort
about proffering his suggestion and his readiness to listen to and
accommodate himself to his superior's wishes. The key indicator is
the repeated professions of incapability or "humbleness." Take for
instance *bu xiaode* 'I'm not sure' in line 40. As Chinese see it, the
speaker has adopted a show of conciliatory non-committedness to
the very issue he proposes:

It is used [here] to downplay your idea, to play low key, not to be proud,
to be humble a little bit, let the listener judge. He had offered his solution
and believed in it, but downplayed his idea by hinting that he didn't know
if the boss would agree to it or whether, indeed, it has much worth.

He also humbles his capability in the ellipted utterance *Nin
juede zhei yangzi huibuhui bijiao...* 'Do you (honorific) think
that this method might be somewhat...' followed immediately by
Wo bu zhidao 'I don't know.' All respondents recognized that the
speaker had negatively tinged his suggestion here. Voiced in a
lingering manner and delivered in a low pitch, these words work
to counteract signs of indecorous or impertinent behavior; they
allow the speaker to de-emphasize his opinion, disclaim responsibility, and ultimately develop – perhaps drop to – a low posture.
But ellipsis is also a natural sign of evocative suggestion. Its use at
a critical juncture enables him to politely invite the superior to
complete his thought, all the while fudging or fuzzifying his own
contribution, in effect, effacing – but not erasing – his role in the
communication. For our Chinese informants, leaving things

unsaid is advantageous in a number of ways since it illuminates the Chinese virtues of modesty:

It might mean he doesn't want to say *hao* ['good'], because that would be him judging his own words and therefore he kind of leaves it hanging. He doesn't want to make a judgment upon himself. He himself, of course, supports this idea, but he's modest in leaving that part out. The structure of the sentence implies *nin juede zhei yangzi huibuhui bijiao hao yidian* ['Do you (honorific) think that this method might be a little better?'] but he doesn't even want to include *hao yidian* ['a little better'].

This sentence is cut short. One would have expected "good" or "save money" to have ended it. In other words, by following his idea, it would be "good" or has the prospect of saving the firm some money. However, he cut short his sentence and said, "I'm not sure" to emphasize his modesty. That is, it may have been too bold to push the benefits of his idea; to allude to it would have been much more effective.

deferential restraint:

In this sentence, he is supposed to finish it with *shengqian* 'save money' or something. In other words, by following his idea it would save money or something. But he cut short his sentence and said *bu zhidao* ['I don't know'] to emphasize that "I'm not sure." He hesitates to come to a conclusion because to follow his way is to save money. That would be too rude; the boss would have a bad opinion of you because you have to play the role of the subordinate. He has to act like he is not smarter than the boss.

and hesitant reserve:

This seems to be a kind of hesitancy. So he mentioned his solution and then he kind of undermined it and said "I don't know really if this is that good," kind of implying that "I don't know if you would agree with this or whether you think this is worth anything." So, he kind of put a negative slant to it. On the one hand, he really believes in his solution, but then the way he presented it was to say "maybe not" – *bu zhidao* ['I don't know'].

For these informants, it seems the situation and the contents of his discourse make it mandatory for the subordinate to speak with hesitation and reserve as a mark of his refinement and good manners. In contrast, to speak fluently and assuredly here might seem vulgar and ill-mannered. In particular, their responses stress the liability of speaking with undue competence and authority and, instead, encourage a communicative strategy that modifies

direct expression and individualistic displays of personal competence or talents. To communicate ideas in a way that draws attention to the person as a unique and distinct being runs the risk of
egocentricity. It creates distance, not bonds. It reinforces the
appearance of an unseemly separation – as opposed to the possibilities of a congenial integration – between self and other.
Similarly, to close an argument firmly and confidently might also
seal oneself off from another. As a result, the ritual parameters of
a relationship might be shortchanged. Accordingly, a strong
closure is discouraged in favor of a more conciliatory, noncommittal stance.

Then again the utterance itself contains a number of other
hedging or softening devices to neutralize assertive nuances. For
one thing, an informant fixed attention on the qualifier *bijiao*
'somewhat,' commenting that "Instead of saying, for example,
'Do you think this way is good?,' he is saying, 'Do you think this
way is a little better?'." Another informant observed that *huibuhui*
'know how or not know how/can or cannot' adds an important
deferential nuance. As this informant puts it: "*Huibuhui* [here]
implies 'Would it be too presumptuous for me to say [what I
have said]?'." In addition, all Chinese explained that the respect
honorific *nin* 'honorable you' had replaced the ordinary *ni* 'you,'
which, by elevating the listener, is yet another way of humbling
oneself.

What clinches our argument that the subordinate seeks to
convey a negotiable openmindedness comes from one other
informant who explored more delicately the utterance *Wode
xiangfa shi zhei yangzi* 'This is my opinion.' She explains that the
speaker was careful to efface his role – that is, he had "put himself
down one rung by restricting the scope of his opinion to himself":

In this sentence, he's saying that "I'm not really sure that I have the final
solution, but this is what I think." By saying "*my* opinion," he has, in
effect, implied that there might be other solutions. He could have been
implying that the boss had another way of looking at it. If you say
"*everyone's* opinion" or "this is the solution," he might have had the
backing of authority that his opinion has the power to persuade everyone
that it's really good. So by limiting it to his opinion seems to me that he's
kind of putting himself down one rung. *Dajia* ['everyone'] is more neutral
sounding than to say *wode xiangfa* ['my opinion']. When you say everyone thinks this way, you don't need to say everyone, you just generally

state, "This is the solution." Then you're implying that your opinion has the power to persuade everyone it's really the truth. But when you say this is just one person's opinion, you're implying that there's a plurality of opinions, that there might be other solutions, so he was implying that maybe the boss had another way of looking at it.

Why should this be? How is it that the singular form 'my opinion' *wode xiangfa* is seen as less assertive than the plural 'everyone's opinion' *dajia de xiangfa*? To answer, consider what sociologist Richard Wilson has to say in *Learning to Be Chinese* (1970: 29): "Chinese generally refer to their actions and thoughts in the plural, emphasizing their relation to the group. 'We Chinese' (*Women Zhongguo ren*)... they will say when expressing their *own* opinions" (emphasis mine). As in the case of *dajia* 'everyone' above, the use of the pluralizer *men* in *women* 'we' broadens the locus of responsibility and authority from one's self to include others. Just as a Chinese person's social standing has traditionally depended on group membership in a kin-based society, so, too, Chinese opinions are more strongly asserted under communal rather than personal auspices.

More importantly, the expression "my opinion" here reinforces the show of deference and receptivity to another's view; it functions as a cooperative device to elicit the listener's view and to indicate the negotiable flexibility of the speaker as well. In short, the utterance politely seeks bidirectional input in meaning-making; it works in combination with the other devices discussed to signal to the listener the following message:

I do not know if you share my assumptions and my view of the situation and so I encourage you to draw an interpretation from what I have said and to give your opinion. What I have given is merely my opinion – a perspective, a point of orientation – available for further negotiation and modification. I am eager to take my cue from your lead in due (and deferential) regard for your status and expertise.

The subordinate's hesitant reserve appears in still other ways. For example, some Chinese insisted that, despite an ill-disguised zeal in speech and voice noted earlier, the speaker had been "suitably afraid" throughout. After I asked for further clarification, one stated that "It's not a direct presentation, not straight" and that "You feel more secure when you talk small things initially." Others pointed out that the speaker had carefully laid out his ideas for the listener, i.e., "always showing what he's thinking and explaining." All were emphatic that:

The boss won't talk this way. Usually the boss will be the last person to speak and he would only make comment, make judgment and pass on orders. He won't explain to his subordinate about okay, why I choose this one, why I make this decision. It's just not the style.

Talking "this way" refers to the fact that, as the less powerful partner in the relationship, the subordinate is anxious to include the superior in his reasoning process while demonstrating his own sense of place as well. Thus, when one Chinese informant heard the tape, she recognized and interpreted some subtle signs of superior and subordinate rank:

So many times [the speaker] has to show the way he's thinking, how he come to his idea. A boss would not say "weishenme ne" ['Why is that?' in line 7]. He just says it; he won't bother explaining. The subordinate is saying, "I'm going to reveal to you my way of thinking." The boss doesn't have to do that. If it's a superior, you won't bother explaining to your subordinate why you have to do something like that, why you make certain decision. You don't have to gain approval. This question is a kind of way leading to persuade the other party, convince them.

And, earlier:

[For example, take] haoxiang hua qian bijiao duo yidian. ['It seems we are spending a little too much money' in line 6.] Then he went on to give the explanation; he was going to explain what he was going to do, how the company benefits from it. It seems to me to be a way of leading to gaining approval or try to persuade the other party of what he thinks.

We could say that in presenting ideas gradually (some might say "fearfully"), the speaker makes sure his words sink in; he also makes way for his listener to chime in. This shows consideration and respect for his listener and, in Chinese thinking, is therefore polite. In developing his argument step by step, the speaker pays special attention to the listener's attitude and regard about his ideas. As one informant observed: "I think the way the presentation is structured kind of leaves way for the boss to interrupt at any time. He had a lot of as, mas (see, for example, lines 6, 10, 13, 15, 20) and so on." It seems the use of such pause particles (see Li and Thompson 1981: 86) – together with, I suspect, the breath-group and idea unit pauses peculiar to Chinese as

compared to Japanese (84) or English – give ample opportunity
for the speaker to monitor the listener's understanding and for the
listener to interrupt at will. At the same time, we could also say
that presenting one's ideas gradually draws the listener into the
reasoning process as a joint enterprise and helps minimize the
aggressive overtones so actively discouraged in many Chinese
interactions.

Conversely, too little information can mystify or make others
feel left out. It can become a distancing mechanism used to reinforce ritual boundaries in the workplace. In this regard, it is
interesting to note Robert Silin's observation that Chinese superiors frequently write opaquely. One of business management
expert S. Gordon Redding's informants, an Overseas Chinese
manager, reinforces this:

It's the art of ruling that I [as a Chinese boss] put you in a situation where
you have to keep guessing what I'm thinking. So I put you in a role where
you are always trying to please me... In the older Chinese style, quite
often what is not said is more important than what is said – and they just
deliberately leave little hints without being explicit – to test you. And this
is said to be the highest art of leadership and management. (Redding
1990: 163)

Together, the honorific address, hedging, ellipsis, pitch change,
step-by-step development, and, if we are disposed to accept an
informant's account, the strategic reference to another contribute
to a well-developed mode of self-humbling and circumspect
action. Far from being simply ceremonial signals of rank and
relation, things said and unsaid are artfully and versatilely employed to counteract what might otherwise be construed in Chinese
thinking as an interactional transgression; further, they work to
engage the other in participatory meaning-making. Offering
his superior the formal expressions of respect and regard, the
subordinate backs off from a committed stance. He thus deftly
reaffirms the superior's place in the hierarchy and assures his
involvement and authority in the communication. Throughout,
the piling up of these devices and strategies not only leaves the
door of communication and accommodation open, but also gives
an oblique thrust to the subordinate's presentation, conveying a
strong sense of restraint according to the high Chinese valuation
of moderation, conciliation, and cooperation. Seen in this light, it

is not improbable that the gentle demurrals, oblique thrust, and demure stance contribute to the conspicuous sense of "passivity," "reluctance" and general negative nuance detected by mystified Americans in the Chinese budget requests of chapter 2.

Taking a different look, we can say that piling up these devices and strategies consistently helps blur the roles between speaker and listener – communicator and communicant – as they engage in mutual meaning-making. In Confucian thinking, ritual humanizes and harmonizes. Ritual keeps people at a distance, but ritual is also the means by which people engage and relate while pursuing their personal ends. And, since the gap between superior and subordinate is traditionally great, then acts of deference and yielding in recognition of their socially distant, yet reciprocal relationship is correspondingly great. As part of Chinese facework, communication on the part of a subordinate becomes even less one-sided and even less self-contained than Westerners might expect.

We have one final point to make about our informants' assessments of superior–subordinate relations. For the most part, while acknowledging the suggestion's deferential nuances, some Chinese informants asserted that subordinates in English-speaking settings would approach and express matters to their superiors in like manner. For example, one informant said: "It's a natural thing to fear one's boss in a Chinese employment situation. In the US, you would fear your boss, too... You always have to respect rank boundaries." That there may be some real cultural differences in *how* one respects rank boundaries quickly became apparent when, as in chapter 2, I inquired whether the subordinate's suggestion might have been introduced in a slightly revised form which would perhaps be more compatible with some American discourse habits – i.e., "Mr. Yang, I have an idea that might save our company some money..." Nearly all the Chinese resisted that alternative and then went on to explain and often with great concern and with great length, its drawbacks:

It seems rude. Maybe it's just show-off or something or maybe people will suspect this is just plain talk, because you don't give any reason why you can save money. I think this is very typical of the way Chinese present a case. You explain first the idea and then conclude what this idea would lead to, what kind of conclusion. Maybe people in the middle [of listening to the passage] way will begin to understand what he wants to talk [about].

It's sort of aggressive. In the Chinese way, you start off by talking something first, start maybe talking the problem first, and then you switch to the meat.

You need to feel your way and test your boss's mood. If you suspect any negative feedback, you can retreat. Westerners can tolerate failures, but Chinese are traditionally trained in terms of saving face.

To "feel your way" – to explore the line of least resistance while gaining access to the listener's ear, to approach obliquely or indirectly while taking measure of the other, to position yourself for quick maneuver – demands both sensitivity and flexibility. It requires antennae-like alertness to every cue and nuance as well as agility in facework's subtle art of adjusting and accommodating. At the same time, the open-ended exploration for points of convergences and common ground is partly a protective maneuver; it insulates the speaker from a sense of discomfort and allows for strategic retreats and conflict avoidance in the event of negative feedback. Given the cooperative dimensions of Chinese discourse, a more forthright approach can be off-putting and offensive and so risk disharmony. Hence, Chinese feel a need for "talking about small things" first.

The social acuity, the anticipatory perception, the sensitive exploration of another's intention and attitude – all this comes under the *cha yan guan se* 察言觀色 of facework, which means 'examining a person's words and observing his or her countenance.' One hangs on to every word, catching shades of intonation or cadence, staying alert to every move. One cultivates a kind of social savvy in sensing how people will react. As a Chinese explains: "You look at the face of your boss – the little actions that he does – and you pick up the hints, you know" (in Redding 1990: 163). Taken together, the indirection and obliquity, the restraint and respect all bear the deep imprint of Confucianism and its distinctive emphasis on human relationships and the natural hierarchy therein. In playing out these relationships, Chinese are perpetually on-stage.

The compelling, even assertive, overtones of the subordinate's argument bear on this point. According to informants, venturing forth with a proposal together with its solution, takes pluck. But perhaps it is just a sign of the times and reflects increasing changes in Chinese ways of dealing with issues. A previous mentioned report comparing US and Taiwanese companies lends credence to this view: "In Taiwan, many Chinese are becoming more issue-oriented and less person-oriented or 'face'-oriented in handling human relations" (Chang 1985: 148). Nevertheless, we should emphasize that the subordinate's assertive posture is more than offset by his suggestive option-giving. He cloaks assertion with an aura of uncertainty. In Chinese thinking, this shows respect. More than that, it shows the vigor of Confucian relational ethos. More immediately, it settles the subordinate's predicament: "He has to speak, he dare not to speak in front of authority."

In this regard, assigning a non-face-threatening intent to the comunication is a way to redress the (im)balance and restore the (a)symmetry. The nurturant "pull" of a diffident close combines with the jabbing "push" of an otherwise vivid, spirited, and zealous delivery. Through modest words, the subordinate gains access to the superior's ear. Assuming a highly apologetic tone, he humbles himself and relinquishes responsibility for the communication and decision. That his voice also becomes as tentative as his judgment signals respect to his superior. He thereby recognizes the distribution of power and authority in a system that has traditionally required daily acknowledgment of rank differences.

The Chinese concern with good form in interactions is reflected in their writing system. Of the four characters showing the phonetic *li* 豊 'ritual/sacrificial vase,' two include the one for 'ritual action' (*li* 禮) and the one for 'body' (*ti* 體). Observing this, Peter Boodberg (1953) suggests that *li* 禮 and *ti* 體 overlap in their connotation of "organic" form. Ritual actions, like integral organisms, seek rebalance in situations of distress or disorder. Or, if we consider form, Chinese public manners ensure the aesthetics of proportion and harmony in hierarchical–deferential relations. For both, transgressions or failures of facework can result in shame. And, given the fact that one's conduct, bearing, and disposition are functionally interdependent and so potentially at risk in Chinese thinking, facial features might sink and posture might droop under the weight of shame.

The Chinese concern for face and form or appropriate conduct within the bonds of an established relationship – without, Chinese can be discourteous and even discordant – hardly represents undue emphasis on behavioral niceties, empty formalisms, or external trappings as some Westerners might imagine; rather, one's conduct – and the reverence and regard that supposedly infuse and guide it – is a great part of what makes a relationally constructed person *human* in Confucian thinking. When it comes to actually and directly constructing their relations – Chinese will otherwise (and prefer to) rely on established network ties or third party intermediaries to facilitate this construction – Chinese aspire in their discourse and facework to elicit and nurture resonantial responses, to (re)produce the ties that bind. The binding power of talk is apparent in the literature on US–China negotiations: Chinese negotiators often greet their American counterparts with familiar fragments from their previous encounter as if to continue the rapport established there or, at least, to recall an established link. The binding ties of talk also figure in Lucian Pye's comparison of the characteristics of American and Chinese commercial negotiators (although he certainly did not have them in mind when writing it):

Americans generally believe that human relations cannot stand still; if they are not being reinforced and progressing toward greater intimacy, they will stagnate and wither. The Chinese accept that relations can remain on the same level for indefinite periods of time. What they want is a sense of reliability, not just greater warmth. Above all, the Chinese seem to want the negotiation process to produce a relationship with the aura of permanence. (1992: 106)

and, more specifically, that:

Although the Chinese objective may be, indeed usually is, to establish a personal relationship, their approach tends to be far more guarded than that of Americans. At the same time, however, they seem to have longer memories for early casual exchanges and will be quick to suggest at a later date that a relationship had been established in a situation the American may not recollect. (1992: 90)

Henry Kissinger said much the same thing about his lengthy negotiations with the late Chinese Premier Zhou (or Chou) Enlai: "Chou's reference to our earlier conversation, as if we were engaged in a continuous dialogue, was a characteristic touch, one of the most insinuating Chinese skills ... subjects were carried forward between meetings months apart as if there had never been an interruption" (1979: 778).

Adroit facework and surefooted adjustments become the delicate balancing mechanisms by which the ritual order is achieved. In one estimation, strategies of face-redress contribute to "the *social* grace which smooths out social conflict ... and which will weld a sense of community" (Cheng 1986: 341). In another estimation, they are "the 'oil' which keeps social relations running smoothly" (Redding and Ng 1982: 218). Hence the latter's view, following Erving Goffman, of a Chinese person as a "ritually delicate object." Facework then is not just putting on a mask nor just a matter of polishing or presenting a cultured surface; it is, rather, an earnest articulation and vigorous pursuit of harmonious attunement. Face-redress recognizes and dignifies another's state and status. In turn, the greater sensitivity to others is encouraged by the greater social interdependence of human existence in Chinese thinking. Links between utterances may be obscured but social links must be honored. Like facework, so with significant social links, they must be put "on record." Correspondingly, just as Chinese search for links and points of convergence in written discourse, they make it a point to seek and demonstrate acts of cooperation at numerous points in their face-to-face communications.

It would be a mistake for Westerners to misread actions of yielding and ceding as examples of a "submissive compliance," a "meek servitude," or a "conforming obedience" to ritual standards. These are stereotypical characterizations of Chinese personality and behavior that Westerners have held for centuries. Besides, personality – together with traits and attributes – represents the visible aspects of behavior; a focus on personality is consonant with some modern Western interests in what is tangible, measurable, or readily identifiable. Chinese, on the other hand, are more concerned about appropriate interpersonal conduct, less with individual behavior; they have traditionally focused on becoming human rather than human be-ing. Moreover, personality suggests a fixed, reified state of being that ignores the possibilities for personal change, malleability, and transformation assumed in *ren*-cultivation and appropriated in modern Chinese political campaigns of self-criticism and personal rectification.

Notably, personality's root sense is "persona," which originally meant a "mask" whose appearance can deceive or differ from what a person is really like deep inside. Accordingly, Western skeptics accustomed to a reality-appearance dichotomy might regard Chinese ritual facework as mere masked performance, a persona encrusted by layers of social and role obligations, giving little real indication of the person within. In their eyes, face then becomes only a matter of surface appearance, a "front," so to say, and a false front at that. But Chinese, on the other hand, are more concerned with showing respect to others than in revealing their own inner reality. If they do don a "face," it is to prevent the direct expression of emotions and feelings so as not to court embarassment, if not censure. And if they do camouflage their intentions and sense of personal resolve and initiative, it is due to their respect for the ideals of mutuality and attunement inspired by the dominant ethos of personal cooperation and social harmony.

Yet, by persistently parading respect in their yielding, receptive ways and reticent, cautious speech, well-mannered Chinese have found themselves stereotyped "mostly in terms of avoidance and restraint" (Singer 1973: 151). There is a ring of truth to this observation that is still reverberating nowadays, but it is only half an understanding, and the point is that those untutored in Chinese ways would not know which half is the right one. Their view that Chinese ways of relating are dependent rather than independent is a misplaced focus that ignores the overriding Chinese emphasis on "inter-dependence."

For all the social, economic, and political changes among Chinese populations, the traditional ideals of respect and face-redress make a deeper claim on their interactions than heretofore realized or admitted. The social delicacy and keen sensitivity to another's state and status is best realized in dialogic encounters that enhance the feeling tone and lingering melody of a well-attuned interaction. For the "faceless Chinese," putting one's (and others') best face forward remains a central concern.

6

Mistaking turns

Earlier chapters have delineated the conflicting expectations and cultural nuances that can enter into and affect the interactive experience between Chinese and Americans. They stressed in particular the variety of obstacles that can make smooth and satisfactory interactions between them difficult to realize. Close examination of the communicative import of culturally based discourse conventions has shown how Chinese stereotypical characteristics can take shape and become perpetuated in cross-cultural interactions. I want to pursue this theme by analyzing here two nearly identical instances of interactions between Chinese and American participants. In particular, I shall fit together the pieces of Chinese inscrutability dissected and examined in the previous chapters to give a clearcut demonstration of the evolving stages of American perceptions of Chinese inscrutability.

The strikingly different assumptions and perceptions with which Chinese and Americans often approach each other contribute to a remarkable instability in their relationship. As I have argued throughout, this instability has been accentuated by a tension created in part by the misreading of subtle cues in conversational encounters and an unfamiliarity with culturally based communicative strategies. What seem to be unproblematic and straightforward moments in their interactions are in fact troubling ambiguities which can create unanticipated misunderstandings and distortions.

When not tested for depth, instances of mismatched responses between Chinese and Americans are manageable. Consider, for example, the following exchange (which I have reconstructed from memory) of two ordinarily congenial roommates conversing in their kitchen:

AMERICAN   Should we put some water in the refrigerator?
CHINESE   You don't have to ask my permission.
AMERICAN   I'm not asking you for permission. I just want to know if we should fill up the bottle of water in the refrigerator.

The Chinese misreading of what, in the American cultural schema, is a taken-for-granted convention in the making of a suggestion triggered the American's retort and attempt at clarification. A subsequent interview with the Chinese, on the other hand, revealed his puzzlement as to why his roommate would bother to ask his permission for such a simple matter. It is worth noting, moreover, that the power of culturally based communicative conventions is such that both responses – the misinterpreted remark by the Chinese and the clarifying statement by the American – reflect the sort of automatic reply that occurs when an unanticipated remark is made. In this situation, the interactants were able to establish the source of the confusion. In many instances, however, special problems crop up that can take a serious turn, depending on the circumstances and the individuals involved. Conversational strategies have a way of backfiring or of generating unwanted side effects. Particularly in interactions between Chinese and Westerners, where efforts to obtain straight answers to straight questions often seem futile, the distinction between a seemingly straightforward strategy gone awry and the perception of a deliberate evasion is confounded.

At times, the misunderstanding may be fixed from the start and can make for some comical moments. Conversations can go in parallel with no real communication; sometimes, they can slip out of control and take on a life of their own. Consider the following example, in which the author indicates that, given the rhythms of Chinese life, his opening query should have been "When will you finish supper?" and a precise response should not have been expected:

When asked a seemingly "strange" question, Chinese tend helpfully to answer the one that *should* have been asked, but only that question, without trying to divine the real intent or volunteering more; thus, they can appear entirely unhelpful. After finding a Chinese cable office dark

early one evening, despite the sign giving its hours as 8:00–22:00, a
visitor discovers two staffers in a back room inhaling their evening noodles.
Question: "Is your office open?" Answer: "We're eating supper." "Ah,
yes, I see that, but when will you be open?" Answer: "When we've
finished supper." "But when will that be?" Answer: "Don't know, but
not too long." "Well, is it likely to be before 6:00 p.m.?" Answer: "Yes,
probably, please come back then."   (Murray 1983: 21)

The author, a former director of Stanford University's United
States–China Relations program, goes on to comment that "Except for the cheerfulness of the replies, one could readily have
assumed that these Chinese workers were more committed to
secrecy or dissembling than to 'serving the people.'"

At other times, the confusion feeds into the considerable repu-
tation of the Chinese for adeptness in avoiding giving information
as well as in creating misinformation. Explanations too often
sound like evasions; and sometimes they are. Consider now the
following two specimens provided by a Canadian China scholar
who, in the early years of China's *rapprochement* with Western
countries, had been in charge of negotiating and administering
all cultural, scientific, technological, and educational exchanges
between Canada and the People's Republic of China (Frolic 1976:
23 and 26):

CANADIAN   Why are all the wall posters and slogans which we saw here
           three weeks ago suddenly gone from the walls and buildings?
           (In some places we could still see the workmen with scrapers
           trying to get rid of the large painted Chinese characters.)
CHINESE   We had some heavy rains recently which caused them all to
           be washed off. (I decide that the rains must be the Fourth
           People's Congress washing the political slate clean.)

CANADIAN   Why can't we stay in the new wing of the Tung Fang Hotel?
CHINESE   Because the new wing has no heat and no proper air condi-
           tioning. (But neither does the old wing.)
CANADIAN   Why can't we stay in the Ren Min Hotel in the center of
           Canton?
CHINESE   Because it isn't as nice as the Tung Fang. We have built a
           new addition to the Tung Fang making it the best hotel in
           Canton.
CANADIAN   Oh, then are we staying in the new wing of the Tung Fang?
CHINESE   No, the old wing.

In this chapter, we shall be pinpointing the signalling detail and nuanced interpretation of some of these strategies-gone-awry. Again, the because...so...construction emerges as a prime source for the consequent interactional discord and communication breakdown between Chinese and American participants. Our discussion profits from work by conversation analysts who argue that conversations go smoothly when interactants share an overall understanding of the interactive goal which, in turn, is jointly achieved by the moment-by-moment, turn-by-turn reading of an assortment of communicative cues embedded in the conversation. Ordinarily, the subtlety and amazing complexity of this coordinated activity is not noticed. However, in cross-cultural exchanges, crossed signals and misinterpretations of a speaker's communicative intent can be so wide of the mark, that they can cause considerable distortion. Unfortunately, participants' efforts at repair misfire and further conversation only compounds the miscommunication. Often enough, when faced with systematic differences in language use and cueing conventions, participants tend to fall back on convenient explanations which reduce the issues to linguistic inadequacy and social incompetence or, worse, to stereotyping and stigmatization.

The data to be examined here come from an audiotaped role play enacted in Hong Kong in a special class for members of Hong Kong's police force who have to be able to speak English in dealing with their English officers and some of the English-speaking general public. The role play was jointly decided upon by the teacher and the police officers as representing some of the communication problems the police officers frequently encountered in their work. Among these problems were the way in which the police phrased their responses and the way they were frequently misconstrued.

There are altogether five participants in the role play, one of whom is a white male, a guest speaker to the classroom from the United States; the other four, one of whom is a female, are Chinese. The four Chinese officers are paired off while the American plays a member of the public. Thus, there are actually two nearly identical role plays, one executed immediately after the other, with two Chinese appearing in each, whereas the American appears in both episodes. The police have the task of stopping the American from approaching and entering a building which apparently houses his office, the reason being that there has just been a fire in the building. After being apprised of the situation, the American keeps asking why he is denied entrance to the building. As such, the entire interaction is organized along question-and-answer lines, with the American asking the questions and the Chinese providing the answers.

Without recourse to the original participants, I relied on a different group of American and Chinese-speaking informants to help analyze the episodes. (Among these informants were a Canadian and an Englishman; for convenience, I have subsumed all Anglos under the term "American.") There were several advantages to this approach, the primary one being that I was able to capture important cultural assumptions and expectations that might otherwise have been overlooked or ignored.

My interviews with the Chinese and the American informants listening to the tape proved illuminating. The Americans were initially sympathetic to the Chinese police officers, finding the American interactant to be somewhat over-insistent as the interchange began. However, as the Americans listened further, their sympathies quickly switched over to the side of the American interactant, as they considered the Chinese responses to be vague, indirect, deferential, and evasive. In stark contrast, the Chinese listeners found the Chinese responses both straightforward and appropriate for the situation. The task here is to isolate and identify the sources of ambiguity and friction in the interaction, to account for the discrepant assessments by the American and Chinese listeners, and to consider how culturally different ways of constructing and presenting information influence face-to-face encounters between Chinese and Americans.

Let me state at the outset that, while the two episodes are simulated sessions, they nonetheless dramatically illustrate how the very real differences in linguistic and cultural backgrounds triggered confusing sets of signals and interpretations. That there is serious disagreement in interpretive conventions is apparent in the outcomes of the episodes themselves as well as in the interviews I subsequently conducted with the Chinese and American informants. In this regard, let me reiterate that the two episodes represent situations of a kind which the police officers routinely encounter in their work. Moreover, the responses they give to the American interactant are in fact similar to the kinds of responses they ordinarily give in real-life situations. Explained in this way, then, the episodes are plausible candidates for the analysis I have in mind. Let me also state that both episodes are, in fact, the first halves of longer exchanges. For purposes of analysis, however, I have eliminated the second halves, as the conversations then shift to a different topic. Finally, where there is a potential for misidentification in the analysis, the participants in the taped episodes are identified as "Chinese police officer(s)" and "American interactant," and those who listened to and discussed the taped episodes with me are, more often than not, identified as "Chinese informants" and "American informants."

I shall first present the two episodes before launching into the analysis. Character A below represents the American interactant. C1, C2, C3, C4 identify the four Chinese police officers. For reasons which soon become apparent, I have deliberately held off putting final punctuation marks in some of these responses. The symbol [indicates speaker overlap, and the empty parentheses (   ) indicate that this portion of the tape was unintelligible.

EPISODE A

1.C1: Yes, sir. Can I help you, sir?
2.A: What's the matter? This is my office.
3.C1: Oh, because this on fire and this area is closed.
4.A: But it's my ⌈ office.
5.C1: ⌊ Yes.
6.A: What happened? Tell me.
7.C1: There's been fire.
8.A: What did you say?
9.C1: There's been fire .. on this ⌈ off-
10.A: ⌊ In my office?
11.C1: No. In this building.
12.A: Oh, but is my office all right?
13.C1: I don't know, but this building is on fire.
14.A: But I must go in and see .. because if .. I've got my papers there and I've got work to do. You can't keep me out. That's my office.
15.C2: Yes, I see. We are very sorry that ... Because uh that is very dangerous
16.A: Well, I don't care but I have some papers there that's very

important for me. It's important business. And if I don't get
those papers, then I'm going to lose a lot of money.

17.C1: ⌈ Yes, I see. Because the building is closed
18.C2: ⌊ Uh w
19.A: You mean . . you mean to say I can't go in?
20.C1: Yes. Nobody allowed to enter the building because the building
        is very dangerous.
21.A: Well, can you . . can you call the other officer? You call the other
        officer and tell him that I have to get into my office. Can you do
        that?
22.C1: I'm afraid I can't do it. I'm afraid . . .
23.C2: Or . . . or we suggest you uh . . . Because it is by the court order
        closed it. Closed it by court order.
24.A: Why, why can't I come in?
25.C2: Because uh it is to prevent theft ⌈ and
26.A: ⌊ But how can it be a court
        order if the fire happened right now? How can you have a . . How
        can you have a court order? You can let me in right now. Just a
        few minutes. Then I'll be . . I'll be back in about fifteen minutes.
        Then I'll be out.
27.C2: No, I'm sorry. There's ⌈ uh
28.A: ⌊ Why can't I just go in? I'm just going to
        get my papers. It's absolutely urgent. ( ) I've got an urgent
        phone call and I've got to get back in there.

EPISODE B

1.C3:   Uh, can I help you, sir?
2.A: Oh, I just want to go to my office.
3.C3:   Uh, this building is uh closed.
4.A: Why? What's happened?
5.C3:   Uh, there has been a fire.
6.A: Fire? In my office?
7.C3:   Uh, in this building.
8.A: In my office?
9.C3:   I don't know, sir.
10.A: But uh I have to find out what happened to my office. Uh,
        I . . I've got to get in there.
11.C3: Uh, I'm sorry uh because this cl . . this building is closed by court
        order uh I can't help you.
12.A: What do you mean, court order? You said there's been a fire.
        How can there have been a court order? When was this fire? I
        was here . . . I was here just a while ago. Couldn't have been . . .
        couldn't have had a court order. You must be wrong.
13.C3: Uh because uh this road is blocked . . . ⌈ was bl
14.A: ⌊ But why is it blocked?
15.C3: Because this road is very dangerous

16.A: But, why...Why can't...I just want to go into my office. I have some important papers there.

17.C4: I'm sorry. Because the building is in dangerous condition...

18.A: Well...

19.C4: Nobody allowed to enter the building.

20.A: Well, how can I get in? I must have my papers. They're very important. I need to work on them today.

21.C4: I suggest you go to..go to the magistrate court and get the permission.

When we examine many of the exchanges in isolation, we see immediately that the Chinese responses are remarkably similar in construction. They follow the because...so...construction discussed in earlier chapters. To be more specific, the American interactant's questions are answered in a roundabout fashion by replies which start with a justifying or reason clause before proceeding to another clause containing an answer. Again, it seems that the Chinese police officers, like the other Chinese in the preceding pages, are transferring their native Chinese discourse patterns into English.

(1) AMERICAN What's the matter? This is my office.

CHINESE 1 Oh, because this on fire and this area is closed.

(2) AMERICAN Well, can you..can you call the other officer? You call the other officer and tell him that I have to get in my office. Can you do that?

CHINESE 1 I'm afraid I can't do it. I'm afraid...

CHINESE 2 Or...or we suggest you uh...Because it is by the court order closed it. Close it by court order.

(3) AMERICAN But uh I have to find out what happened to my office. Uh, I..I've got to get in there.

CHINESE 3 Uh, I'm sorry uh because this cl..this building is closed by court order uh I can't help you.

Recall that in Chinese, the because...so...construction is distinguished by a number of features. According to Chao (1968: 115) and others, a reason clause seldom occurs as the second clause in a Chinese sentence. Moreover, as stated in chapter 3, one or both of the morphological markers connecting the two clauses are optionally omitted in speech. Occasionally, the two clauses are simply juxtaposed to each other, leaving it to the listener, from knowledge of the situation and from what has already been acknowledged, to infer the speaker's intent that the two clauses

are connected, and, furthermore, are connected in a specific
way. In essence, there is a set of co-occurring features in the
because ... so ... construction which differs from English in some
significant respects.

How far do these differences in the signalling and organization
of linguistic material affect the course and outcome of the interaction between speakers of such dissimilar linguistic and cultural backgrounds? How do they influence the way Chinese and
Americans evaluate such encounters?

To return to the analysis, we note a great deal of overlap
between the two sets of speakers. Specifically, the Chinese police
officers are frequently interrupted in their responses. The interruptions occur precisely at the juncture where the clause containing "because" ends, leaving the Chinese response in (4), for
example, awkward and incomprehensible.

(4) AMERICAN   What do you mean, court order? You said there's been
                 a fire. How can there have been a court order? When
                 was this fire? I was here ... I was here just a while ago.
                 Couldn't have been .. couldn't have had a court order.
                 You must be wrong.
     CHINESE 3   Uh because uh this road is blocked ... ⎡ was bl
     AMERICAN   ⎣ But why is it
                 blocked?
(5) AMERICAN   Why, why can't I come in?
     CHINESE 2   Because uh it is to prevent theft ⎡ and
     AMERICAN   ⎣ But how can it be a
                 court order if the fire happened right now? How can
                 you have a .. How can you have a court order? You
                 can let me in right now. Just a few minutes. Then I'll
                 be ... I'll be back in about fifteen minutes. Then I'll be
                 out.

There is some evidence that the American interactant misconstrued the Chinese police officers' responses. In the first place, it
seems that the pauses in the responses of the Chinese police
officers were mistakenly viewed by the American to indicate a
finished statement; that is, the American assumed that the Chinese
had completed their answers. We shall take up this issue below.
Secondly, it seems that the Chinese officers' responses deviated
from what many Americans would expect as standard ways of
responding. Take, for example, the Chinese response in example

(4). In response to the American's question of "What do you mean, court order?" an American would typically start his answer with reference to the court order. However, the Chinese officer's response makes no overt reference to any court order; thus, it seems to have a focus which is different from the original query. Similarly, in example (5), there is a shift in perspective in the Chinese officer's response insofar as it relates to the preceding query. Let me briefly expand on this point. In the American interactant's question of "Why can't I come in?" the focus is on the actor and what the actor can or cannot do. Accordingly, an American would probably expect a response which makes some reference to the actor or the actor's action. Yet, the Chinese officer's response makes no overt reference to the actor. Instead, the focus has inexplicably shifted from the actor or the actor's action to the situation.

Let us now turn to the misconstrued pausing phenomenon mentioned above, and let us assume that the American interactant has misperceived the juncture or the brief interval of silence after a clause which begins with "because" to be a completed turn (Sacks, Schegloff, Jefferson 1974), when in fact it may not be. Viewed from this perspective, a sort of interactional asynchrony arises when, for example, a pause between clauses is misread as a signal for one's turn to talk. There is another issue at stake here: assuming that there is a Chinese tendency to frame responses differently from Americans, a pause or juncture between clauses provides a vulnerable point of entry for the American interactant to unwittingly or deliberately interrupt, particularly when the surface form of the Chinese responses bears a strong resemblance to certain kinds of English replies and particularly when the responses appear irrelevant and unsatisfactory as well. This issue needs to be stressed because cutting short someone's responses is generally considered a serious violation of the cooperative principle that guides conversational behavior. It is viewed, therefore, as offensive. As we shall see, the Chinese and the American informants uniformly agreed that the American interactant had been interrupting the Chinese police officers. However, the reasons for and the appropriateness of the interruptions were viewed differently. These differences, in turn, are culturally based.

To return to our analysis, then, if we accept the fact that the

Chinese had been packaging their responses in a pattern unfamiliar to the American and consequently were not given a chance to complete their statements, we see that the difference in language backgrounds and signalling conventions may have lent an unrecognized dimension of confusion to the interaction. Accepting this line of reasoning, notice now how the fourth Chinese speaker deals with the apparent interruption:

(6a) AMERICAN   But why... Why can't... I just want to go into my office. I have some important papers there.
(6b) CHINESE 4 I'm sorry. Because the building is in dangerous condition...
(6c) AMERICAN   Well...
(6d) CHINESE 4 Nobody allowed to enter the building.

The last response (6d) by the Chinese police officer reflects the completion of her thought begun earlier in (6b). However, the American interactant, apparently unaware, or by this time, unwilling to recognize, that the Chinese police officer was actually pausing at a juncture between two clauses, rather than what he assumed to be completing her turn at talk, broke in with "Well." The Chinese officer, in turn, prevented the American interactant from expanding on what he had intended to say by finishing what she had wanted to say in the first place. Note that none of the interruptions examined so far contributes information to the previous response of the Chinese speakers. Note as well that the American interactant interrupted with a single word followed by a slight pause in example (6) as compared to his full-sentence responses in (4) and (5), thereby shifting the focus of talk.

In this example, moreover, there is a recognizable suspense intonation in the first Chinese response which alerts most American listeners to the fact that the utterance has not been completed. On the other hand, there is a protracted pause after this first clause which the American interactant either did not recognize as merely a pause or, if he was aware of it, nonetheless took the opportunity to interrupt. Both possibilities are conceivable, since the truncated Chinese response "because the building is in dangerous condition" seems to follow directly from the American's truncated question "But, why... why can't [I go in]." In actuality, the two Chinese clauses, dependent and independent, are linked.

In other instances, however, the American perceptions of a

linkage between two clauses were blocked by the different use of prosodic cues which led to the mistaken inference that two separate statements had been intended. Whereas Americans would expect a slight rise at the end of the first clause to indicate a sort of suspense–conclusion intonation, what emerged instead, in the case of example (1), was a falling stress on the word "fire." Upon hearing the Chinese response, some American informants momentarily assumed that two separate statements had been uttered.

These American informants indicated other difficulties with the Chinese response in example (1). For one thing, they expected an immediate answer to the effect of "There's been a fire" or some sort of official pronouncement such as "There's been a fire, the area's closed off, and no one can go in." Since they did not reply in accordance with the American's expectations, the Chinese seemed to them unnecessarily indirect and ineffective. From the American perspective, it was "as if the Chinese had been giving an excuse rather than making an authoritative statement." Furthermore, the American listeners were momentarily sidetracked, as the construction of the response did not immediately follow from the American interactant's question "What's the matter?" in line 2 of Episode A. As one American commented:

When you say "What's the matter?" you're not supposed to say "Because anything." You're supposed to *say* what's the matter. [It's] not a logical answer to a "what" question. "Because" is generally the answer to a "why" question. You'd expect an answer like "The building's on fire." "Because" doesn't plug you in, doesn't answer what's the matter.

He went on to say that:

"Because the building is closed" sounds like the answer to the question and it's a syntactical nonsequitur. And so just in the way my mind processes it, that throws me off because I think I have an answer to my question but it doesn't make sense. And so then the person continues with more or less the intonation of a separate sentence "This area is closed." So I've already reacted to the fact that I've thought he answered my question in a funny way.

When I next asked the Chinese informants to listen to the Chinese police officer's response in example (1), they replied that the form of the response was typical of the way in which many Chinese speak. To be more specific, they regarded the two clauses

of example (1) as a well-formed, conjoined utterance, and, furthermore, explained that the Chinese response reflected features
most clearly derived from Chinese. The following is a representative approximation in Chinese:

(7) *yinwei   dalou   qi   huo le   (suoyi) zheige*
    because building start fire aspect so   this

    difang guanbi le.
    area   closed aspect

    Because the building is on fire and this area is closed.

They proceeded to explain the Chinese antecedents of examples
(2), (3), and (6) as well. Again, the following are representative
approximations in Chinese:

(8) *yinwei   fayuande mingling (suoyi zheige dalou)*
    because   court   order   so   this   building

    fengbi le.
    closed aspect

    Because it is by the court order, closed it.

(9) *yinwei   fayuan xia   ling   guanbi zhei dalou*
    because   court   issue order closed this building

    (suoyi) wo bu   neng bang ni
    so   I   not   can   help you

    Because this building is closed by court order, I can't help
    you.

(10) *yinwei zhei dalou   you   daotade weixian (suoyi)*
     because this building exist collapse danger   so

     ren   bu   neng jin   qu
     person not   can   enter go

     Because this building is in dangerous condition, nobody al-
     lowed to enter the building.

In order to determine the stylistic options available to the
Chinese interactants, I next asked the Chinese informants whether
what Chao calls the reason clause could appear as the second
clause in an utterance – i.e., "Because the building is very dangerous, I can't help you" versus "I can't help you because the

building is very dangerous." Their explanations indicated that, while the because . . . so . . . construction is appropriate for written Chinese, the situation is less clear for everyday, spoken Chinese. Some of the Chinese informants, particularly those in their twenties, found both utterances acceptable whereas others considered the occurrence of the reason clause in second clause position to be stylistically odd, if not grammatically awkward. What was noteworthy about their comments, nevertheless, was a consensus that the pattern of the Chinese police officers' responses sprang from Chinese discourse practices.

In this regard, they observed that the acquisition and practice of English for many Chinese is an artificial experience at best, and largely limited to classroom exercises. One individual reached back to his childhood experience to remark that when Chinese teachers presented Chinese sentences to the students to translate into English, they would provide the sentences in standard Chinese, which followed a because . . . so . . . format. In his reckoning, the Chinese police officers had been "translating Chinese sentences into English words," which then accounted for the preponderance of the because . . . so . . . construction in the interaction between the Chinese and the American. His explanation hinged on what, following Weinreich (1968), applied linguists have called interference, where the linguistic features of one's native language intrude in the production of a second language. More to the point, his explanation of the phenomenon hews close to what Lin Yutang (1935: 81), in writing about some Chinese versions of English, once characterized as "English meat with Chinese bones." By this he means that the words may be English, but the understanding and intention they carry remain Chinese. Here is what this informant had to say:

All native born Chinese, when they speak English, they are not speaking English, they are constructing English sentence in head. So in a way they are creating English, not speaking English. How he construct English sentence? He construct English sentence by Chinese way. [The Chinese police officer] use Chinese way to express English. I don't think Americans would say that [way].

On the other hand, another person claimed that she was less inclined to use the because . . . so . . . construction in spoken discourse. What is curious about this statement is that the day following the interview, the informant did not appear as scheduled for another interview. When I called to inquire about the matter, I began the exchange with "Hi, I thought we were going to meet at one [o'clock]." Her immediate response was "Oh. Because Alice called me to this [other] office, so I cannot meet you."

Interestingly enough, in spite of her earlier claim, her response, beginning with the use of "Oh" and combined with the because ... so ... construction, echoes the police officer's opening response in example (1). In this incident, we see a personal discrepancy in judgment between matters of habit and matters of performance. Individuals are often simply not aware of their own speech habits in contrast to what they think they have learned or do.

Still another person commented that when the utterance is short, both choices are unmarked in Chinese. However, he reflected that, in his experience, in longer utterances there is a general tendency for the Chinese to launch into a wholesale display of reasons before coming to the "result" or main point; even then – and significantly, given the evocative–participatory bent in Chinese rhetoric – the "result" may not be explicitly stated. This person, who is a native of Beijing, went on to explain that, in his view, the infusion of Western writings into Chinese has perhaps influenced Chinese short responses of this type whereas the longer responses remain unaffected. His explanation clarifies in part the equivocal position of those Chinese informants, notably the younger ones, who were unclear as to the regular placement of the reason clause in native Chinese utterances.

Finally, and most enlightening, one individual declared that the Chinese police officers overused the fixed Chinese *yinwei* ... *suoyi* ... construction. To her mind, responses (1), (2), (3) and (6) in the context under discussion would sound too stilted to be typical Chinese responses. She commented that it is not unusual for native Chinese speakers to overgeneralize certain native discourse patterns into English, and she herself, being a native of Canton, constantly monitors herself on this issue. By way of explanation, she provided an illustration using another fixed Chinese construction: *budan* ... *erqie* ... 'not only ... but also ...' According to her, the Chinese might say in English, for example, "He not only bought [ordinary] apples but he also bought [special] Tianjian apples." (Let me just say that the nuances here, which I have tried to indicate by the bracketed material, are somewhat analogous to "He didn't just buy canned ham; he got prosciutto ham.") Essentially, Chinese use *erqie* to focus on what follows. Sometimes, depending on the context, *erqie* simply connotes "moreover, in addition" as our English "but also" translation might suggest; other times, *erqie* connotes "and even better yet" as illustrated by our informant. In other words, the "but also" as used in our examples does not follow native English discourse conventions in that it is not meant to be a transition device; it can mean something else entirely and something which derives from native Chinese discourse conventions to indicate a special fixed construction with an altogether different meaning from what the literal English translation would indicate. It appears, then, that the original connection and the intended nuances of the Chinese fixed "not only . . . but also . . ." construction often remain intact in the Chinese version of English. For Americans, however, the nuances are lost.

The point is that responses which American informants perceived as stylistically odd and "syntactically awkward" are often simply matters of convention in Chinese discourse; the pattern of message construction has a cultural rather than an idiosyncratic basis. These conventions are interesting in and of themselves, of course, and earlier chapters have discussed them at some length, but their empirical import arises particularly when they contribute to instances of ambiguity and discord in cross-cultural exchanges. As we have seen, confusion on this issue lent itself to mistimed interruptions. And yet, there are other side effects which are decidedly more intriguing. In the first place, the Chinese responses apparently caused the American interactant to want to argue back. According to the Americans interviewed, the Chinese appeared to be rationalizing or offering arguments about the situation, and, from their perspective, the natural response would be to offer arguments back, and, indeed, the American interactant did so. Viewed from this perspective, then, the way in which the Chinese police officers responded to the American's questions provided considerable room for confusion and disputation and so contributed to his repeated attempts at clarification. Second, the American informants claimed that the use of "because" to start a statement effectively weakened the Chinese police officers' stance.

That is, to issue a firm statement by beginning with a reason or qualification clause gave the statement the appearance of an afterthought and also provided an opening for the American interactant to interrupt and dispute the situation. The American observations are illustrated as follows:

This reversed structure where they always say "because" something – I don't know whether we're going to get to the second half of the sentence as the American was always interrupting . . . I think they had more to say, but the American understood what they had to say. And they started out saying it by sort of trying to give an explanation for it rather than issuing it as an order, and so he knew sort of what they were going to say and they were sort of opening an argument with him and so he was going to argue back.

The behavior of the policemen tends to be deferential to the American, and, because it's deferential, they offer him the chance to rebut and that's what he's doing.

The American informants made similar comments about Episode B. In contrast to Episode A, the Americans noted that the Chinese started with much stronger or firmer, hence "appropriate" responses. On the other hand, it seemed to them that the third Chinese police officer fell back on native discourse patterns beginning with (B:11) and (B:13), when the American interactant began exhibiting signs of disagreement. What is interesting is that these unconventional response patterns of the Chinese police officer were interpreted by the American informants to be a language deficiency rather than simply the consequence of a different discourse style:

His command of English seemed to decrease and he seemed to revert to what we heard in the first segment of making weaker statements using "because" at the beginning of the statement, and this just gave the American more chance to argue and insist.

In short, whether due to Chinese style or intention, the primary effect of a different pattern of message construction, itself the product of a difference in syntactic and/or pragmatic conventions, inadvertently fostered an illusion of Chinese weakness or deference in American eyes. This weakness, in turn, apparently provoked resistance and further dispute on the part of the American interactant. By contrast, Chinese informants viewed the Chinese police officers' responses as straightforward statements with little deferential intent involved: "[It's] just Chinese way of saying it." Again, the construction of the Chinese police officers' responses was viewed as a matter of convention in Chinese discourse.

Another aspect of the confusion stemmed from the fact that the Chinese did not come straight out with the message "You cannot enter the building." From the American viewpoint, the Chinese had been talking around this issue at some length; in fact, explicit acknowledgment of this issue only came about midway through the exchange in both episodes, and, in the case of Episode A, only after the American interactant himself verbalized it. As a case in point, note the following excerpt from Episode A:

(11a) AMERICAN   But I must go in and see . . . because if . . . I've got my papers there and I've got work to do. You can't keep me out. That's my office.

(11b) CHINESE 2   Yes, I see. We are very sorry that . . . Because uh that is very dangerous.

(11c) AMERICAN   Well, I don't care but I have some papers there that's very important for me. It's important business. And if I don't get those papers, then I'm going to lose a lot of money.

(11d) CHINESE 1   ⎡ Yes, I see. Because the building is closed
(11e) CHINESE 2   ⎣ Uh w

(11f) AMERICAN   You mean . . you mean to say I can't go in?

(11g) CHINESE 1   Yes. Nobody allowed to enter the building because the building is very dangerous.

As far as the American informants were concerned, the Chinese response in (11b) is less informative than the situation requires. Similarly, the Chinese response in (11d) seemingly bears little connection to the preceding remarks by the American. In contrast to the examples examined earlier, it would be difficult to draw any confident conclusion as to whether the Chinese responses are completed or truncated responses. Hints from prosodic cues are negligible in both instances. In any event, both the American and the Chinese informants perceived that the implicit message conveyed by the police officers from the outset of the interchange took the form of "you cannot enter" which, indeed, the American interactant confirmed in *his* following response of (11f) "You mean, you mean to say I can't go in?"

Let me here point out as well that the Chinese response in (11g) provided yet another source for ambiguity. Throughout the interchange, the Chinese police officers apparently sought to convey the message that entrance to the building was prohibited. From the American perspective, the use of "yes" is odd as it contradicts this inference. The ambiguity is quickly cleared up when we attend to the fact that the Chinese have an opposite way of answering negative questions. Specifically, a "no" response by a Chinese to a negative question does not mean the negation of the question's assumption. On the contrary, it signals agreement (see Cheung 1974). Thus, to the question of "You mean to say I can't go in?" many native English speakers would reply "No [you can't go in]" whereas a typical Chinese response would appear exactly as in the example above "Yes [you can't go in]" (see Gumperz 1982b, chapter 10, for a similar ambiguity in "yes–no" responses in the discourse habits of a Filipino doctor). Philosopher Nakamura Hajime's explanation of an analogous situation for Japanese is instructive here: "The Japanese reply refers to the opinion and intention of the interrogator, whereas the Western reply refers to the objective fact involved in the interrogation. In short, a Japanese replies to his interrogator, not to the fact involved" (1964: 407). It was, in fact, one of the Chinese informants who first alerted me to the Chinese use of "Yes" here to illustrate his contention that the Chinese police officers had been addressing the American interactant using the Chinese version of English. And it was he who exclaimed, after listening to the taped episodes, "That's very American way. Never allow anyone to finish. Always cut in!"

Let me also note that the Chinese response in (11g), where the reason clause appears in second clause position, demonstrates that the officer's earlier responses, which largely adhered to the because . . . so . . . construction (i.e., example [1]), are not just mechanical gestures stemming from a lack of familiarity with other stylistic options; it is not the case that second language learners always follow native discourse patterns in all second language situations.

The American informants also indicated that the use of "because" in the Chinese response in (2), as in (1), was unusual in that it gave the appearance of answering an underlying question that had not been asked; that is, it had little reference to anything occurring earlier in the interchange. More importantly, the Chinese response also appeared to avoid specifics, as in (1), by omitting directives to the American interactant altogether. Instead of telling the American he should go to the court because the building has been closed by court order, if such is the case, the Chinese simply mentions the court order, as if expecting the American interactant to fill in with the message "you should go to the court" or, as one American remarked "as if the court order is sort of the magic word that is supposed to make the American go away." Once again, then, the Chinese response is vague; instead of telling the American what to do, the issue is worked around by indirection. Put otherwise, there seems to be a Chinese tendency to swallow the explicit part of utterances – what we noted earlier as a matter-of-fact reliance on a listener's ability to complete the meaning-making – whereas Americans would expect to hear more specific "on-record" responses such as "You can't go in because there's a court order" or "You can't go in because there's been a fire."

Still another source of confusion for the American informants invited judgments which coincide with the stereotypical behavioral characteristics commonly associated with the Chinese. Specifically, the American informants found it problematic to reconcile the response of the Chinese police officer in (5), i.e., "Because it is to prevent theft and," with the earlier statements that the building was in a dangerous condition. For the Americans, the Chinese response in example (5) appeared abruptly and did not fit in with the previous responses of the police officers. It is difficult in this instance to determine the original intent of the Chinese police officer's response. Part of the difficulty stems from the fact that his response may have been cut short. Whatever the case, the American informants saw the police officer's response as "coming from nowhere" and as "evasive."

By themselves, none of the aforementioned ambiguities and oddities are significant. The cumulative effect of a series of mismatched responses, however, left the American listeners with a profound sense of dissatisfaction, to the disadvantage of the Chinese interactants. The issue did not lie in the American comprehension of individual Chinese utterances. Rather, the difficulty resided in fitting together the utterances and comprehending the conversational strategies of the Chinese. The situation was sufficiently problematic that it caused the Americans to ultimately side with the American interactant. Yet when I put the matter before the Chinese informants, it rapidly became clear that there are cultural and stylistic differences for putting "off record" what many Americans would assume to be matter-of-fact "on-record" responses. In the first place, apart from basic cultural differences in attitudes to authority in general, all the Chinese informants were at pains to make clear that white foreigners are treated with slightly more decorum than is the ordinary Chinese citizen in Hong Kong. Beyond this consideration, however, certain facts stand out. The Chinese informants observed that the American interactant had already been informed that the area had been closed off due to a fire. Given that the American interactant understood the area was off limits, they further observed that the cultural assumptions of the Chinese would preclude the sort of direct action which Americans would take for granted as natural. In other words, what seem to be mysteriously vague omissions are instead the elements of a different cultural style at work, one which leans on a tacit understanding and leaves it to the listener to fill in the information from what has already been acknowledged. Whereas the frequent acts of explanation led Americans to assume that the Chinese were amenable to discussion or persuasion, the Chinese informants viewed the statements rather as firm signals conveying the opposite intent. The tenor of the Chinese informants' responses is conveyed in such statements as:

You try to explain and avoid the strong words. The American get the idea he cannot get in. If I know he get the idea, I want to be polite. Give him the understanding of the condition but not the order "so you cannot go in."

In Chinese we always say things not straight, try to be more polite to people. If he [the policemen] will be more straight and say "you cannot go in," they will argue and make the American angry.

American police would say "Hey, I cannot let you in. Sorry." We don't have that kind of mind, law mind. Chinese mind, they say when enforce, not enforce law. They are from personal view. Explain it to him: because [of] danger.

Their responses reflect a Chinese social outlook that prefers indirect to direct means of interaction. In their aesthetic of indeterminacy and open-endedness, there is greater emphasis on shunning or deflecting face-to-face confrontation and greater reliance on allusive reference and suggestive statement. To repeat, Chinese traditionally go to great lengths to avoid a humiliating outcome in face-to-face encounters, and prefer instead to influence another by reasoning with the person and appealing to his or her self-interest.

These different cultural ideals of personal interaction are consonant with preferences for indirect expression and for delicate understatement which are reflected throughout the language. Thus, linguist Timothy Light (1983: 38) observes that:

> In negotiation, an agreement to a proposal may be given as *wenti buda* which literally means "The problems are not great." This tendency is related to formulaic expressions in Chinese such as *bucuo* "no error" = "right you are," *bushao* "not few" = "a lot," *chabuduo* "off not much" = "approximately." Similarly, a denial may take the form of "Perhaps it's not convenient" or "Possibly the time isn't right" when refusing to respond to a proposal that is seen as impossible to implement.

Likewise, educator Douglas Murray (1983: 20) notes that "'Perhaps' and 'maybe' are cultural stock-in-trade. 'Maybe I will come with you' usually means 'I'm not coming.' 'Perhaps it is too far for you to walk' means 'There's no way I'll let you walk.' When something is 'inconvenient,' it most likely is impossible." Similarly, political psychologist Lucian Pye (1992: 91) in his discussion of Chinese negotiating practices, states that "In responding to proposals from the other side, the Chinese frequently appear to be agreeing when they respond by saying that it is 'possible.' The answer, however, is often an ambiguous way of saying 'no.'"

Writing about the verbal strategies of minor officials in China, Chinese literature scholar Perry Link (1992: 188–189) also points out that:

> Answers of "yes," "no," or "maybe" are usually delivered in standard codes that leave a margin of ambiguity through which the official can escape if the answer turns out to be wrong ... [A] "no" answer will often be ... "there are some difficulties" (*you xie kunnan*) ... The most famous of the standard answers are the "maybes": *yanjiu yanjiu* ("we'll study the matter") or *kaolü kaolü* ("we'll think it over"). These normally mean that the small official will refer the matter to higher-ups ... To the ordinary citizen, an answer of *yanjiu yanjiu kaolü kaolü* also means "you will have to come back and press that matter again at a later time." Without such pressure, the phrases amount to a "no."

Explained in this way, we see that the intricate blend and interplay of stylistic conventions and politeness strategies guiding Chinese discourse differ from American expectations in essential particulars. Moreover, they are realized in strikingly different ways, and these differences, in turn, allow room for misplaced interpretation and erroneous judgments. As such, the comparative ease with which the American and Chinese informants diverged in their interpretations and evaluations is not too hard to understand, and the reasons for the interactional discord as analyzed here become transparent.

A part of the ambiguity lay in the fact that the interactants saw the situation within different frameworks for interpretation. An unfamiliarity with each others' communicative conventions coupled with significant cultural differences of emphasis and expression in their politeness systems contributed to the ambiguity. By American standards, many of the Chinese responses not only seemed indeterminate, ineffective, and weak but also appeared stylistically odd or incomplete, if not bewildering. And, as the interchange progressed, they appeared irrelevant and evasive as well, leaving the American informants with the strong impression that the Chinese police officers were bent on concealing information. That the information emerged in piecemeal fashion merely reinforced this general impression. As such, the communicative force of the police officers' responses was considerably dampened, if not subverted.

The communicative effects are far subtler, however. To the Americans, the construction of the Chinese officers' responses gave them the incongruous appearance of having to argue and justify their position, thus putting themselves in a more subservient position than should have been the case. And, because the Americans interpreted such responses to be deferential as well, they pointed out that the American interactant was given the opportunity to rebut, as indeed he did many times, to the consternation of the Chinese police, as adjudged by the Chinese informants. Thus, the continued and delicate efforts by the Chinese to accommodate and explain led the American interactant to surmise mistakenly that there was room for argument. Likewise, American misconstruals that Chinese are unaccountably servile stem from their cultural unfamiliarity with the dynamics of Chinese discourse; recall here the double-sided aim of Chinese to redirect the communication's authorship to involve others and to efface the speaker's impositional role as well. In short, the Chinese police officers' responses boomeranged on them; the way they phrased their replies only provoked the American to dispute the situation and redouble his efforts to gain entry. By contrast, the Chinese informants pointed out that the American interactant had peremptorily disregarded the authority of the police, had repeatedly ignored their warnings of the building's dangerous condition, and continually intruded on their attempts at explanation. From the Chinese viewpoint, the Chinese police had been hard-pressed to dissuade the American from entering the building without provoking a confrontation.

In sum, it seems that the Chinese and the American had approached the situation from contradictory standpoints. As such, the interactants had lost contact with each other from the outset. The American interactant rarely obtained satisfactory answers to his questions, and the Chinese police officers were foiled in their efforts at explication. The American's attempts to achieve clarification were rebuffed by responses that appeared uninformative or far-fetched and had no immediate bearing on his concerns. In short, the Chinese police officers and the American interactant were not just talking at cross-purposes but ended up talking right past each other. As one American informant observed after listening to the taped episodes, "They were like two ships passing in the night."

Apparently, neither side recognized that subtle incongruities in communicative behavior led them astray. Neither side realized that their understandings rested on false certainties. And because so much happens on a subconscious level while conversing, they remained oblivious to serious misperceptions that ultimately widened the differences between them. Believing that they shared the same linguistic code, they erroneously assumed that they also shared the same conceptual worlds. Thinking they were speaking the same language, they mistakenly expected that each could read the other's intentional signals loud and clear. Instead, to their chagrin, they found themselves locked in an escalating cycle of mutual bewilderment and confusion from which they were not able to extract themselves. Such misjudgments and misconstruals

– the different cultural presuppositions and conflicting social expectations entering into them – will no doubt continue to invite and invigorate American perceptions of Chinese inscrutability.

It is often said that people keep talking to increase understanding. This is not always the case. It is just as easy for them to lose their way through talk. Especially between unsuspecting Chinese and Americans, seemingly insignificant details can turn into huge dilemmas and conversational wrong turnings can lead to interactional deadends.

7

Parting words

Scrutinizing the inscrutable Chinese has been the aim of this inquiry. Its sociolinguistic analysis has brought to light some vital areas of discord and distortion in the cultural interchanges between Chinese and Americans. Using different empirical examples and drawing together scraps of information from a wide variety of sources, we were able to look at the puzzle of Chinese inscrutability from a variety of perspectives, and form a coherent analysis of its origins and resilience. Our intent was not so much to scuttle the image of Chinese inscrutability but, rather, to see how such stereotypes can unwittingly arise, subtly sabotage interactions, and quickly establish cultural barriers.

We saw that Chinese on the one hand and Americans on the other bring to their face-to-face interactions certain unstated cultural expectations and customary ways of perceiving and responding which do not coincide at all. The two cultures differ crucially in their approach to talk, what they expect from talk, and how they respond to talk. This arises in large part from their different ways of viewing the world, their different ways of relating to people, their different communication goals and politeness strategies, their different sets of communicative conventions and signalling devices, their different ideals and strategies of rhetoric, and their different methods of generating meaning and eliciting response. As we have seen, many of these differences go unrecognized or undergo serious misreadings in the routine of talk, sometimes in an obvious fashion, sometimes more subtly.

We moved from harmony-in-the-making in chapter 2 to dissonance-in-the-making in chapter 6. We saw that what Americans and others take for granted as a proper beginning, middle, and end in discourse gets turned upside down in their encounters with the Chinese. Just where they expect Chinese to appear definitive and confident, Chinese become suggestive and tentative, just where they expect Chinese to appear clear and precise, Chinese become vague and ambiguous, and just where they expect Chinese to appear open and forthcoming, Chinese become circumspect and reticent. Often, Chinese abruptly stop short just when some sort of punchline, wrap-up, or enlightenment would seem warranted. Likewise, they sell themselves short in instances where greater assertion seems necessary. Even their turn-taking assumes turn-sharing or turn-giving dimensions. The topsy-turvy pattern prevails, from the surface signs of pitch and prosody to the underlying sense of order and causality. All this and more contribute to the puzzle of Chinese inscrutability.

One key to the puzzle is differing cultural conceptions of a created world and an uncreated world. The latter had such an all-pervasive influence on ancient Chinese thinking that its echoes are still heard everywhere. The ancients saw the cosmos as self-generating and spinning in endless rounds of bipolar oscillation and division. It was a dynamic, process-oriented outlook, one defined by repeated transformations and interlocking phenomena among diverse, concrete particulars. It emphasized living rather than static wholes, "becoming" rather than "being," relatedness rather than autonomy, interdependency rather than agency, multiple influences rather than initiating source. Even today, particulars are not viewed in their isolation or separateness but always with a view as to how they relate to a larger scheme. Parts are more than just parts; parts are not just there to serve the whole. On the contrary, part and whole are inextricably intertwined; each establishes and articulates the other. Each part, moreover, is embedded in a web of significant intersections; like yin and yang, each empowers and energizes the other. Each part is sensitive to the vibrations and resonances generated by the other parts.

Similarly, a person is primarily understood as a person-in-community, a person-in-context, a member of something bigger than his or her self. Each person is enmeshed in a network of social relationships and interdependencies that is fairly permanent, albeit often circumscribed and localized. Each person's identity, moreover, is firmly derived from and established within this network. Correspondingly, self is broadened to include the advancement and wellbeing of significant others in the network as part of one's own advancement and wellbeing; benefits and rewards, prosperity and profits accrue collectively rather than individually. At the same time, while individual selves ought to maintain an integral consistency and an unambiguous identity in interaction, persons are seen as forever malleable, their humanity capable of greater and constant development. In short, quality persons ought to behave in an open-minded and non-dogmatic way. They are expected to function in a profoundly relational manner, to be sensitive to and influenced by their social environment, and to show a high degree of responsibility for generating order among and within themselves.

So also in communication, participants act and react as responsive interactants and, while communicating, become dynamically one. Communication is construed as an agent of harmony and mutuality, relations are conducted with an aim towards congeniality and continuity, and interactants work together to make communication a joint effort. Given a cultural disposition towards participatory meaning-making, boundaries between persons are effaced and theses frequently deferred as participants strive for a greater harmony of shareable views. Discourse here often assumes a dynamic, outward movement that redirects or broadens the focus to include the other in the communication. Its construction not only shifts the spotlight off one's self, but it also requires another's interpretation for its full realization; communicant must meet communicator halfway.

For the most part, ideas and utterances are put together to build a picture, give an impression, configure an image, develop a field of conditions, promote a perspective, or provide a point of orientation; they lure, move, transmit, suggest, stimulate, prod, or guide. Foregrounding background information helps to create a mood or atmosphere that encourages fruitful engagement, to set up a context in which a joint understanding can be nurtured, to demonstrate a need while giving the other room for reflective, independent judgment, or to soft-pedal intent while allowing for a felt-soled progress. At the least, given the cultural emphasis on unmediated experience, Chinese try to resist thinking for or pushing ideas onto another. Alternatively, Chinese might use

this emphasis to their advantage – in particular, to sidestep accountability, to shift responsibility for final decisions, to suggest a
regretted inability, or to cast themselves as helpless victims of
circumstances. More often than not, individual positions and intentions are left open-ended, ideas and images are loosely clustered,
and words and utterances are tenuously connected. Likewise,
context and contiguity, correlation and conjunction take on keen
significance as Chinese routinely search for links and points of convergences while conscientiously interpreting meaning from trifles.

Yet, communication for Chinese also occurs in a fairly formalized social world in which status and power distinctions predominate and must be visibly signalled and respected in sundry
ways. People come together in communication to build bonds of
cooperation, yet they are kept apart by ritual forms of restraint. In
Chinese rituals of social deference, self often takes on a subdued
presence and force while honoring the precedence, prestige, or
power of the other. In particular, those assuming subordinate
status are eagerly attentive and accommodating: they might
elevate the other with increased honorifics or they might allow the
other more leeway. Alternatively, they might forego their initiative
and efface their role in the communication by subtly reshaping its
authorship. Sometimes, they simply remain quiet and peripheral
to show respect. In short, they variously yield, relinquish, or cede
their standing while bolstering the standing of others. In situations
defined as especially face-threatening, they rely more on hints and
indirection, negotiate and conciliate with greater frequency, and
make greater show of a humble, accommodative pliancy. Even in
situations of formal discourse where interactants are of the same
standing, each aggressively elevates the other as part of Chinese
strategies of facework; just as yang is deemed superior to yin, so
also is addressee to speaker. The point to remember, however, is
that what gets nurtured and honored is the relationship between
the particulars. The world of the average Chinese is a network
of relationships and interdependencies in which forging links,
making connections, nurturing bonds, assuring collaboration, and
striking mutual resonances are never-ending processes. Relationships are personalized and pursued for the long term. The underlying dynamic is mutual cooperation; the dominant imperative is
avoiding conflict.

These are some of the aims and means by which Chinese focus their interactional energies and achieve their communicative ends. When the ability to understand and recognize such aims and means disappears, then the Chinese will be very different people indeed. Conversely, in cross-cultural contexts, such aims and means can be misread and so exacerbate cultural differences, polarize peoples, and encourage stereotypical characterizations.

And here we come to our final point. The because...so... construction provided us with the thread that unravelled part of the puzzle of Chinese inscrutability. We explored its etymological and grammatical underpinnings and examined it in instances of explanation, persuasion, and "turn-taking." It allowed us the opportunity to discuss diverse issues that arise in cross-cultural conflicts between Chinese and others. Notably, it persists in Chinese rhetorical strategies despite the crossings of oceans and languages. On the face of it, the construction seems deceptively similar to English and so its different nuances and implications can slip by unnoticed or cause no more than a ripple of unease in cross-cultural exchanges. But, as we have seen, cultural conflicts intensify and worsen precisely when these microscopic misunderstandings go unrecognized. When people lack awareness of alternative cues and conventions or overgeneralize their own, their interpretive strategies can go awry and their intentions misrepresented as their attempts to converse repeatedly misfire.

People don't always enter cross-cultural exchanges with stereotypes. Stereotypes can be generated unwittingly within conversations. Mismatched expectations can quickly turn into cultural biases, and, in the case of the Chinese, originate or reinforce their image of inscrutability.

If this were the end of it, inscrutability would be no more than a manageable irritation, not a major threat to East–West endeavors or a menace to peoples' well-being. But, inscrutability can – and has – jeopardized the cohesion of collaborative efforts, from joint ventures (Mann 1989) to marital adventures (Sung 1990), from diplomatic negotiations to across-the-table price talks. It can inflict crippling self doubt (Klein, Miller, and Alexander 1981) or leave a permanent taint of inferiority. It can constrict opportunity and block access to prized resources (Tsai 1986); alternatively, it can cause talented minorities to spurn opportunities that would force them to adopt mainstream lifeways (Tom 1988). Inscrutability is an old problem but it takes on new urgency and new forms in this age of global business, accelerated communications technology, and the multi-cultural work force and student body.

East may be East and West may be West. But, contrary to Rudyard Kipling's ode, the twain certainly do meet – in increasing numbers and under varying circumstances. On the whole, people's intentions and messages do carry across cultural boundaries. But, sometimes, imperfect mappings and misplaced interpretations cause gaps in translation. It is not just that things get lost in translation; translating itself gets people lost.

This inquiry has opened some avenues of perception to heretofore unexamined, intersecting factors which may contribute to the special character of Chinese discourse. As a result, some vital pieces in the puzzle of Chinese inscrutability should fall into place for readers.

References

Abegg, Lily   1952. *The Mind of East Asia*. London: Thames and Hudson.
Ahern, Emily M.   1981. *Chinese Ritual and Politics*. Cambridge University Press.
Albert, Ethel   1972. "Cultural patterning of speech behavior in Burundi." In *Directions in Sociolinguistics: The Ethnography of Communication*. John J. Gumperz and Dell Hymes, eds. New York: Holt, Rinehart, and Winston.
Atkinson, John M. and Heritage, John (eds.)   1984. *Structures of Social Action: Studies in Conversation Analysis*. Cambridge University Press.
Ball, James D.   1903. *Things Chinese*. Hong Kong: Kelly and Walsh, Limited.
Bauman, Richard and Sherzer, Joel (eds.)   1974. *Explorations in the Ethnography of Speaking*. London: Cambridge University Press.
Becker, Alton L.   1979. "The figure a sentence makes: an interpretation of a classical Malay sentence." In *Syntax and Semantics, Vol. 12: Discourse and Syntax*. Talmy Givon, ed. New York: Academic Press.
Birdwhistell, Ray L.   1970. *Kinesics and Context: Essays on Body Motion Communication*. Philadelphia: University of Pennsylvania Press.
Bloom, Alfred H.   1981. *The Linguistic Shaping of Thought: A Study in the Impact of Language on Thinking in China and the West*. Hillsdale, N.J.: Lawrence Erlbaum Associates, Publishers.
Bodde, Derk   1991. *Chinese Thought, Society and Science: The Intellectual and Social Background of Science and Technology in Pre-Modern China*. Honolulu, Hawaii: University of Hawaii Press.
Boodberg, Peter A.   1953. "The semasiology of some primary Confucian concepts." *Philosophy East and West* 2(4): 317–332, January.
Brown, Penelope and Levinson, Stephen   1987. *Politeness: Some Universals in Language Usage*. Cambridge University Press.
Cao, Xueqin   1982. *The Story of the Stone, Vol. 4: The Debt of Tears*. Appendix II. Trans. by John Minford. London: Penguin.
Caudill, William and Weinstein, Helen   1969. "Maternal care and infant

behavior in Japan and America." *Psychiatry* 32(1): 12–43.

Chafe, Wallace L. 1976. "Givenness, contrastiveness, definiteness, subjects, topics, and point of view." In *Subject and Topic*. Charles Li, ed. New York: Academic Press.

    1980. "The deployment of consciousness in the production of a narrative." In *The Pear Stories: Cognitive, Cultural, and Linguistic Aspects of Narrative Production*. Wallace L. Chafe, ed. Norwood, N. J.: Ablex Publishing Corp.

    1985. "Linguistic differences produced by differences between speaking and writing." In *Literacy, Language and Learning: The Nature and Consequences of Reading and Writing*. David R. Olson, Nancy Torrance, and Angela Hildyard, eds. Cambridge University Press.

Chan, Wing-tsit 1955. "The evolution of the Confucian concept *jên.*" *Philosophy East and West* 4(4): 295–319, January.

Chang, Hui-ching and Holt, G. Richard 1991. "More than relationship: Chinese interaction and the principle of *kuan-hsi.*" *Communication Quarterly* 39(3): 251–271, Summer.

Chang, Kang-i Sun 1983. "Chinese 'lyric criticism' in the six dynasties." In *Theories of the Arts in China*. Susan Bush and Christian F. Murck, eds. Princeton University Press.

Chang, Samuel K. C. 1985. "American and Chinese managers in U.S. companies in Taiwan: a comparison." *California Management Review* 27(4): 144–156, Summer.

Chao, Yuen Ren 1968. *A Grammar of Spoken Chinese*. Berkeley, Calif.: University of California Press.

Cheek, Timothy 1981. "Deng Tuo: culture, Leninism, and alternative Marxism in the Chinese Communist Party." *China Quarterly* 87: 470–491

Chen, Hongwei 1986. "Teaching translation in China." In *American Translators Association Conference: Proceedings of the 27th Annual Conference of the American Translators Association*. Karl Kummer, ed. Medford, N.J.: Learned Information, Inc. Cleveland, Ohio, October 16–19.

Chen, T. Hsi-en 1976. "Chinese intellectuals in America." In *The Chinese in America*. Paul K. T. Sih and Leonard B. Allen, eds. New York: St. Johns University Press.

Cheng, Chung-ying 1986. "The concept of face and its Confucian roots." *Journal of Chinese Philosophy* 13(3): 329–348, September.

Cheng, François 1986. "Some reflections on Chinese poetic language and its relation to Chinese cosmology." In *The Vitality of the Lyric Voice: Shih Poetry from the Late Han to the T'ang*. Shuen-fu Lin and Stephen Owen, eds. Princeton University Press.

Cheng, Peggy 1982. "Contrastive rhetoric: English and Mandarin." Paper presented at conference on Rhetoric and Composition. Pennsylvania State University.

Cheung, Fanny M. 1985. "An overview of psychopathology in Hong

Kong with special reference to somatic presentation." In *Chinese Culture and Mental Health*. Wen-shing Tseng and David Y. H. Wu, eds. Orlando: Academic Press, Inc.

Cheung, Yat-shing 1974. "Negative questions in Chinese." *Journal of Chinese Linguistics* 2(3): 325–339, September.

Chow, Rey 1991. *Woman and Chinese Modernity: The Politics of Reading Between West and East*. Minneapolis, Minn.: University of Minnesota Press.

Clancy, Patricia 1982. "Written and spoken style in Japanese narratives." In *Spoken and Written language: Exploring Orality and Literacy*. Deborah Tannen, ed. Norwood, N. J.: Ablex Publishing Co.

Clyne, Michael 1981. "Culture and discourse structure." *Journal of Pragmatics* 5: 61–66.

Condon, John C. and Ogsten, D. 1969. "Speech and body motion." In *Perceptions of Language*. P. Kjeldergaard, ed. Columbus, Ohio: Charles Merrill.

Cragnin, John P. 1986. "Management technology absorption in China." In *The Enterprise and Management in East Asia. Center of Asian Studies Occasional Papers and Monographs 69*. Stewart R. Clegg, Dexter C. Dunphy, and S. Gordon Redding, eds. Hong Kong: The Chinese University Press.

Creel, Herrlee G. 1979. "Discussion of Professor Fingarette on Confucius." *Journal of the American Academy of Religion Thematic Studies* 47(3): 373–405, September.

   1983. "On the Opening Words of the *Lao-Tzu*." *Journal of Chinese Philosophy* 10(4): 299–329.

Cua, Antonio S. 1985. *Ethical Argumentation: A Study in Hsun Tzu's Moral Epistemology*. Honolulu, Hawaii: University of Hawaii Press.

DePauw, John W. 1981. *U.S.–Chinese Trade Negotiations*. New York: Praeger Publishers.

DeWoskin, Kenneth J. 1982. *A Song for One or Two: Music and the Concept of Art in Early China. Center for Chinese Studies. Michigan Papers in Chinese Studies 42*. Ann Arbor, Mich.: University of Michigan Press.

Dollar, Bruce 1985. "Child care in China." In *Anthropology 85/86*. Elvio Angeloni, ed. Guilford, Conn.: The Dushkin Publishing Group, Inc.

Eberhard, Wolfram 1965. "Chinese regional stereotypes." *Asian Survey* 5(12): 596–608, December.

Eggington, William G. 1987. "Written academic discourse in Korean: implications for effective communication." In *Writing Across Languages: Analysis of L_2 Text*. Ulla Connor and Robert B. Kaplan, eds. Cambridge, Mass.: Addison-Wesley Publishing Co.

Elvin, Mark 1985. "Between the earth and heaven: conceptions of the self in China." In *The Category of the Person: Anthropology,*

Philosophy, History. Michael Carrithers, Steven Collins, and Steven Lukes, eds. Cambridge University Press.

Erickson, Frederick and Schultz, Jeffrey 1982. *The Counselor as Gatekeeper: Social Interaction in Interviews*. New York: Academic Press.

Farrell, Thomas J. 1979. "The female and male modes of rhetoric." *College English* 40(8): 909–921, April.

Fingarette, Herbert 1972. *Confucius: The Secular as Sacred*. New York: Harper and Row.

1980. "Reply to Professor Hansen." *Journal of Chinese Philosophy* 7(3): 259–266, September.

Fox, James J. ed. 1988. *To Speak in Pairs: Essays on the Ritual Languages of Eastern Indonesia*. Cambridge University Press.

Frolic, B. Michael 1976. "Wide-eyed in Peking: a diplomat's diary." *New York Times Magazine*, January 11, p. 16–33.

Gernet, Jacques 1985. *China and the Christian Impact: A Conflict of Cultures*. Trans. by Janet Lloyd. Cambridge University Press.

Giles, Howard and Powesland, Peter F. 1975. *Speech Style and Social Evaluation*. New York: Academic Press.

Gilligan, Carol 1982. *In a Different Voice: Psychological Theory and Women's Development*. Cambridge, Mass.: Harvard University Press.

Goffman, Erving 1967. *Interaction Ritual: Essays on Face-to-Face Behavior*. Garden City, N.Y.: Anchor Books.

Graham, Angus C. 1959. "'Being' in Western philosophy compared with *shih / fei* and *yu / wu* in Chinese philosophy." *Asia Major*, new series 7(1–2): 79–112.

1981. *Chuang-tzu: The Seven Inner Chapters and Other Writings from the Book Chuang-tzu*. London: Allen and Unwin.

1989. *Disputers of the Tao: Philosophical Argument in Ancient China*. La Salle, Ill.: Open Court Publishing Company.

Grice, H. Paul 1975. "Logic and conversation." In *Syntax and Semantics, Vol. 3: Speech Acts*. Peter Cole and Jerry L. Morgan, eds. New York: Academic Press.

Gumperz, John J. 1982a. *Discourse Strategies*. Cambridge University Press.

1982b. *Language and Social Identity*. Cambridge University Press.

1990. "Conversational cooperation in social perspective." In *Proceedings of the Sixteenth Annual Meeting of the Berkeley Linguistics Society*, p. 429–441. Berkeley, Calif.: Berkeley Linguistics Society.

1992. "Contextualization and understanding." In *Rethinking Context: Language as an Interactive Phenomenon*. Alessandro Duranti and Charles Goodwin, eds. Cambridge University Press.

Gumperz, John J. and Roberts, Celia 1991. "Understanding in intercultural encounters." In *Selected Papers of the International Pragmatics Conference, Antwerp, August 17–22, 1987, Vol. 3: The*

Pragmatics of Intercultural and International Communication. Jan Blommaert and Jef Verschueren, eds. Amsterdam: J. Benjamins Publishing Co.

Haiman, John and Thompson, Sandra A. 1984. "'Subordination' in universal grammar." In *Proceedings of the Tenth Annual Meeting of the Berkeley Linguistics Society*, p. 510–523. Berkeley, Calif.: Berkeley Linguistics Society.

Hall, David L. and Ames, Roger T. 1984. "Getting it right: on saving Confucius from the Confucians." *Philosophy East and West* 34(1): 3–23, January.

    1987. *Thinking Through Confucius.* Albany, N.Y.: State University of New York Press.

    1991. "Rationality, correlativity, and the language of process." *Journal of Speculative Philosophy* 5(2): 85–106.

Hall, Edward T. 1959. *The Silent Language.* Garden City, N.Y.: Doubleday.

Hansen, Chad 1985a. "Individualism in Chinese thought." In *Individualism and Holism: Studies in Confucian and Taoist Values.* Donald J. Munro, ed. Center for Chinese Studies. Michigan Monographs in Chinese Studies 52. Ann Arbor, Mich.: University of Michigan Press.

    1985b. "Chinese language, Chinese philosophy, and 'truth.'" *Journal of Asian Studies* 44(3): 491–518, May.

Hart, James 1984. "The speech of Prince Chin: a study of early Chinese cosmology." In *Explorations in Early Chinese Cosmology.* Henry Rosemont, ed. Chico, Calif.: Scholars Press.

Hendry, Joy 1990. "Humidity, hygiene, or ritual care: some thoughts on wrapping as a social phenomenon." In *Unwrapping Japan: Society and Culture in Anthropological Perspective.* Eyal Ben-ari, Brian Moeran, and James Valentine, eds. Manchester University Press.

Henricks, Robert 1981. "Hsi K'ang and argumentation in the Wei, and a refutation of the essay 'residence' is unrelated to good and bad fortune: nourish 'life' (by Hsi K'ang)." *Journal of Chinese Philosophy* 8(2): 169–223, June.

Hinds, John 1983. "Contrastive rhetoric: Japanese and English." *Text* 3(2): 183–195.

Hofstede, Geert H. 1984. *Culture's Consequences: International Differences in Work-Related Values.* Beverly Hills, Calif.: Sage Publications.

Holcombe, Chester 1895. *The Real Chinaman.* New York: Dodd, Mead, and Co.

Hoosain, Rumjahn 1986. "Perceptual processes of the Chinese." In *The Psychology of the Chinese People.* Michael H. Bond, ed. Hong Kong: Oxford University Press.

Hsia, Jayjia 1988. *Asian Americans in Higher Education and at Work.*

Hillsdale, N.J.: Lawrence Erlbaum Associates, Publishers.

Hsiung, James C. 1969. "Chinese ways of thinking and Chinese language." *Journal of the Chinese Language Teachers Association* 4(2): 41–54, May.

Hsu, Francis L. K. 1981. *Americans and Chinese: Passage to Differences.* Honolulu, Hawaii: University Press of Hawaii.

Hu, Hsien Chin 1944. "The Chinese concepts of 'face.'" *American Anthropologist* 46: 45–64.

Hwang, Kwang-kuo 1987. "Face and favor: the Chinese power game." *American Journal of Sociology* 92(4): 944–974, January.

Hynes, Maureen 1981. *Letters from China.* Toronto, Ontario: Women's Press.

Ide, Sachiko 1989. "Formal forms and discernment: two neglected aspects of universals of linguistic politeness." *Multilingua* 8(2/3): 223–248.

Ikegami, Yoshiko 1989. "Introduction (to special issue of discourse analysis in Japan)." *Text* 9(3): 263–273.

Irvine, Judith T. 1979. "Formality and informality in communicative events." *American Anthropologist* 81(4): 773–790.

Isaacs, Harold R. 1958. *Images of Asia: American Views of China and India.* New York: Capricorn Books.

Jiang, Yiping 1983. "Topic establishment: Chinese data in conversation and discourse environments." Paper presented at conference on Discourse and Conversation. University of Missouri, April 10.

Kaplan, Robert B. 1966 (1&2). "Cultural thought patterns in intercultural education." *Language Learning* 16: 1–20.
   1968. "Contrastive grammar: teaching composition to the Chinese student." *Journal of English as a Second Language* 3(1): 1–13.
   1987. "Cultural thought patterns revisited." In *Writing Across Languages: Analysis of L₂ Text.* Ulla Connor and Robert B. Kaplan, eds. Mass.: Addison-Wesley Publishing Co.

Kawasakiya, Tsuneo 1979. "Organizing for China trade: the view from Japan." Address to seminar on Doing Business with People's Republic of China. Business International Institute/Asia. Hong Kong, April.

Kim, Elaine H. 1978. "English and the Asian American college student." *Education and Urban Society* 10(3): 321–336.

King, Ambrose 1991. "Kuan-hsi and network building: a sociological interpretation." *Daedelus* 120(2): 63–84.

King, Ambrose and Bond, Michael H. 1985. "The Confucian paradigm of man: a sociological view." In *Chinese Culture and Mental Health.* Wen-shing Tseng and David Y. H. Wu, eds. Orlando, Fla.: Academic Press, Inc.

Kissinger, Henry A. 1979. *White House Years.* Boston, Mass.: Little, Brown, and Co.

Klein, Marjorie, Miller, Milton H. and Alexander, A. A. 1981. "The

American experience of the Chinese student: on being normal in an abnormal world." In *Normal and Abnormal Behavior in Chinese Culture*. Arthur Kleinman and Tsung-yi Lin, eds. Dordrecht: D. Reidel Publishing Company.

Kondo, Dorrine K.   1990. *Crafting Selves: Power, Gender and Discourses of Identity in a Japanese Workplace*. University of Chicago Press.

Lakoff, George and Johnson, Mark   1980. *Metaphors We Live By*. University of Chicago Press.

Lakoff, Robin T.   1975. *Language and Woman's Place*. New York: Harper and Row.

Lang, Olga   1946. *Chinese Family and Society*. New Haven: Yale University Press.

Latourette, Kenneth S.   1964. *The Chinese: Their History and Culture*. Fourth edn. New York: MacMillan Company.

Lau, Dim Cheuk   1979. *The Analects (Lun Yu)*. Harmondsworth, Middlesex: Penguin Books.

Lee, Wai-chun   1973. "Intrusions from Chinese in composition by Hong Kong students." Master's thesis. University of California, Los Angeles.

Li, Charles N.   1984. "From verb-medial analytic language to verb-final synthetic language: a case of typological change." In *Proceedings of the Tenth Annual Meeting of the Berkeley Linguistics Society*, p. 307–323. Berkeley, Calif.: Berkeley Linguistics Society.

Li, Charles N. and Thompson, Sandra   1976. "Subject and topic: a new typology of language." In *Subject and Topic*. Charles Li, ed. New York: Academic Press.

   1978. "An exploration of Mandarin Chinese." In *Syntactic Typology: Studies in the Phenomenology of Language*. Winfred P. Lehmann, ed. Austin, Tex.: University of Texas Press.

   1981. *Mandarin Chinese: A Functional Reference Grammar*. Berkeley, Calif.: University of California Press.

   1982. "The gulf between spoken and written language: a case study in Chinese." In *Spoken and Written Language: Exploring Orality and Literacy*. Deborah Tannen, ed. Norwood, N.J.: Ablex Publishing Co.

Li, Frances C.   1977. "Communicative function in Chinese syntax." *Journal of the Chinese Language Teachers Association* 12(2): 128–135.

Li-Repac, Diana   1980. "Cultural influences on clinical perception: a comparison between Caucasian and Chinese-American therapists." *Journal of Cross-Cultural Psychology* 11(3): 327–342, September.

Light, Timothy   1979. "Word and word order change in Mandarin Chinese." *Journal of Chinese Linguistics* 7(2): 149–180, June.

   1983. "The Chinese language: myths and facts." In *Communicating with China*. Robert A. Kapp, ed. Chicago, Ill.: Intercultural Press.

Lin, Yü-sheng   1974–1975. "The evolution of the pre-Confucian mean-

ing of *jen* 仁 and the Confucian concept of moral autonomy."
Monumenta Serica 31: 172–204.

Lin, Yutang   1935. *My Country and My People*. New York: Reynal and
Hitchcock.

Link, Eugene Perry   1992. *Evening Chats in Beijing: Probing China's
Predicament*. New York: W. W. Norton and Co.

Lipman, Jonathan and Harrell, Steven (eds.) 1990. *Violence in China:
Essays in Culture and Counterculture*. SUNY Series in Chinese
Local Studies. Albany, N.Y.: State University of New York Press.

Liu, James J. Y.   1962. *The Art of Chinese Poetry*. University of Chicago
Press.

Longacre, Robert E.   1985. "Sentences as combinations of clauses." In
*Language Typology and Syntactic Description, Vol. 2: Complex
Constructions*. Timothy Shopen, ed. Cambridge University Press.

Lord, Betty B.   1990. *Legacies: A Chinese Mosaic*. New York: Alfred A.
Knopf.

Maltz, Danny N. and Borker, Ruth A.   1982. "A cultural approach to
male–female miscommunication." In *Language and Social Identity*.
John J. Gumperz, ed. Cambridge University Press.

Mann, Jim   1989. *Beijing Jeep: The Short, Unhappy Romance of
American Business in China*. New York: Simon and Schuster.

Matalene, Carolyn   1985. "Contrastive rhetoric: an American writing
teacher in China." *College English* 47(8): 789–808.

Matthiessen, Christian and Thompson, Sandra A.   1988. "The structure of discourse and 'subordination.'" In *Clause Combining in
Grammar and Discourse*. John Haiman and Sandra A. Thompson,
ed. Amsterdam: John Benjamins Publishing Co.

Miyazaki, Ichisada   1981. *China's Examination Hell: The Civil Service
Examinations of Imperial China*. New Haven: Yale University
Press.

Moore, Charles A., ed.   1967. *The Chinese Mind: Essentials of Chinese
Philosophy and Culture*. Honolulu, Hawaii: East–West Center
Press.

Moser, Leo J.   1985. *The Chinese Mosaic: The Peoples and Provinces of
China*. Boulder, Colo.: Westview Press, Inc.

Mote, Frederick W.   1971. *Intellectual Foundations of China*. New York:
Alfred A. Knopf, Inc.

Mun, Kin-chok   1986. "Characteristics of the Chinese management: an
exploratory study." In *The Enterprise and Management in East
Asia. Center of Asian Studies Occasional Papers and Monographs
69*. Stewart R. Clegg, Dexter Dunphy, and S. Gordon Redding, eds.
Hong Kong: The Chinese University Press.

Murray, Douglas P.   1983. "Face to face: American and Chinese interactions." In *Communicating with China*. Robert A. Kapp, ed.
Chicago: Intercultural Press.

Nakamura, Hajime   1964. *Ways of Thinking of Eastern Peoples: India,*

China, Tibet, Japan. Honolulu, Hawaii: East–West Center Press.

Needham, Joseph 1956. *Science and Civilization in China,* vol. II. Cambridge University Press.

Obenchain, Diane 1989. "Japanese and Chinese women as emerging selves: some encouraging differences." Paper presented at conference on Perceptions of Self: China, India, and Japan (An Interdisciplinary Inquiry into Concepts and Practices), East–West Center, Honolulu, Hawaii, August 14–18.

Oliver, Robert T. 1971. *Communication and Culture in Ancient India and China.* New York: Syracuse University Press.

Ong, Walter J. 1982. *Orality and Literacy: The Technologizing of the Word.* London: Methuen.

Owen, Stephen 1985. *Traditional Chinese Poetry and Poetics: Omen of the World.* Madison, Wis.: University of Wisconsin Press.

1990. "Poetry in the Chinese tradition." In *Heritage of China: Contemporary Perspectives on Chinese Civilization.* Paul S. Ropp, ed. Berkeley, Calif.: University of California Press.

Perlmutter, Howard V. and Heenan, David A. 1986. "Cooperate to Compete Globally." *Harvard Business Review* 64(2): 136–152. March–April.

Peterson, Willard J. 1979. *Bitter Gourd: Fang I-chih and the Impetus for Intellectual Change.* New Haven: Yale University Press.

Plaks, Andrew H. 1977. "Towards a critical theory of Chinese narrative." In *Chinese Narrative: Critical and Theoretical Essays.* Andrew H. Plaks, ed. Princeton University Press.

Porter, Edgar A. 1990. *Foreign Teachers in China: Old Problems for a New Generation, 1979–1989.* New York: Greenwood Press.

Potter, Sulamith H. and Potter, Jack M. 1990. *China's Peasants: The Anthropology of a Revolution.* Cambridge University Press.

Pye, Lucian 1968. *The Spirit of Chinese Politics: A Psychocultural Study of the Authority Crisis in Political Development.* Cambridge, Mass.: M.I.T. Press.

1992. *Chinese Negotiating Style: Commercial Approaches and Cultural Principles.* New York: Quorum Books.

Redding, S. Gordon 1990. *The Spirit of Chinese Capitalism.* Berlin: W. de Gruyter.

Redding, S. Gordon and Ng, Michael 1982. "The role of 'face' in the organizational perceptions of Chinese managers." *Organization Studies* 3(3): 201–219.

Richards, Ivor A. 1932. *Mencius on the Mind: Experiments in Multiple Definition.* London: K. Paul, Trench, Trubner.

Rosener, Judy B. 1990. "Ways women lead." *Harvard Business Review* 68: 119–125, November–December.

Rubin, Vitaly A. 1976. *Individual and State in Ancient China: Essays on Four Chinese Philosophers.* New York: Columbia University Press.

Sacks, Harvey, Schegloff, Emanuel A. and Jefferson, Gail 1974. "A simplest systematics for the organization of turn-taking for conversation." *Language* 50(4): 696–735.

Sante, Luc 1990. "Unlike a virgin." *The New Republic*, August 20 and 27, pp. 25–29.

Schachter, Jacquelyn and Rutherford, William 1979. "Discourse function and language transfer." *Working Papers in Bilingualism* 19: 1–12, November. Toronto, Ontario: Institute for Studies in Education.

Schiffrin, Deborah 1987. *Discourse Markers.* Cambridge University Press.

Schneider, Michael J. 1985. "Verbal and nonverbal indices of the communicative performance and acculturation of Chinese immigrants." *International Journal of Intercultural Relations* 9(3): 271–283.

Schwartz, Benjamin I. 1985. *The World of Thought in Ancient China.* Cambridge, Mass.: Harvard University Press.

Shapiro, Sidney 1979. *An American in China: Thirty Years in the People's Republic of China.* New York: New American Library Inc.

Shiraishi, Bon 1965. "The Chinese way of thinking." *Japan Quarterly* 12(1): 87–92.

Silin, Robert H. 1976. *Leadership and Values: The Organization of Large-Scale Taiwanese Enterprises.* Cambridge, Mass.: Harvard University Press.

Singer, Kurt 1973. *Mirror, Sword, and Jewel: A Study of Japanese Characteristics.* New York: G. Braziller.

Smith, Richard J. 1983. *China's Cultural Heritage: The Ch'ing Dynasty 1644–1912.* Boulder, Colo.: Westview Press.

Solomon, Richard H. 1971. *Mao's Revolution and the Chinese Political Culture.* Berkeley: University of California Press.

Song, Weizhen 1985. "A preliminary study of the character traits of the Chinese." In *Chinese Culture and Mental Health.* Wen-shing Tseng and David Y. H. Wu, eds. Orlando: Academic Press.

Sung, Betty L. 1990. *Chinese American Intermarriage.* New York: Center for Migration Studies.

Tannen, Deborah 1990. *You Just Don't Understand: Women and Men in Conversation.* New York: Morrow.

Thompson, Paul M. (n.d.) "The Shen Tao fragments." Ph.D. dissertation. University of Washington, Seattle.

Tobin, Joseph J., Wu, David, and Davidson, Dana 1989. *Preschool in Three Cultures: Japan, China, and the United States.* New Haven: Yale University Press.

Tom, Gail 1988. "The bifurcultural world of the Chinese American." *Asian Profile* 16(1): 1–10, February.

Tsai, Shin-shan Henry 1986. *The Chinese Experience in America.* Bloomington, Ind.: Indiana University Press.

Tsao, Ding-ren 1985. "The persuasion of Ku Kuei Tzu." Ph.D. dissertation. University of Minnesota.

Tu, Ching-I 1974–1975. "The Chinese examination essay: some literary considerations." *Monumenta Serica* 31: 393–406.

Tu, Wei-ming 1976. *Centrality and Commonality: An Essay on Chung-yung*. Monograph of the Society for Asian and Comparative Philosophy, no. 3. Honolulu, Hawaii: University Press of Hawaii.

  1981. "*Jen* as a living metaphor in the Confucian Analects." *Philosophy East and West* 31(1): 45–54, January.

  1986. "Profound learning, personal knowledge, and poetic vision." In *The Vitality of the Lyric Voice: Shih Poetry from the Late Han to the T'ang*. Shuen-fu Lin and Stephen Owen, eds. Princeton University Press.

Tung, Rosalie L. 1982. *U.S.–China Trade Negotiations*. New York: Pergamon Press.

Vernon, Philip E. 1982. *The Abilities and Achievements of Orientals in North America*. New York: Academic Press.

Waley, Arthur 1938. *The Analects of Confucius*. London: G. Allen and Unwin, Ltd.

Weinreich, Uriel 1968. *Languages in Contact, Findings and Problems*. The Hague: Mouton and Co.

Wilson, Richard W. 1970. *Learning to be Chinese: The Political Socialization of Children in Taiwan*. Cambridge, Mass.: M.I.T. Press.

  1981. "Conformity and deviance regarding moral rules in Chinese society: a socialization perspective." In *Normal and Abnormal Behavior in Chinese Culture*. Arthur Kleinman and Tsung-yi Lin, eds. Dordrecht: D. Reidel Publishing Company.

Yang, Mayfair 1989. "The gift economy and state power in China." *Comparative Studies in Society and History* 31(1): 25–54, January.

Yu, Pauline 1987. *The Reading of Imagery in the Chinese Poetic Tradition*. Princeton University Press.

Yu, Shiao-ling 1983. "Voice of protest: political poetry in the post-Mao era." *The China Quarterly* 96: 703–719, December.

Index of subjects

Index of authors

Lightning Source UK Ltd.
Milton Keynes UK
22 March 2011

169656UK00001B/48/A